GEROPSYCHOLOGY

GEROPSYCHOLOGY

THE PSYCHOLOGY OF THE AGEING PERSON

Edited by Lars Larsen

Aarhus University Press

Geropsychology. The psychology of the ageing person
© Aarhus University Press and the Authors 2011
Cover photo: Tom Hussey, ©Tom Hussey Photography
Cover design: Jørgen Sparre
Translation: Nick Wrigley
Printed by Narayana Press, Denmark, 2011
ISBN 978 87 7934 574 4

Aarhus University Press
Langelandsgade 177
8200 Aarhus N, Denmark
www.unipress.dk

White Cross Mills
Hightown, Lancaster, LA1 4XS, United Kingdom
www.gazellebookservices.co.uk

ISBC
70 Enterprise Drive
Bristol, CT 06010
USA
e-mail: ian@isbookcompany.com

With sincere thanks to the Velux Foundation
for financial support.

CONTENTS

PREFACE

This anthology contains ten chapters dealing with various aspects of the psychology of ageing, an area which is known as "geropsychology" among professionals in the field.

The composition of the anthology reflects the editor's attempt to produce a book which covers the most important topics in geropsychology. The ten chapters have been written by Scandinavian experts in either general or clinical geropsychology.

The contents unavoidably reflect the priorities made by the editor, and some psychologists may well feel that other topics should have been preferred. If this is the case, I hope that as well as increasing the amount of interest shown in geropsychology, the book will also inspire others to publish articles and books dealing with other aspects of this field.

This publication, *Geropsychology*, consists of three main parts:
Part I deals with geropsychology as an object of study and research, and contains an introduction to the field as well as a discussion of research-methodological challenges.

Part II deals with the normal psychology of ageing, and contains chapters on personality, intelligence, social participation and life satisfaction. And part III deals with the psychopathology of ageing, containing chapters on diagnosis, dementia in a psychological perspective, the psychiatry of dementia, depression and paraphrenia.

I hope you enjoy reading this book.

Lars Larsen
Aarhus, October 2011

PART I

GEROPSYCHOLOGY AS AN OBJECT
OF STUDY AND RESEARCH

INTRODUCTION: GEROPSYCHOLOGY

Lars Larsen

Summary

The object of the study of geropsychology can be described as the study of both normal-psychological and psychopathological age-related variation, change and continuity in adulthood. Today geropsychology has consolidated its position as part of modern psychology. There is plenty of research in this field, and as the number of elderly people increases the need for clinical geropsychologists will increase significantly in the years ahead. Historically speaking, psychologists have shown only a limited interest in geropsychology, and in future an acute shortage of geropsychologists must be expected. This problem will probably be particularly serious in Europe, where geropsychologists have not been integrated into the field of practice to the same extent as in the US (for instance).

The demographic challenge

In terms of the average age of its population, Europe is the oldest continent in the world. At the start of the last century average life expectancy was about 40, and no more than 5% of the population was more than 65 years old. By the turn of the present century life expectancy had almost doubled, and about 17% of the population was more than 65 years old. Since 1950 the proportion of the population aged 65 or more has doubled, the proportion aged 80 or more has increased four-fold, the proportion aged 90 or more has increased eight-fold, and the proportion aged 100 or more has increased twenty-fold (Jeune, 2002). The reduction in mortality of the elderly seems to be connected with better living conditions and better medical treatment.

It is estimated that one-quarter of the European population will be more than 65 years old in the year 2025 (Fernández-Ballesteros, 2006). For this reason alone, the field of psychology needs to acquire far more specialist knowledge about the psychology of ageing. There is no reason to suppose that the elderly have any less need for the services provided by psychologists than other age groups – in fact the reverse may be true. We are living longer, so we will also be forced to live longer with what could be called the diseases of long life such as osteoarthritis, arteriosclerosis, heart failure, high blood pressure and various forms of neuropathology (Vidiik, 2002). This situation constitutes a major challenge to our healthcare system, including the services provided by psychologists for the elderly.

The scientific study of ageing

Even though geropsychology is a clearly delimited, specialised field of psychology, it is also very much an interdisciplinary area with a great number of interfaces with the other sciences of gerontology, including geriatrics and geropsychiatry.

The term 'gerontology' means the study of old age; and it is used as a general term applying to sciences whose area of focus is old age – including geropsychology. Geriatrics involves the study of illness in old age. The term is derived from the Greek words geras (meaning old age) and iatrikos (meaning medical treatment): Ger(as)iatri(kos).

Unlike geriatrics, geropsychiatry is a special field limited to mental illness in the elderly and its treatment.

In the publication entitled Krankheiten des höheren Alters und ihre Heilung in 1839, the German doctor C.F. Canstatt presented the first overall study of the diseases of the elderly (Canstatt, 1839; Kirk, 1995). The term gerontology was introduced by the Russian-French biologist Elie Metchnikoff in a book entitled *Etudes sur la nature humaine* (Studies of Human Nature) in 1903, and the term geriatrics was used for the first time in 1914 in Nascher's textbook entitled *Geriatrics – The diseases of old age and their treatment.*

The earliest book on the psychology of ageing is G.S. Hall's *Senescence: The Last Half of Life*, published in 1922. In this book Hall predicted many of the themes of psychology that have been (and still are) the focus of interest for geropsychologists. One central and even almost prophetic theme in the book concerned the threat of ageing in the 20th century: Hall predicted that the combination of longer life expectancy, changing family patterns and expulsion from the labour market would lead to the social isolation of elderly citizens and limit their participation in public life (Cole, 1984). The first handbook on the psychological aspects of ageing was not published until 1959, 28 years after the first handbook on child psychology was published – a fact which illustrates the low priority allocated to late adulthood in the specialist literature on psychology.

The object of study of geropsychology

Geropsychology is the psychology of ageing. The term is derived from the Greek word geron (meaning 'old man'), and in one sense it is misleading because geropsychology does not only focus on old age – and of course it does not focus solely on men, either. Even though some geropsychologists define the field as life-span psychology covering people's entire life from the cradle to the grave, the object of study in this book will be adulthood in general – and late adulthood in particular.

The focus of geropsychology can be defined as the study of both normal-psychological and psychopathological age-related variation, change and continuity in adulthood. In general it is not possible to distinguish precisely between normal and pathological ageing; but in late life such distinctions become even less clear. In late life illness is the rule rather than the exception, and the same is also true to some extent with regard to mental health.

Even though the framework of psychological ageing is ultimately linked to the biological ageing processes, it is not sufficient to define the psychology of ageing solely as a bio-psychological discipline. The decline of most biological functions starts in the 30s (Stuart-Hamilton, 2006, chapter 1). But in normal circumstances psychological development is possible for the entire course of a life – although a reduction in mental reserve capacity in late life places increasingly severe restrictions on our development potential. So biological development does not parallel psychological development precisely, which means that the psychology of ageing must also be described at levels other than that of bio-psychology. As a result, geropsychology covers a wide variety of possible approaches ranging from neuropsychological, individual-psychological and social-psychological approaches to culture-psychological ones.

Research and practice

If we take our point of departure in the perspective of an adult life course, it is surprising that relatively few psychologists demonstrate an interest in the ageing psyche. This limited interest may be the result of ignorance or at worst gerontophobia (the fear of ageing). Geropsychology has found it hard to gain a permanent foothold on the psychology degree programmes at Danish universities; but at the moment this situation does seem to be changing. The low professional status allocated to this area must be regarded as an expression of a short-term, ageist discrimination of the elderly part of the population (Solem, 2005; Larsen & Solem, 2010).

Despite this slightly bleak picture from a historical point of view, interest in geropsychology is fortunately on the increase. Geropsychology research is flourishing on the international stage. A comprehensive bibliometric study of the occurrence of geropsychology publications in the period 1920-1972 showed that the rate of publications on geropsychology increased during these years, accelerating after the Second World War and culminating in 247 publications in 1969 (Riegel, 1977). Krampen & Wahl (2003) have carried out a bibliometric study of developments in the frequency of geropsychology publications during the last quarter of the 20th century (1977-2000). The scale used for this involved the number of publications cited in PsycINFO and PSYNDEX. The volume of literature on geropsychology increased consistently during this period, particularly in German-speaking countries. In relative terms geropsychology publications account for 1-3 per cent of all psychological citations since 1978, so geropsychology must be regarded as a small but well established subsidiary area within the science of psychology.

However, trained geropsychologists are in short supply (Dittmann, 2003). Almost 70 per cent of American psychologists treat all age groups in their clinics, with only 3 per cent naming the psychology of the elderly as their primary area of treatment. Approximately one-fifth of the elderly have various diagnosable psychiatric illnesses (Gatz & Smyer, 2001), so the need for geropsychology expertise will almost explode as a result of the major demographic changes occurring at present. It is estimated that in 2020 the US will need 5,000 geropsychologists, which is more than seven times as many full-time geropsychologists as the number registered by the American Association of Psychologists in 2002.

Unfortunately, European psychologists do not focus on the elderly to the same extent as their American colleagues – despite the fact that the European research environments are among the most active in the world (Fernández-Ballesteros & Caprara, 2003; Fernández-Ballesteros, 2006). As a result, in 2004 the European Federation of Psychologists' Associations (EFPA) set up a special task force for geropsychology comprising participants from six different countries (including Denmark). The aim is to register all the existing knowledge and education activities in the field of geropsychology in Europe, and to provide recommendations regarding ways of raising the profile of geropsychology (www.efpa.eu/working-groups).

REFERENCES

Canstatt, C.F. (1839). *Die Krankheiten des höheren Alters und ihre Heilung.* Erlangen: Ferdinand Enke.

Cole, T.R. (1984). The prophecy of Senescence: G. Stanley Hall and the reconstruction of old age in America. *Gerontologist*, 24:360-366.

Dittmann, M. (2003). Geropsychologists are badly needed. *Monitor 5* (34), 51.

Gatz, M. & Smyer, M.A. (2001). Mental health and aging at the outset of the twenty-first century. In: J. Birren (Ed.), *Handbook of the psychology of aging.* San Diego, CA: Academic Press.

Fernández-Ballesteros, R. (2006). Geropsychology – An Applied Field for the 21st Century. *European Psychologist, 11* (4), 312-323.

Fernández-Ballesteros, R. & Caprara, M. (2003). Psychology of Aging in Europe. Editorial. *European Psychologist, 8* (3), 129-130.

Hall, G.S. (1922). *Senescence: The Last Half of Life.* New York: Appleton.

Jeune, B. (2002). Aldrings demografi og det lange liv. In: C. Swane, A.L. Blaakilde & K. Amstrup (Eds.), *Gerontologi – livet som gammel.* Copenhagen: Munksgaard Danmark.

Kirk, H. (1995). *Da alderen blev en diagnose – Konstruktionen af kategorien "alderdom" i 1800-tallets lægelitteratur.* Copenhagen: Munksgaard Danmark.

Krampen, G. & Wahl, H-W. (2003). Geropsychology and Psychology in the Last Quarter of the 20th Century. *European Psychologist, 8* (2), 87-91.

Larsen, L. & Solem, P.E. (2010). Alderisme. In: J. Bjerg (Ed.), *Gads Psykologileksikon. 3rd edition,* p. 26-27.

Metchnikoff, E. (1903). *Etudes sur la nature humaine.* Paris: Masson et Cie éd.

Nascher, I.I. (1914). *Geriatrics – The diseases of old age and their treatment.* Philadelphia, PA: Blakiston.

Qualls, S.H. (2002). Psychologists and practise with older adults: Current patterns, sources of training, and need for continuing education. *Professional Psychology: Research and Practise, 33(5),* 435-442.

Riegel, K.F. (1977). Theory of psychological gerontology. In: J.E. Birren & K.W. Schaie (Eds.), *Handbook of the psychology of aging.* New York: Van Nostrand Reinhold.

Solem, P.E. (2005). Alderisme, aldring og sosial deltakelse. Nordisk Psykologi, 57 (1), 47-63.

Stuart-Hamilton, I. (2006). *The Psychology of Ageing – An introduction.* London, Jessica Kingsley Publishers, 4th edn.

Viidik, A. (2002). Den biologiske aldringsmodel. In: H. Kirk & M. Schroll (Eds.), *Viden om aldring – veje til handling.* Copenhagen: Munksgaard Danmark.

RESEARCH METHODOLOGICAL ISSUES IN GEROPSYCHOLOGY

Lars Larsen & Peter Hartmann

Summary

This chapter underlines how important it is that geropsychologists keep up to date with current geropsychology research, for instance by reading the latest empirical studies with a view to ensuring that geropsychology practice is evidence based. However, it is sometimes difficult to distinguish between good and poor research. The aim of the following presentation of a series of basic research methodological issues is to try and make it easier for our colleagues in this field to read and interpret the research literature on geropsychology.

Modern geropsychology involves studying the age-related variation, change and continuity of psychological variables during adulthood. In other words: What effect does the passage of time have on the human psyche? In order to find qualified answers to this question, empirical research must be structured in the form of a research-methodological process consisting of four general, consecutive stages. These stages concern operationalisation, psychometrics, research design and forms of stability respectively. Assessing the quality of empirical research requires thorough knowledge of this research-methodological process.

If theoretical and practical geropsychology is to continue to develop in a positive fashion, it must be evidence based. No matter how obvious and true a theory or clinical practice seems to be intuitively, it is worthless from a strictly academic point of view unless it can be based on evidence. Without evidence one theory or practice is just as good (or bad) as any other, so deciding which theory or practice to choose becomes a question of faith. It is the demand for academic evidence that distinguishes serious geropsychology from a variety of alternative pseudo-psychological theories and forms of treatment.

Consequently, both present and future geropsychologists must continue to keep up to date with the latest research in their area. One way to keep up with evidence-based knowledge is to read the latest empirical research, but unfortunately not all this research is equally good. However, it may be difficult to distinguish between good and poor research. It is our hope that the presentation of a series of basic research-methodological issues below will make it easier for our colleagues in this field to read and interpret the research literature on geropsychology.

Modern geropsychology involves studying the age-related variation, change and continuity of psychological variables during adulthood. What effect does the passage of time have on the human psyche? The answer to this question may seem easy to the reader, but this is by no means the case. An adequate answer requires the clarification of a range of methodological issues. How should we delimit and define the phenomenon? How should we make it measurable? Are these measurements valid and reliable? What kind of research design has been used, and what form of change or continuity can be identified as a result?

Some of these issues apply to all psychology research, while others are more typical of studies of ageing.

The vast majority of geropsychology research is done by using a quantitative approach, so this chapter will focus solely on the quantitative study of the connection between age and psyche. However, many of the methodological issues considered also apply to qualitative research.[1]

If we wish to give a qualified answer to the question of what happens to the human psyche with the passage of time, it is vital that we carry out a research-methodological process consisting of four general, consecutive stages. These stages concern operationalisation, psychometrics, research design and forms of stability respectively.

Let us start by warning practical geropsychologists that the following presentation of research-methodological process may sometimes seem exceptionally theoretical and perhaps even tedious. However, without a sound empirical foundation it is not possible to achieve a sound practice, and a sound foundation is only possible if the empirical data on which it is based satisfies a number of basic methodological quality requirements.

Having appealed to the reader's patience, let us commence our presentation of the research-methodological process.

Operationalisation

The first point to make is that it is vital to set limits to the definition of the concept you wish to study. There is far too much research presenting the results

1 Readers interested in qualitative research method are referred to Denzin & Lincoln (2005), Fog (2002) and Kvale (1997).

of poorly defined psychological phenomena. This can easily result in unclear research results that are difficult to test and highly divergent. The problem can be illustrated by considering the available geropsychology research regarding personality. This research area is characterised by a wide range of definitions which are more or less unclear, resulting in a highly fragmented picture (Ryff, 1989) from which it is difficult to derive any coherent conclusions. However, if a more precise definition is used it becomes possible to obtain a clear picture of the connection between age and personality (Larsen & Winsløv, 2005). A clearly delimited definition of a psychological phenomenon will strengthen any study of the area concerned, although naturally it will also mean that some aspects have to be omitted. In other words, such a definition makes it possible to derive precise conclusions about a small area rather than imprecise conclusions about a larger area. However, a precise definition of a given psychological phenomenon is only the start, since the phenomenon defined must subsequently be operationalised with a view to making it measurable (Popper, 1937). Operationalisation can only be achieved if the general theory and associated definitions are converted into specific hypotheses which can be tested directly. In principle, a flimsy theory can be broken down into fragments that can then be tested and confirmed or denied. This is a laborious task resulting in fragmented knowledge which must subsequently be synthesised with a view to evaluating whether the theory on which it is based should be accepted, revised or perhaps rejected altogether. The dialectic process by which hypotheses are verified or falsified, thereby forming the background for new theories leading in turn to new hypotheses, is a convoluted and sometimes exhausting process. But the interchange between the differentiation of theory and the integration of data is the essence of all academic work whose purpose is to reveal correlations in the real world.

Psychometrics

The next step in the academic process is to ensure that the hypotheses being put forward can be tested with good measuring equipment, since the use of inaccurate tools always leads to imprecise or even incorrect results. For this purpose it is necessary to use psychological tests whose value can be estimated based on two fundamental principles involving reliability and validity. Degrees of reliability and validity are classical indicators of the effectiveness of any given test[2] (see for instance Elsass, P.; Ivanouw, J.; Mortensen, E.L.; Poulsen, S. & Rosenbaum, B.; 2006).

---

2 For a very brief introduction to psychometrics, please see Larsen & Hartmann (2005).

Reliability

In general terms, the reliability of any test reflects the consistency of measurements of a given phenomenon. A high degree of consistency indicates a high degree of measuring precision. There are various ways of measuring reliability, but the four most common of these are presented below (Jensen, 1980, p. 259; Zachariae, 1998, p. 100).

Internal reliability reveals the extent to which individual questions or tasks (also known as items) measure the same phenomenon – in other words, whether each item illustrates the phenomenon being investigated from a variety of angles. Internal reliability is sometimes indicated using a coefficient of reliability known as Cronbach's alpha, which reveals something about the internal consistency of a test in relation to what you are trying to measure. The principle behind Cronbach's alpha is that if all the items in question point in the same direction, the total result must be free from any unsystematic measuring defects and must therefore be reliable.[3] One problem with this form of reliability coefficient is that the size of the test concerned (the number of items) may increase the reliability coefficient. The same thing might occur if a large number of almost identical items are involved, or if an extremely narrowly defined area is involved. So although a high degree of internal reliability may be due to the fact that the test concerned is reliable, it may also arise because the test is unnecessarily long, because the questions involved overlap to a large extent, or because the phenomenon being studied has been defined extremely narrowly.

Test-retest reliability reveals the extent to which a measurement taken at one given point in time is the same as a measurement taken at a later time. In other words, it reveals whether a test result is stable. The main principle is that if a test is not influenced by temporal changes and the test result remains stable, the result of the measurements is independent of the time of measurement and can therefore be regarded as reliable. However, there are two problems here.

Firstly, the time interval must be defined. If it is too short the question is whether two separate measurements have actually been taken at all. But if it is too long there is a risk that any instability in the phenomenon being measured is misinterpreted as reflecting low reliability. In other words: if the time interval is long the test may be regarded wrongly as having low reliability because real changes have occurred in the phenomenon being measured.

And secondly, it may be assumed *a priori* that there is a high degree of stability in the phenomenon measured and in the test over short time intervals,

---

3   Please note that the reliability coefficient for internal reliability is a variance ($r_{xx} = r^2$); so it is *not* a correlation like those of the other forms of reliability, but the square of the correlation coefficient between the test result and the hypothetically correct score.

which is not necessarily the case. For instance, owing to natural hormonal fluctuations a hormone test of the oestrogen level in women will result in low test-retest reliability unless it is carried out at identical points in women's menstruation cycle. And in this example we even know about the kind of cyclical changes involved. It is easy to imagine a situation in which such variations are unknown or unsystematic. In such circumstances any indication of test-retest reliability will be underestimated, appearing to be lower than it actually is.

Parallel form tests measure the degree of conformity between two tests which resemble each other sufficiently to measure exactly the same phenomenon in exactly the same way, but which are also so different that they cannot be regarded as identical. The idea is that if respondents give the same answer to "the same questions" expressed in two different ways, the test is reliable. However, the obvious problem with this method is finding questions which measure exactly the same thing but which are expressed in two different ways.

Inter-rater reliability reveals the degree to which the results of one rater match those of other raters. The basic principle involved in this type of reliability analysis is that if two independent measurements of the same phenomenon lead to the same result, the result of these measurements must be correct. However, this principle relies on the assumption not only that the two measurements are independent (so that the true reliability is not concealed), but also that they actually estimate the same phenomenon. It is assumed that different raters observe the same phenomenon with the same precision; but it is common knowledge that observations depend on the eyes that see them. Another difficulty involved in self-reporting is that the people being tested do not necessarily report their results truthfully. They may provide the answer that they think is expected of them, or they may wish to present themselves in an excessively positive light. As a result, there is a risk that the subjective impressions of the observer and the motives of the people being tested may "contaminate" the degree of reliability measured in such cases.

In other words, evaluating the reliability of a measuring technique and thereby the level of consistency in the phenomenon being measured is no easy task. In principle it is not possible to say that any one form of reliability is better than any other. The choice of how to measure reliability depends on the type of test and study in question. The reliability tests outlined above reflect various form of reliability, and it is important to remember that this means that they cannot be compared directly with each other. Some tests may be useful as long as one form of reliability has been covered satisfactorily. It depends on what you wish to measure. Consequently, the focus should be placed not on a naïve idea that the classical 0.7 limit of reliability applies in general, but on deciding which form of reliability is important for the study in question.

Validity

As mentioned above, reliability reflects the consistency of the object being measured. Validity, on the other hand, reflects the relevance of the object being measured. As is the case with reliability, an indication of the validity of any test can be based on several approaches, the four most central of which will be dealt with here (Jensen, 1980, p. 297).

Validity of content reflects validity in relation to the theory behind it, and is linked to the relationship between the test result and the phenomenon you wish to study. The validity of content of any test shows whether it can be said to contain the central aspects of the phenomenon being measured in terms of semantics/content. For instance, if you want to measure the general cognitive abilities of human beings, a reading test will be too narrow an approach. And if you want to measure reading abilities, an IQ test will be too broad. In other words: the test, test result and object being studied all have to match each other.

Unlike the validity of content, which is concerned with the theory that lies behind it, *construct validity* is connected more closely to empirical considerations and is concerned with the extent to which a test result reflects anything interesting about the phenomenon in question: for instance, whether our test of reading abilities does actually distinguish strong readers from weak readers. Construct validity is strongly linked to the testing of simple hypotheses presented on the basis of theory and the associated definitions of concepts. The construct validity of a test is regarded as being high if the test result reveals something about the concept in question and its associated domains.

Validity of convergence and divergence reflects the extent to which a test resembles other tests studying the same phenomenon (validity of convergence) and can be distinguished from tests studying non-identical phenomena (validity of divergence). If the test result of a given "unknown" test is identical to the test results of other known tests studying the same phenomenon, it is assumed that all the tests are measuring the same thing and the "unknown" test is therefore valid. Naturally, tests of other phenomena must not be related to the test result. In other words, what is being tested here is whether a test is identical to known measurements of the same phenomenon and different from known measurements of another phenomenon. However, the problem with this is that it only works if there are one or more known tests that can be regarded as valid. So this form of validity is only useful when introducing new tests in an area which has already been studied.

Criteria or practical validity resembles construct validity to some extent because it examines the connection between test results and concrete abilities/ skills. But whereas construct validity remains within its own narrow domain in relation to theory and definitions, criteria validity extends beyond any narrow theoretical delimitation and reflects the practical application options of test results. Notwithstanding the reliability or theoretical validity of any test, criteria validity focuses on the predictability value of the test results obtained. For instance, can our test of reading abilities predict the future educational achievements of the person being tested, or his/her future earnings, or the risk that he/she might become a criminal? In this way, criteria validity extends beyond the narrow framework of theory and focuses on what test results can actually be used for in practice.

Hopefully, the points raised above have demonstrated that the problems involved in determining the validity of a test are largely identical to those associated with the concept of reliability. So validity is not just a question of the extent to which a test is relevant – it is also a question of the way in which it is relevant.

In other words, the validity of a given test depends on whether it is consistent and relevant. In order to comply with these two basic conditions, a test must be able to measure a relevant psychological phenomenon, it must be consistent in its measurements of this phenomenon, and finally the test results must have theoretical and/or practical significance. Good measuring tools can potentially increase our knowledge of the world around us, thereby increasing our ability to act appropriately and constructively in relation to our psychological reality. So a good test can be compared with an accurate tool that makes it possible to measure the individual elements of a larger theory correctly. Inaccurate tools produce poor results which will (at worst) be useless. Poor psychological measuring tools produce poor research results.

Research methods

The third step in the academic process involves choosing a suitable research method/design. Estimating the extent to which a method can be regarded as qualified requires elementary knowledge of the advantages and disadvantages of various test designs. Such knowledge makes it possible to assess potential sources of error which might "contaminate" the test results and thereby lead to erroneous conclusions. When unpredicted sources of error lead to erroneous conclusions, the tests involved can be categorised as being confounded. In other words, tests are confounded if it is assumed (for instance) that the results are due solely to age, whereas in fact they are due to another distorting variable (Hamilton, 2001, p. 55). Normally such problems are solved using experimental control, but geropsychology studies cannot be dealt with using classical experimental techniques because age is a "locked" variable which cannot be manipulated experimentally (Schaie, 1996, p. 26). As a result, geropsychology research must use alternative methods that are also known as quasi-experimental methods (Campbell & Stanley, 1963).

There are several different methodological approaches to geropsychology research, so there are also several ways in which sources of confounding can be eliminated. All these methods have advantages and disadvantages (McCrae & Costa, 2003). Unfortunately, there is no one perfect method. The most frequently used methods are the cross-sectional and the longitudinal methods (Schaie & Willis, 2002). The advantages and disadvantages of a range of different methods are outlined below (see figure 1): the cross-sectional method, the longitudinal method, different variations on the sequential method, and finally the cross-cultural method.

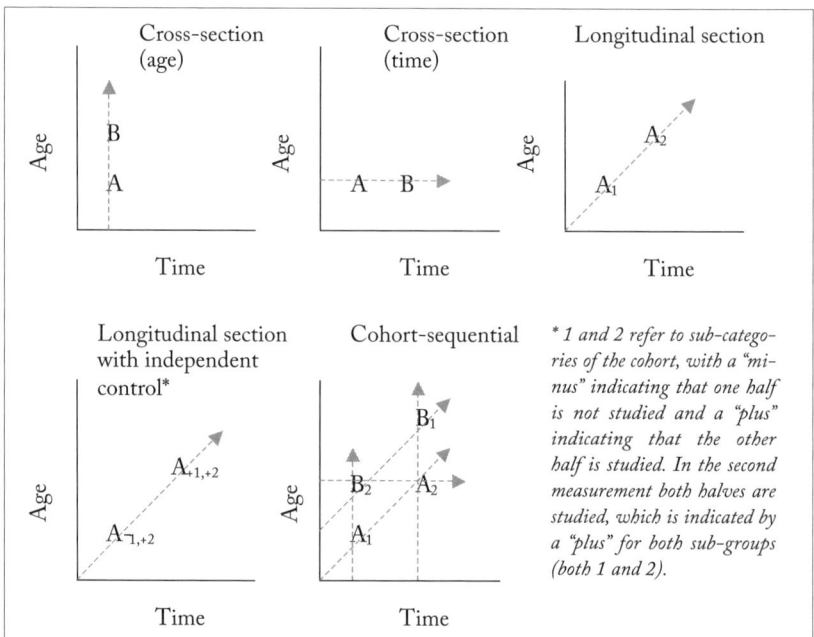

FIGURE I. Quasi-experimental research design. A = first cohort, B = second cohort.

The most obvious and simple method by which the connection between age and a specific psychological variable can be studied involves measuring and comparing various age groups at a given point in time. This approach is called the *cross-sectional method*. The advantages of this method are that it saves time and resources, makes it possible to include a large representative number of participants, and generates results after the first data collection. The primary problem of the cross-sectional method is that the results may be confounded by what could be called "group-historical" differences which are not caused by age-related change. There may simply be such a large difference in the background of the groups that it influences the results. Confounding caused by unknown "group-historical" differences is also referred to as cohort effects. Cohort effects may (for instance) be due to differences between generations. Let us assume that we wish to study the extent to which people's verbal skills are reduced with age, so we compare the verbal skills of a group of 20-year-olds with those of a group of 70-year-olds. The result is that the young group performs much better than the older group, so the conclusion is that there is a large age-related loss in verbal skills. However, we have not allowed for the fact that the level of education has increased considerably during the 50 years that divide the two groups. In addition, many of the older generation were once employed in jobs requiring hard physical work (agriculture, fishing and craftsmanship), while many of the younger generation are employed in trade, clerical work or the service industry – where verbal communication plays a more central role. The actual age-related loss of verbal skills is small, so the large differences are due not to age but to cohort differences. The generation effect is just one example of a cohort effect – there are many other cohort differences that can confound studies comparing two groups (health-related differences or differences in socio-economic status, for instance).

In order to estimate the significance of such generation effects, we need to carry out a simple *time-delay* study involving the comparison of individuals who come from different generations but who are the same age – which means that the time of testing is not the same for both groups. For instance, we could compare individuals born in 1930 and individuals born in 1950 by testing them when they reach the age of 70 (in 2000 and 2020 respectively). Any differences between the two groups will be due to generation differences, perhaps related to whether they were born before or after World War Two. However, simple time-delay studies do not measure either differences between age groups or change.

Many geropsychologists prefer to use the *longitudinal method* to study age-related change or continuity. Longitudinal studies study one specific cohort (or generation if you prefer) several times, often involving a pre-defined interval of time. This means that the same individuals are measured at different ages, making it possible to estimate changes at individual level rather than at group level. Some of the potential effects of cohort differences are eliminated in this way because everyone being studied belongs to the same generation with the same general "group-historical" background, which means that differences between individuals cannot be caused by generation differences. However, it is important to remember that the results generated by one cohort are not necessarily representative of other cohorts. So longitudinal studies may generate valid data about changes in one study group that would not be reproduced by a study of another group: the solution of one cohort problem leads to a new one (Stuart-Hamilton, 2001, p. 57).

Apart from the problem of representativity, the longitudinal method is slow and expensive because it typically lasts a great number of years. Researchers might die before extremely long studies have been completed, as was the case with Sol Seim's life-long study of intelligence and personality (Haugen & Krüger, 1999). However, this does not mean that such studies are a waste of time. Good longitudinal studies generate valuable results on an ongoing basis.

A third major problem is the repetition effect. When the same individuals are measured several times using the same test (or tests of a similar type), a repetition effect can be observed in some cases. This repetition effect is well known in studies of intelligence in which the subjects being studied grow familiar with the test or type of test involved, helping them to improve their performance. This phenomenon is also known as test smartness. The repetition effect may also be a problem when using personality tests – the test subjects may be able to remember their previous answers and will be influenced by this.

A fourth potential problem is the drop-out rate. There is a danger that the weakest and/or least motivated participants will drop out of the test so the test population eventually consists of an elite group which grows increasingly unrepresentative. For instance, in some longitudinal tests of age and intelligence it is possible to gain the impression that the participants grow wiser over the years, even though this tendency is actually due to test smartness and the fact the weakest participants have dropped out. In fact the connection between intellectual abilities and ageing is far more complex than this because changes in these abilities do not become uniform until the late stages of ageing, when all cognitive abilities become reduced (Brody, 1992). A fifth problem with the longitudinal method is connected with the test tools that are used. The longitudinal method requires the use of the same test tools in all tests; but the ongoing development of theory and method in any given field may lead to the abandonment of a given theory or test, making the test tools and test results obsolete, hard to convert into the dominant terminology of the field, or (at worst) simply meaningless. For instance, the Five-Factor Model of personality has gained a dominant position in the field of trait psychology (McCrae & Costa, 2003; Hartmann, 2006b); making test tools based on the previous Three-Factor Model (e.g. Eysenck, 1991) seem less interesting in the light of the latest dominant paradigm. The situation is even worse with regard to personality studies which have used test tools that are difficult to "translate" into more modern terminology. In Seim's life-long study of personality the Rorschach test is used as a test tool (Haugen & Krüger, 1999). This test is hardly ever used in research these days, and it has also been shown to contain a series of serious defects (Eisdorfer, 1963).

A final problem is due to major unforeseen social events occurring during the study period. This phenomenon is known as a period effect. Let us assume that we wish to study whether or not people grow more worried and nervous as they get older. We study our cohort in 1957, 1962 and 1967 respectively, and discover that our test group has grown much more nervous and worried during the study period. So we conclude that nervousness and worry increase with age. However, we have failed to allow for the Cuba Crisis, which occurred in the middle of the study period. The marked increase in insecurity is not necessarily age related – it may be due to the historical event in October 1962 when the world was minutes away from a nuclear war. The truth is that there is no empirical evidence for claiming that people grow more nervous and worried with age – on the contrary, in fact (Larsen & Winsløv, 2005). In other words, our study has been confounded by a period effect.

An attempt has been made to solve these cohort problems by using more sophisticated *sequential designs* (Baltes, Reese & Nesselroade, 1977; Schaie, 1977).

The *cohort sequential method*, which is also known as the overlapping longitudinal study method, measures several different cohorts (generations, for instance) several times over a short or long period. This makes it possible to gain the advantages of the longitudinal study method but still measure and adjust for any differences between the cohorts. The latter point increases the probability that the results will be representative. As was the case with the simple time-delay study, the cohort sequential study makes it possible to compare different generations of the same age, thereby measuring generation effects directly. In cohort sequential studies it is also possible to control any period effects to some extent. This is because it is possible to register the influence of unforeseen historical events by comparing the scores of the cohorts of various generations at a given age (some cohorts before, some during and some after the occurrence of the historical event in question). This might sound rather complicated, but it can be illustrated using the above-mentioned historical example of the Cuba Crisis.

Let us assume that we follow three cohorts over an 11-year period from the beginning of 1957 to the end of 1967. The three cohorts are measured in 1957, 1962 and 1967 respectively, and are 35, 40 and 45 years old respectively when first measured in 1957. So the Cuba Crisis in 1962 occurs in the middle of the study period and may therefore potentially influence the results of the measurements and give us the mistaken impression that significant age-related changes occurred during the period which might actually have been due to the Cuba Crisis instead.

If we compare the results of the three cohorts at a specific age on conclusion of the study (for instance at the age of 45), we will have three cohorts of the same age who reached the age of 45 before, during and after the Cuba Crisis respectively. The first cohort were 35 in 1957 and 45 in 1967 (after the crisis); the second cohort were 40 in 1957 and 45 in 1962 (during the crisis); and the third cohort were 45 when the study started in 1957 (before the crisis). So the differences between the three cohorts at the age of 45 might be due to the major political event that occurred during the study period. However, the problem is that it may be difficult to distinguish the period effect from previous generation effects unless we have already identified the generation differences in a previous study period.

Despite the many strengths of cohort sequential studies, they also have their difficulties. Like longitudinal studies, they demand a lot of time and resources and are vulnerable to drop-out rates. Finally, the method is not free of confounding due to possible repetition effects, and it cannot control period effects with any guarantee because it is not possible to know in advance which cohorts should be studied in order to counteract all conceivable period effects.

The repetition effect can be controlled using another sequential method to compare the results of so-called *dependent* and *independent* groups from the same cohort. The dependent groups are measured several times using the same test tools, so the results are inter-dependent. The independent groups are only measured once, so the results are independent of previous measurements. This method could also be called a *longitudinal study with an independent control group*. The point of departure is a longitudinal design, but an attempt is made to control any repetition effect by constructing two identical groups and testing group 1 at a given point in time (t1), while group 2 is not tested. After a given period both groups are tested (t2). The first group has now been tested twice, so this part of the study is identical with a simple longitudinal design. But the second group has only been tested once (at t2); and since both groups have experienced the same historical period (since t1), the test results for the two groups at t2 should be identical apart from the possible effect of having taken the test previously. Differences between the two groups at t2 are therefore attributed to the effect of having taken the test previously (the repetition effect), and must be "deducted" from the change observed for group 1 between the two test points (t1 and t2). Only then is it possible to determine the "true" longitudinal effect.

There is also a simpler way to transfer the principle outlined above to all types of study in which the same individuals are measured more than once. At any time during such studies it is possible to include a new group from the original cohort which has not been tested previously. This makes it possible to control the repetition effect even though this was not allowed for at the start of the study. However, it can only be done if both groups are representative of the cohort in question.

It should be possible to achieve the most "bullet-proof" design by combining the various methods outlined above (Schaie, 1996, pp. 29-31; Schaie & Willis, 2002, pp. 116-120), making it possible to control the cohort effects, representativity problems, repetition effects and period effects. Several different cohorts could be studied, each divided into randomly selected sub-groups of equal size. The first measurement measures some of the trial subjects in each cohort, while the others function as a control group. The second measurement re-examines the first group as well as testing some of the control group for repetition effects. The third measurement re-examines the two groups tested previously (group 1 being tested for the third time and group 2 being tested for the second time). At the same time more individuals from the control group are included and tested with a view to controlling the repetition effect. And this continues until you have carried out the pre-defined number of measurements (2, 3 or more).

This design makes it possible:

1. To control cohort effects, because each of the cohorts is measured separately at several different points in time.

2. To partially measure representativity by comparing the longitudinal results from the various cohorts of the study.

3. To control the repetition effect, because you do not test every individual in the cohorts every time.

4. To carry out cross-sectional comparisons between the cohorts.

5. To partially control period effects, because the cohorts reach the same age at different points in time.

Apart from being very costly, a complex research design like this one will require a great number of participants in order to ensure the necessary number of study subjects in the individual sub-groups. And finally it is worth remembering that the vulnerability of empirical studies vis-à-vis the drop-out rate of participants increases as the complexity of design increases. The greater the number of different sub-categories, the smaller the number of individuals in each group – so even if only a few participants drop out there are major problems.

One far less complicated and also safer way to avoid period effects and/or repetition effects is to carry out all the measurements at the same time – but this brings us back to the cross-sectional study with its associated problem involving the risk of cohort confounding. One solution to this problem might be to compare results from a series of cross-sectional studies of different cohorts. If the results from a series of cross-sectional studies carried out in different populations and at different times all point in the same direction, the importance of cohort differences in each study will be limited. One example of this approach involves the so-called *cross-cultural studies*, in which cross-sectional results from different cultures are compared (Costa & McCrae, 2003). Some researchers have accused the cross-cultural method of being the source of discrimination against certain cultures and races, pointing out with some justification that variation within cultures is larger than variation between them (Coolican, 2004). However, this merely indicates that confounding caused by cultural differences seems to have a limited extent in many cross-sectional studies.

Various concepts of stability

The focus of geropsychology on stability and change is not as simple as we might assume, since the concept of stability can be understood in a variety of ways. In addition, the specific design of each study determines which form of stability can be identified. Consequently, at the start of each new study it is necessary to decide which form of stability you wish to investigate. The identification of stability is the fourth and last stage in the research-methodological process.

Some of the most frequently used concepts of stability (Caspi & Bem, 1990) are outlined below.

Absolute stability concerns the degree of quantitative constancy of a given psychological characteristic. Conceptually speaking it is linked with the stability of psychological characteristics in individuals, but in practice it is often measured at group level. Change is typically measured directly using a longitudinal design in which the same phenomenon is measured several consecutive times in the same individuals. Alternatively, change can be estimated indirectly using the cross-sectional design, in which test results from two different age groups are compared at a given point in time instead. However, it is important to remember that the latter method actually only measures presumably age-related differences between two groups, and that conclusions regarding change in individuals therefore rest on a qualified estimate.

It is not possible to obtain valid measurements of absolute stability using different measurements of the "same" pheno-typical expression. This is because if you do this it is impossible to decide whether changes in the pheno-typical expression are involved, or whether the apparent changes are due to differences between the measuring tools used.

Differential stability concerns the consistency of individual differences within a population measured at several different points in time. Or in other words, it concerns the extent to which individuals retain their respective positions in relation to each other over a certain period (via longitudinal design). The degree of differential stability is normally expressed in terms of correlation coefficients, which are also known as stability coefficients. Such coefficients reflect general relative connections, thereby ignoring the absolute scores. In this connection it is worth remembering that it is possible to find both differential stability and absolute change if the individuals in the study population change absolutely but retain their relative positions in the population. On the other hand, at group level it is also possible to find a high degree of absolute stability and a low degree of differential stability. Hypothetically this may occur if some of the participants in the study improve their performance while the performance of a similar number grows correspondingly poorer. In such circumstances the absolute group level has not changed even though the participants do not retain their relative positions.

Structural stability concerns patterns in the relations of psychological variables within and between different general dimensions or factors over time. Such structural patterns can be identified using advanced correlative statistics such as factor analysis, in which variables can be grouped in different dimensions depending on their mutual relations. Given variables will then belong primarily to specific dimensions, and it will be possible to express the strength of their relationship using a measure of factor loading. The higher the factor loading, the better the variable in question is as an indicator of the dimension concerned. Structural stability can thus be measured by comparing the factor loading of the individual variables on two or more occasions. If the variables retain their relative positions in the dimensional structure, we can talk of structural stability. In other words, the issue is whether the internal structure of a test or phenomenon is constant. Do the individual variables retain their relative positions? For instance, is the structure of a general measure of intelligence the same for both old and young people? If this is not the case, it is in principle impossible to compare general measures of intelligence for the two age groups. Doing so would be like comparing apples and pears.

Whereas absolute, differential and structural stability are based on the statistical properties of a group of individuals, *ipsative stability* relates to the individual-specific level. What is involved here is the continuity of different personal characteristics and their configuration in one specific individual over a period of time (via longitudinal design). Unlike the other variable-focused and inter-individual concepts of stability dealing with the position of individuals across a series of variables, ipsative stability can be defined as an individual-focused concept because it deals with the consistency of intra-individual characteristics and their mutual relationships over time (for more details on ipsative testing, please see Hartmann & Larsen, 2005). Ipsative stability is measured using the idiographic method, in which specific characteristics are tested in a single individual several times. So in principle the results only apply to the specific individual concerned, although average figures based on several ipsative results in different individuals may reveal something about the general ipsative stability of a population.

In practice the differences between different forms of stability can be illustrated using examples taken from intelligence research. The identification of the type of stability you wish to study is an important prerequisite if you wish to interpret your results correctly. Without this kind of identification you may obtain some interesting answers, but they will not necessarily be answers to the questions that you asked. The problem could be summarised as follows: Here is the answer, but what was the question?

If you want to measure the absolute stability of intellectual abilities, it is necessary to carry out at least two measurements of the same individuals using exactly the same cognitive test; or alternatively to use two different groups and compare their results – and then assume that these group differences reflect individual differences that lie behind them. The degree to which the two results resemble each other is a measure of absolute stability.

However, if you want a measure of differential stability, at least two measurements must be taken of the same individuals – but not necessarily with identical tests even though this would be preferable. However, differential stability does not preclude absolute instability. If one individual retains his/her relative position in a population but all the individuals in the population change their intellectual competence, the population will show both absolute instability (or development if you prefer) and differential stability (Larsen, Hartmann & Nyborg, 2007).

To decide whether it makes any sense to calculate absolute and differential measures of stability in intelligence, it is necessary to study structural stability. The study of structural stability within general intelligence, also known as g, constitutes an independent area of research known as *Spearman's Law of Diminishing Returns* or *the hypothesis of differentiation* (Jensen, 1998; Hartmann & Teasdale, 2004; 2005; Hartmann & Reuter, 2005; Hartmann, 2006a). The study of structural stability is based on advanced statistics (factor analysis), the aim of which (as mentioned above) is to determine whether the relations between items in an IQ test or between sub-tests in an IQ test battery are identical despite the age factor.

Ipsative stability is present when individual intellectual skills retain their strength in relation to each other over time for a specific individual. For instance, are the verbal competences of an individual still better than the person's visual competences, or have they changed in relation to each other?

As shown in this presentation, it is not possible to refer to "stability" as a single, unambiguous concept. The interpretation of results from geropsychology studies of stability will always be determined by the definition of stability that has been used. Different forms of stability are measured in different ways, so they illustrate different aspects of stability or change.

Concluding remarks

The lesson to be derived from this presentation of methodological problems associated with the study of age-related stability and change must be that categorical conclusions based solely on studies of the same type should be avoided.

Instead, it is an advantage to piece together the connection between age and a given psychological phenomenon based on the results of studies with different research designs. If a great number of studies with identical, valid and reliable operationalisations and using different methods find the same general tendency, it must be regarded as constituting the basis of qualified answers. However, it is important to remember that the interpretation of the results of geropsychology studies of stability (or the lack of stability) depend on the definition of stability that has been used.

REFERENCES

Baltes, P.B.; Reese, H.W. & Nesselroade, J.R. (1977). *Life-span developmental psychology: Introduction to research methods*. Oxford, England: Brooks/Cole.

Brody, N. (1992). *Intelligence*. 2nd ed., San Diego, CA: Academic Press.

Caspi, A. & Bem, D.J. (1990). Personality Continuity and Change across the Life Course. In: L.A. Pervin (Ed.), *Handbook of Personality. Theory and Research*, 549-575. New York City: The Guilford Press.

Coolican, H. (2004). *Research methods and statistics in psychology*. London: Hodder & Stoughton.

Campbell, D.T. & Stanley, J.C. (1963). Experimental and quasi-experimental designs for research in teaching. In: N.L. Gage (Ed.), *Handbook of research on teaching*, 171-246. Skokie, IL: Rand McNally.

Denzin, N. & Lincoln, Y. (2005). *Handbook of qualitative research*. 3rd ed., Thousand Oaks: Sage Publications.

Eisdorfer, C. (1963). Rorschach Performance and Intellectual Functioning in the Aged. *Journal of Gerontology, 18*, 358-363.

Elsass, P.; Ivanouw, J.; Mortensen, E.L.; Poulsen, S. & Rosenbaum, B. (2006) (Eds.). *Assessment-metoder: Håndbog for psykologer og psykiatere [Assessment methods: Handbook for psychologists and psychiatrists]*. Copenhagen: Dansk psykologisk Forlag.

Eysenck, H.J. (1991). Dimensions of Personality: 16, 5 or 3? – Criteria for a taxonomic paradigm. *Personality and Individual Differences, 12*, 773-790.

Fog, J. (2002). *Med samtalen som udgangspunkt*. 2nd ed. Copenhagen: Akademisk Forlag.

Hartmann, P. (2004). Et århundrede efter Spearmans g. *Nordisk Psykologi, 56 (1)*: 3-18.

Hartmann, P. (2005). Faktoranalyse: En introduktion for psykologer. In: P. Hartmann & L. Larsen (Eds.), *Differentialpsykologi: Tekster i Psykometri; Psykologisk Skriftserie, (26) 1*, 39-58. Aarhus: Psykologisk Institut.

Hartmann, P. (2006a). *Investigating Spearman's "Law of Diminishing Returns" [PhD dissertation, 2006]*. Aarhus: Aarhus University.

Hartmann, P. (2006b). The Five-Factor Model: Psychometric, biological and practical perspectives. *Nordisk Psykologi, 58*, 150-170.

Hartmann, P. & Larsen, L. (2005). Psykometriske egenskaber ved ipsative testformater. In: P. Hartmann & L. Larsen (Eds.), *Differentialpsykologi: Tekster i Psykometri; Psykologisk Skriftserie, (26) 1*, 39-58. Aarhus: Psykologisk Institut.

Hartmann, P. & Reuter, M. (2006). Spearman's "Law of Diminishing Returns" Tested with Two Methods. *Intelligence, 34*, 47-62.

Hartmann, P. & Teasdale, T.W. (2004). A Test of Spearman's "Law of Diminishing Returns" in two large samples of Danish military draftees. *Intelligence, 32*, 499-508.

Hartmann, P. & Teasdale, T.W. (2005). Spearman's "Law of Diminishing Returns" and the role of test reliability investigated in a large sample of Danish military draftees. *Personality & Individual Differences, 39*, 1193-1203.

Haugen, P.K. & Krüger, R.E. (1999). *Din tanke er din skæbne – Sol Seim og hennes forskning*. Tore Mårds: Akribe.

Jensen, A.R. (1980). *Bias in Mental Testing*. New York: The Free Press.

Jensen, A.R. (1998). *The g Factor*. Westport, CT: Prager.

Kvale, S. (1997). *InterViews – en indføring i kvalitativ interviewforskning*. Copenhagen: Hans Reitzels Forlag.

Larsen, L. & Hartmann, P. (2005). Om at måle psyken. In: P. Hartmann & L. Larsen (Eds.), *Differentialpsykologi: Tekster i Psykometri; Psykologisk Skriftserie, (26) 1*, 1-3. Aarhus: Psykologisk Institut.

Larsen, L.; Hartmann, P. & Nyborg, H. (2008). The stability of general intelligence from early adulthood to middle age. *Intelligence*, 36 (1), 29-34.

Larsen, L. & Winsløv, J-H. (2005). Stadig mig selv efter alle disse år. *Nordisk Psykologi, 57*, 21-46.

McCrae, R.R. & Costa, P.T. (2003). *Personality in Adulthood*. 2nd ed., New York: The Guilford Press.

Popper, K.R. (1937). *Logik der Forschung*. New York: Springer.

Schaie, K.W. (1996). *Intellectual development in adulthood – The Seattle Longitudinal Study*. New York: Cambridge University Press.

Schaie, K.W. (2000). The impact of longitudinal studies on understanding development from young adulthood to old age. *International Journal of Behavioral Development, 24 (3)*, 257-266.

Schaie, K.W. & Willis, S. (2002). *Adult Development and Aging*. 5th ed., Upper Saddle River, New Jersey: Prentice Hall.

Stuart-Hamilton, I. (2001). *Aldringens psykologi – grundbog i gerontopsykologi*. Copenhagen: Gyldendals uddannelse, Nordisk Forlag.

Zachariae, B. (1998). *Det vellykkede eksperiment*. Copenhagen: Munksgaard.

II

NORMAL AGEING

THE STABILITY OF PERSONALITY IN ADULTHOOD

Lars Larsen, Peter Hartmann & Jan-Henrik Winsløv

Summary

Based on trait-psychology personality research, this chapter seeks to answer the following questions: What happens to our personality as we grow older? Are personality traits stable, or do they change during adulthood? If they are stable, why is this so? And if they change, how and why do they change?

In order to find qualified answers to these questions, it is necessary to combine the information gained from studies employing various ways of measuring trait psychology and various research designs.

By way of conclusion the implications of the knowledge gained are discussed, as well as the way in which this knowledge can be used in psychology practice for the benefit of the elderly population.

Introduction

The notion that certain personality traits are stable in various situations can be traced right back to Antiquity. For instance, Theophrastus (approx. 372-287 BC) wondered why Greeks born under the same sky who had received the same education had different characters. Hippocrates (460-377 BC) attributed such individual differences to the intervention of the gods; whereas Galen (129-199 AD) believed that they were caused by different bodily fluids such as phlegm, yellow bile and blood causing four types of personality: sanguine, phlegmatic, choleric and melancholic. These four types can be found subsequently in the work of the philosopher Immanuel Kant, the father of phrenology Alfred Combe, and the founder of modern experimental psychology Wilhelm Wundt.

However, although it is true that the idea of stable individual differences in personality traits has deep historical roots, it is quite another matter to prove the point empirically. And even if the point can be proved, what are the issues or factors that explain such stability?

In this chapter we shall seek to answer these questions, taking our point of departure in modern personality psychology. However, the literature and research on personality and ageing is rather fragmented, due not least to the lack of consensus regarding the definition of the concept of personality. In the field of personality psychology the only common denominator is that an attempt should be made to account for the person as a whole (McCrae & Costa, 2003). For instance, ego psychologists choose to focus on more general and integrating whole theories (Erikson, 1998); while trait psychologists focus more narrowly on specific measurable aspects of personality (Eysenck & Eysenck, 1985; McCrae & Costa, 2003). Geropsychological personality research has covered a wide variety of different areas, such as personality traits, executive processes, social clocks, psycho-social development stages, stress adaptation and coping style, psychological wellbeing, feelings, morality, belief and the self (Ryff, Kwan & Singer, 2001). Among other things, this wide variety reflects the use of different definitions and operationalisations of the concept of personality, which are subsequently manifested in different study foci and levels of analysis. The pluralistic nature of personality research makes it difficult to compare different studies with each other, thereby reducing the potential for drawing general conclusions.

In the hope of being able to present a qualified idea of whether (and to what extent) personality changes, and the potential causes of stability and change respectively, we have chosen a delimited approach to the area. The concept of personality is delimited, defined and operationalised within one given paradigm, making it possible to illustrate the issue empirically (Popper, 1935). In other words, the assumption that there are adequate methods of presenting the ageing personality is also a prerequisite.

Based on these requirements, in this chapter we have chosen to take our point of departure in trait-psychology research. Trait-psychology studies are normally well operationalised, and there are a great number of comparative studies. Naturally, our choice involves deselecting a number of other approaches to geropsychological personality research. We are not under the illusion that we can produce an exhaustive presentation of the connection between personality and age or the importance of personality for the course of a life and ageing; we simply hope that we can give the reader some more detailed knowledge of age-related stability and change viewed from the perspective of trait psychology.

After a general introduction to trait psychology, we will touch on some of the issues associated with studies that seek to illustrate stability and change over various periods of time. We will then present some of the results of gerontology trait research, followed by a discussion illustrating some of the problems and weaknesses of the existing studies and trait models. In addition, pathological changes of the personality will be dealt with briefly, and the article concludes by indicating some of the areas which might benefit from the existing knowledge about the ageing personality.

Trait models, personality dimensions and measuring tools

The following presentation might strike the reader as being rather technical and abstract, but the use of personality characteristics is actually a natural part of everyday life for us all. If we are asked to describe ourselves or other people we know well, we tend to resort to descriptive adjectives such as quiet, sociable, nervous, meticulous, ambitious, aggressive, friendly, obliging, matter-of-fact, indecisive or dominating. We characterise each other by using familiar personality traits. This does not mean that we have said everything that there is to say about an individual – instead, we have given a general idea of a person's more or less typical approach to life by describing their feelings, thoughts and behaviour. For instance, we would not expect a person who is characterised as introverted, disobliging, indecisive and passive to be the life and soul of any party. And similarly, we would not expect to find an obstinate, ambitious, extrovert and dominant person at the bottom of a company hierarchy. The everyday language we use to describe ourselves and others – including our feelings, thoughts and behaviour – apparently reflects some identifiable individual differences between human beings. These individual differences in personality traits are the object of study in the trait-psychology approach to personality. However, the question is whether it is possible to identify all existing personality traits.

Within the trait-psychology tradition there have been two predominant approaches to the identification of personality traits: the lexical and the non-lexical approach respectively (McCrae & John, 1992, pp. 181ff).

The lexical approach can be traced back to Sir Francis Galton, who (in the second half of the 19th century) collected about 1,000 words describing personality (John et al., 1988, p. 176). By contrast to Galton's somewhat unsystematic method, in 1926 Ludwig Klages suggested that various works of reference could be used to identify all the words used to characterise a person (John et al., 1988, p. 174). A few years later Baumgarten (1933) followed up on this idea, as did Allport (1937), Cattell (1943), Norman (1963) and Goldberg (1982) (all taken from John, Angleitner & Ostendorf, 1988, pp. 174ff). The rationale behind the lexical approach to personality is that the individual differences that are most significant and socially relevant in people's lives will gradually be embedded in the language; and the larger these differences are, the greater the probability that they will be expressed in single words (John et al., 1988, p. 174). This means that language is an invaluable source of information for the trait-psychology approach to personality. By examining language and finding the words used to characterise personality most frequently, researchers in the lexical tradition assume that it is possible to identify all existing personality traits. In addition, these words embedded in the language can be used to describe the individual and thereby form a basis for the development of personality tests (Hartmann, 2006).

The non-lexical approach to personality traits, on the other hand, is based primarily on questionnaires constructed on a theoretical platform with a view to confirming a personality theory or with a view to practical use (Goldberg, 1971, in McCrae & John, 1992, p. 185). The roots of the non-lexical approach are to be found (for instance) in Jung (1923) and Murray (1938) (both in McCrae & John, 1992, p. 185), each of whom created a personality theory for which a personality test was subsequently constructed with a view to testing the theory. In recent years this method has been used successfully by Eysenck & Eysenck (1991); Zuckermann (Joireman & Kuhlman, 2004); Costa & McCrae (1992) and others.

The most dominant trait-psychology models are Eysenck's Three-Factor Model (PEN) and Costa and McCrae's Five-Factor Model, both of which can be regarded as prototypes of trait-psychology personality models. These models are based on factor analysis, which is a statistical method used to derive general factors from a large number of variables.

In the so-called PEN model Eysenck operated with three basic personality dimensions: Neuroticism (emotionally unstable-stable), Extraversion (extrovert-introvert), and Psychoticism (psychopathology, vulnerability or not). He also employed a Lie scale (detecting the tendency towards inconsistent and untruthful answers to tests).

Eysenck perceived personality as a hierarchical structure whose elements could be ranked according to an increasing degree of cross-situational consistency. At the bottom of the hierarchy are the behaviour or actions that are specific to individual situations, followed by habitual actions, then personality traits, and finally general personality dimensions (Eysenck & Eysenck, 1985). These are not simple categories in which individuals can be labelled (for instance) as either extroverts or introverts – instead, they are dimensions which measure the extent to which an individual is an extrovert. Eysenck's dimensions are measured using the Eysenck Personality Questionnaire (EPQ).

Costa and McCrae's version of the Five-Factor Model (FFM) operates with five basic personality dimensions: Neuroticism (N, emotionally unstable-stable), Extraversion (E, extrovert-introvert), Openness (O, open-minded-conservative), Agreeableness (A, compassionate-antagonistic) and Conscientiousness (C, conscientious-unreliable) (McCrae & Costa, 2003). Like Eysenck, McCrae and

Costa define personality traits as a consistent characteristic in human beings influencing our feelings, thought and behaviour in such a way that it is possible to refer to more or less fundamental patterns of feelings, thoughts and behaviour. These dimensions are regarded as universal because they can be found in people from different cultures. The five dimensions are measured using the Neuroticism, Extraversion, Openness Personality Inventory (NEO PI-R). It is assumed that personality traits have a biological foundation in which genes, neuro-physiology and neuro-chemistry play a central role (McCrae & Costa, 2003). Based on William James's assumptions about personality development and change, Costa & McCrae assume that personality traits are changeable during the first stage of life until the age of 30, after which they become stable and do not change significantly (Caspi & Roberts, 1999). However, it is important to realise that personality traits cannot be used to predict precisely what individuals will do in specific situations – instead, they provide an indication of the action and behaviour tendencies that will be more or less likely.

There are a number of similarities between Eysenck's Three-Factor Model and Costa and McCrae's Five-Factor Model. They both operate with E and N, and the content of Eysenck's P factor corresponds largely to the content of A and C from the FFM – high P corresponding to low A and C. The Openness dimension does not occur in Eysenck's model.

The PEN and FFM models are not the only trait-psychology models that have been used in gerontological personality psychology. A number of different operationalisations occur when considering gerontological personality research, such as the Minnesota Multi Phasic Personality Inventory (MMPI), Cattell's Sixteen Personality Factors Model (16PF), the California Personality Inventory (CPI), the Guilford-Zimmerman Temperament Scale (GTZS), the Personality Research Form (PRF), and the Myers-Briggs Temperament Inventory (MBTI).

To simplify this picture and make it easier to compare these different studies, we will "translate" the empirical results obtained so they correspond with the concepts used in Costa and McCrae's Five-Factor Model. We have chosen to take our point of departure in the conceptual framework of the FFM partly due to the dominant position of the FFM on the stage of trait psychology, and partly because we assume that most psychologists will be familiar with the terminology of the FFM and with Costa and McCrae's NEO PI-R personality test.

Table 1 contains an overview of the measurement systems mentioned, their origins, background and scales. Their dimensions have all been "translated" so they correspond with Costa and McCrae's FFM terminology.

Before we present the results of gerontological trait-personality research, it is important to underline that these studies all use different research designs, and that these design differences may influence the results obtained.

TABLE I

Abbreviation	Full name	Origin	Background	Examples of dimensions and relation to FFM*
NEO-PI	Neuroticism, Extraversion, Openness Personality Inventory	Costa & McCrae (1985)	The Five-Factor Model involves the integration of several decades of Anglo-Saxon personality research, and is now the most widely used model in trait psychology.	Neuroticism (N), Extraversion (E), Openness (O), Agreeableness (A), Conscientiousness (C)
EPQ	Eysenck Personality Questionnaire	Eysenck & Eysenck (1975)	The philosophical roots of this model lie in the theory of the Greek philosopher Galen regarding the four classical humours.	Psychoticism (-A,-C), Neuroticism (N), Extraversion (E)
MMPI	Minnesota Multiphasic Personality Inventory	Hathaway & McKinley (1940)	Constructed to measure the degree of presence or absence of psychiatric symptoms. Originally developed for clinical psychology, but subsequently often used to identify normal personality.	Includes ten clinical scales: Psychastenia (N), Social Introversion (-E), Fantasy (O), Self Control (C) etc.
16PF	Sixteen Personality Factors	Cattell, Cattell & Cattell (1949)	Operationalisation based on 16 factors identified by R.B. Cattell using factor analysis	16 bipolar dimensions: Tension (N), Self-reliance (E), Openness to change (O), Rule consciousness (C) etc.
MBTI	Myers-Briggs Type Indicator	Myers, I. & Briggs, K.C. (Myers & McCauley, 1985)	Based on C.G. Junge's personality typology, which operates with four dichotomous indices. In the MBTI these four are combined into a total of 16 types.	Four dimensions: Extroversion (E), Intuition (O), Feeling (A), Judgement (C)
GZTS	Guilford-Zimmerman Temperament Survey	Guilford & Zimmerman (1948)	Tool developed to measure normal personality and temperament	Ten dimensions of personality and temperament: Sociability (E), Emotional Stability (-N), Thoughtfulness (O), Friendliness (A), Restraint (C) etc.
CPI	California Personality Inventory	Gough, H.G. (1987)	The CPI is constructed by measuring a broad spectrum of personality characteristics, from socially observable qualities to values and motivation. This tool also makes it possible to score three general dimensions.	Three general dimensions: Realisation (-N), Internality (-E), Norm-favouring (C)
PRF	Personality Research Form	Douglas N. Jackson (1984)	Based on Henry Murray's motivation- and need-based personality theory	20 scales: Nurturance (N), Exhibition (E), Need for change (O), Aggression (-A), Ambition (C) etc.

Source: Larsen & Winsløv, 2005, pp. 26-27.

Any attempt to answer the questions posed above about ageing and personality should be made based on the results of studies with a variety of different research designs. If many different studies with different operationalisations and designs generally show the same tendency, this must be assumed to constitute the basis of qualified answers.

Gerontological personality research

We will now seek to give the reader an overview of the results achieved by gerontological personality research, categorised according to the design of the studies in question. And to make it easier for the reader to maintain a clear view of all the many designations of personality traits used, the results will be presented following translation into the terminology of the FFM. We hope to present a general conclusion regarding the relationship between personality and ageing. However, it is important to point out that in this article we are only concerned with general tendencies. This is because most of the studies in question have illustrated the degree of stability at group level. A distinction is drawn between absolute stability and differential stability, with the former referring to whether a study group changes with regard to one or more trait dimensions over time, while the latter refers to the relative positions of the individuals studied in terms of trait dimensions (Caspi & Roberts, 1999). This means that individual variations in terms of behaviour and actions may be concealed beneath these general tendencies, and individual variations may also be concealed in terms of the degree of stability of the various trait dimensions. It is possible to illustrate such aspects using idiographic studies focusing on structural and ipsative stability (ibid). It is true that idiographic studies of personality traits also display stability in their trait configurations (McCrae & Costa, 2003, chapter 6), but we will not deal with this issue in any greater detail in this chapter.

Cross-sectional studies (age differences)

Cross-sectional studies estimate the effect of age differences at a given point in time, but do not necessarily reveal anything about stability. The results of cross-sectional studies may be "contaminated" by generation-specific differences between the age groups you wish to compare. And such differences may be mistakenly interpreted as a sign of change.

In a summary article in 1977, Neugarten considered cross-sectional studies of age differences in personality traits (Neugarten, 1977). The following personality traits were included in her study of the literature: egocentricity, dependence, introversion, dogmatism, rigidity, caution, conformity, ego strength, the willingness to take risks, the need to perform, control, creativity, hope, self-awareness, social responsibility, morality, daydreams and attitude to ageing. There were differences between age groups with regard to all these traits. Indeed, the studies she included revealed extremely different and often contradictory results for the traits in question. For instance, some studies showed that elderly people were more dogmatic than young people, while others showed the opposite. According to Neugarten (1977), introversion (-E) was the only trait that was consistently more in evidence in elderly people. Naturally, since the end of the 1970s a wide range of differently operationalised cross-sectional studies have been carried out.

Using 16PF Siegler, George and Okun (1979) studied 331 men and women aged 54-70 and found no age differences in terms of N-like traits such as vigilance, tension and apprehension. Nor were there any age-related differences in terms of E-like traits such as warmth, self-reliance, boldness and group dependence. And nor were there any differences in terms of O-like traits such as sensitivity, imagination and liberal thinking – or for C-like traits such as ego strength and self-control. 16PF does not operate with traits that can be assumed to belong under A (McCrae & Costa, 2003). In other words, Siegler, George and Okun's study indicates that the personality traits known as O, C, E and N are stable.

Using GZTS Douglas and Arenberg (1978) carried out a cross-sectional study of men who had originally been recruited for the Boston Longitudinal Study of Aging (BLSA). The first group (consisting of 605 men) was studied between 1958 and 1968, while the second group (310 men) was studied between 1968 and 1974. In terms of age the two groups ranged from 17 to 74. Masculinity was slightly lower in the elderly, and personal relations were slightly higher. No differences were found in terms of N-like traits such as emotional stability and objectivity. In terms of E-like traits GTZS revealed that general activity and dominance were lower in elderly people in both study groups, while sociability was lower in the first group but not in the second.

As far as C-like traits are concerned, Douglas and Arenberg found that consideration was more widespread in the elderly, while there were no age-related differences in terms of autonomy and the need to avoid harming others. In terms of A-like traits, friendliness, humility and self-control scored slightly more highly in the elderly, while the need for dominance and aggression scored lower. O-like traits such as thoughtfulness scored more highly in the elderly. In general, this study seems to reveal stability for N and a slight tendency towards lower E and slightly higher O, A and C.

Butcher et al. (1991) found only a few small differences in the MMPI profiles of two male groups aged 40 and 60 respectively. The scales for Depression (+N), Psychopathy (-A and -C), Hypomania (+E and -C) and Social Introversion (-E) showed small but statistically significant age differences: the older group scored higher in terms of Depression and Social Introversion, and lower in terms of Psychopathy and Hypomania.

Among other things, Warr, Miles and Platts (2001) compared CPI and MBTI scores from various British samples with an age range of 16-64. They found significant differences on a range of scales: for instance, older people were more conscientious and conservative but less social, extroverted and motivated for change.

Cummings (1995) used MBTI to study possible age differences in eight different age groups between 15 and 60 years old. Among other things, he found that older people had a greater need for structure and order (+N), and that they were more introverted (-E).

Using the Personality Research Form (PRF), Costa and McCrae (1988) studied correlations between age and personality traits in 296 men and women aged 22-90. This study population consisted of neighbours and friends of participants in the Baltimore Longitudinal Study of Aging.

No differences were found in terms of N-like traits such as the need for social recognition, the tendency to go on the defensive and the need for care. As far as E-like traits were concerned, age was negatively correlated with seeking attention and needing entertainment. There were no age differences as far as the need for social relations was concerned.

In terms of C-like traits – ambition, the need for order, perseverance, the need for cognitive structure (unambiguous categorisable information), low impulsiveness – no age differences were found.

With regard to O-like traits Costa and McCrae found that the need for change and sensitivity was lower in the elderly, while the need to understand the world around them was higher. A-like traits such as aggression and the need to dominate (-A) were less characteristic of the elderly. So the conclusion of this study indicates a slight tendency towards less O and more A, while there was no difference in terms of C and N.

Cross-sectional data from the extensive Berlin Age Study (BASE) indicates that personality traits are also relatively stable in people of great age (Smith & Baltes, 1999). Stability seems to continue until a very great age. However, the results of the BASE showed that Extraversion and Openness were lower in the elderly – while no significant changes were found with regard to Neuroticism.

Cross-cultural studies
Even though some researchers regret the international dominance of the FFM model (Bond, 2000; McCrae & Costa, 2003, p. 88), it does offer new potential for cross-sectional studies of personality traits. NEO PI-R has now been

translated to many different languages, so at the moment a wealth of information is being received from various cultures around the globe (McCrae & Costa, 2003, chapter 5). Among other things, this makes it possible to identify culture-historical influences on personality traits. From a culture-psychological perspective we might expect age-comparative cross-sectional studies from various cultures to show different cohort effects and therefore different results. The varying norms and values of different cultures presumably favour certain qualities at the expense of others, so we might also expect some qualities (and thereby traits) to be more widespread in some cultures than in others (e.g. Bruner, 1990; Gergen, 2001; Cushman, 1996). However, neither major differences in the spread of various traits nor major variation in age-related personality patterns across different cultures have been registered. In a range of different cultures (e.g. the US, Russia, Croatia, Germany, Portugal, South Korea, Turkey, the UK, Japan and China) it has been discovered that O and E fall while A and C increase with age. With the exception of studies in Italy and Croatia, where no age differences were found, studies from the other countries showed an age difference involving lower N in the older age groups (McCrae et al., 1999). Apart from a dubious argument based on increasing globalisation, it is hard to find any explanation other than the fact that FFM traits and their age-related changes seem to be universal, and that all the cross-sectional studies in various cultures support a hypothesis of general stability and minor age-related changes (O, E and N down a little and A and C up a little). This leads to the following questions: are these minor age-related changes related to the actual process of ageing; what are the mechanisms involved; and are the results due to general human changes of personality?

Longitudinal studies
While cross-sectional studies estimate the effect of age differences at a given point in time, longitudinal studies estimate the effect of age changes over time. Longitudinal studies enable us to see whether the personality changes, but not necessarily whether such changes are due to age. Many longitudinal studies suffer from the problem of a major drop-out rate and what is known as "test smartness", as well as demanding a lot of time and considerable cost. In particular, cost is the reason why relatively few personality studies have been carried out with this design. In connection with the National Aging Study (NAS) 1,000 of 2,000 volunteer men aged 25-90 were studied between 1965 and 1967 using 16PF. In 1975 139 of these men were studied again. These 139 men were originally aged 25-82. Only two of the 16 scales – intelligence and social independence – showed any change (an increase), while the other traits were stable (Costa & McCrae, 1976). This increased "intelligence" was probably

due to a design problem (in the first study there was a time limit which was not enforced in the second study) and test smartness (the participants had tried the test before). In addition, many trait psychologists (including the authors of this article) would not categorise intelligence as a personality trait. Social independence (-E) was the only E-related trait that changed, and the tendency has not been registered in other studies. In an eight-year longitudinal study of both men and women using 16PF, Siegler et al. (1979) found no changes for social independence, and increased "intelligence" was also found in this study. As far as guilt (N-related) was concerned, men scored lower as their age increased while women scored higher. Despite these minor differences between studies, the results seem in general to support the stability hypothesis.

Leon, Gillum, Gillum & Gooze (1979) studied the MMPI profiles of a group of physically and mentally healthy men over a period of 30 years from the age of about 50 to 80. Generally speaking these MMPI profiles were remarkably stable. Despite this general stability the participants did tend to score higher in the final test on the N-related scales for Hypochondria, Depression and Hysteria. However, Leon et al. attributed these changes to realistic concerns about age-related physical ailments rather than regarding them as a reflection of underlying personality traits. Stable MMPI profiles have subsequently been confirmed by other longitudinal studies (Pancoast & Archer, 1989; Greene, 1990; Trull, Useda, Costa & McCrae, 1995).

Costa, Herbst, McCrae & Siegler (2000) carried out an extensive longitudinal study of 2,274 participants. The statistical strength of a study involving so many participants is that it is capable of detecting even small changes. The participants were about 40 when the study started, and were studied for the second and third times six and nine years later. No major changes were registered (only minor ones), but a statistically significant decrease was registered in N, E and O while A and C were stable. Changes in the form of a decrease in N and E were also reported in a major Australian study involving the Eysenck Personality Questionnaire (Loehlin & Martin, 2001). Helson et al. carried out longitudinal studies using CPI lasting more than 40 years (Helson, Jones & Kwan, 2002). A relatively small continuous sample was involved, but the study showed significant changes indicating a decrease in N and E, while C increased with age. However, the changes were relatively small, being approximately one-third of a standard deviation.

Using CPI Jones, Livson & Peskin (2003) studied 279 individuals aged 33-75. Six of the 20 CPI scales showed significant linear change over the years. Flexibility (O), sociability (E) and empathy (A) fell; while self-control (C), socialisation (A) and dependence (N) increased.

In Scandinavian psychology the best known study of personality traits is surely Sol Seim's life-long study of a number of individuals who were observed from between 13 and 70 years of age (Seim, 1997; Haugen & Krüger, 1999). Seim's study is not a typical trait-psychology personality study. The traits in question are derived from the projective Rorschach test. In general Seim's studies confirm the findings regarding the stability of personality traits in adulthood (30-70 years old), but minor changes were also registered over the study period. Harmony, tolerance, the ability to make contact, the tendency to be less calculating and a more stable emotional life characterised the participants as they grew older. Some of these minor changes seem to support previous findings regarding increased A and C and reduced N; whereas the tendency towards lower E and O scores was not confirmed. For several reasons the results are difficult to compare with traditional trait studies, and nonconformities may be due to the fact that the traits in Seim's study were found based on a rather uncertain projective test. The fact is that the Rorschach test detects not only personality but also cognitive and perceptual skills as well. There are age-related changes in cognition and perception, so using this test could easily lead to misleading results. This has been convincingly argued by Eisdorfer (1963), who matched young and old people cognitively by using Wechsler's Adult Intelligence Scale (WAIS), according to which the differences revealed by the Rorschach test disappeared. Apart from the problems involved in the measuring tool used, Seim's life-long study only included a rather small number of participants. Confounding due to time and drop-out rates is also a possible explanation. In fact the most important aspect of Seim's study is perhaps that in general she found stability over such a long period of time.

The stability hypothesis is also supported by a relatively new meta-analysis of 81 longitudinal studies and 95 cohorts carried out by Bazana and Stelmack (2004). Based on their extensive analysis, the authors conclude that personality traits show evidence of considerable stability during the course of a lifetime.

Sequential studies
Baltes et al. (1977) and Schaie (1977) constructed a design which can exclude cohort confounding. The cross-sequential design, in which individuals from the same generation are tested at different times in relation to each other, has been used by Douglas & Arenberg (1978) and others. For their purpose they used two successively collected study groups from 1958-1968 and 1968-1974 respectively. All the participants were born at the same time, so there were no generation differences. Both groups were only tested once, so there was no risk of test smartness either. GZTS results from this study showed that older people scored lower than younger people on the scales of emotional stability, personal relations and masculinity (-N) (McCrae & Costa, 2003, p. 56). In other words,

in contrast to cross-sectional studies the result was that N seemed to increase with age. None of the other traits changed. Siegler et al. (1979) used 16PF to study 331 men and women over a period of eight years. The participants were between 54 and 70 years old during the first of a total of four studies. In general the results indicated stability and no significant differences across the cohorts, and no changes over time.

The Seattle Longitudinal Study (Schaie, 1996, 2005) focused primarily on intellectual changes, although it also included a number of personality parameters. The data came primarily from a test called the Test of Behavioral Rigidity, the purpose of which is to identify the degree of flexibility in people's attitudes. This test includes items from CPI's scale of Social Responsibility. Schaie found significant age differences in cross-section, but these could largely be explained by cohort differences. On the other hand, the sequential results also revealed few personality changes, although a moderately significant age-related decrease was found in terms of the personality traits known as ego strength (C) and threat activity (N), while there was a dramatic decline in honesty (C). Affectothymia (A) fell from youth to middle age, but then rose significantly during old age.

Summary
Across various trait-psychology operationalisations and test designs the general picture seems to indicate stability. However, there are some moderate age-related changes, primarily in the form of a tendency towards lower N, E and O and higher A and C.

Stability and causality

We can conclude that personality traits are generally stable during the ageing process. However, some studies spontaneously raise a question about the factors that influence trait stability. We have largely used study results illustrating absolute stability (the average degree of stability for a given population), so studies of differential stability (for instance) may display variations which could have been overlooked in this connection (Caspi & Roberts, 2001).

Stability – when?
McCrae & Costa (2003) have shown that personality traits experience the greatest change during the first part of life up to the age of 30, when they reach maximum stability. After this age there are only minor changes. However, an extensive meta-analysis of 150 cross-sectional studies of differential stability has demonstrated that personality traits do not reach maximum stability at the age of 30 – this point is reached at the age of 50-59 instead (Roberts & DelVecchio,

2000). This analysis also showed that the degree of stability increased in linear fashion with age, and that this occurred in stages: it increased dramatically at the age of 3-6, after which there was a slight decrease. Then it increased until the age of 18-21, with a major increase in early adulthood (22-29) and an even larger increase from the first to the second half of middle age. The degree of stability increased from 0.35 in childhood to 0.57 at the age of 30, and to 0.73 at the age of 50-59. The most stable dimensions were E and A (0.55), closely followed by the other three dimensions (0.50-0.52) (ibid, p. 17).

Stability and causality

It is obviously not possible in this chapter to include a complete discussion of the reasons for trait stability and possible changes. In many ways the complexity of the issue resembles the complexity of the nature-nurture discussion. Consequently, we will only make a few central points here, referring interested readers to Roberts & DelVecchio (2000), Caspi & Roberts (2001) and McCrae & Costa (2003) for a more detailed treatment of the issue.

According to McCrae and Costa's FFM, the gradual change in the degree of trait stability must be attributed primarily to physiological maturity because traits are regarded as being solely biologically determined (McCrae & Costa, 2003, pp. 190-192). However, this reductionistic perspective on the factors constituting traits contains a number of problems. For one thing, it seems difficult to explain the gradual increase in stability, and for another this perspective cannot explain the changes registered owing to environmental factors (in the form of extreme and long-term stress, for instance). In other words, it seems necessary to take our point of departure in a model which adopts a more dynamic and interactional perspective capable of integrating biological, psychological and contextual factors.

However, it is still not clear which biological processes and factors play a central role and how much importance should be attributed to inheritance and environmental factors respectively in relation to continuity and change. The results of longitudinal twin studies seem to be ambiguous. For instance, one study concludes that inheritance is the more important of the two factors (McGue, Bacon & Lykken, 1993); while others have found that the importance of inheritance does not exceed that of the environment, and the degree of stability is best explained using an interactionist model (Pedersen & Reynolds, 1998). The latter study also found that the importance of inheritance generally declined with age: recent events (so-called time-specific unshared environmental effects) should be regarded as the greatest source of variance for two of the dimensions measured (N, E). However, unshared environmental factors of a general nature had major importance for O, and the importance of inheritance did not decline to the same extent for this dimension compared with the other two (ibid).

The fact that recent events seem to influence N and E is confirmed in a longitudinal study in which a group of elderly people was monitored for 6-7 years (their average age was 74 at the start of the study). The aim was to illustrate the stability of personality traits and any connections between the timing of negative events and changes in personality traits (Maiden, Peterson, Caya & Hayslip, 2003). In general, moderate differential stability was found for the personality dimensions studied (N, E and O). Moderate changes were also found, as well as a significant connection between the negative events occurring during the study period and changes in N and E. The N level measured previously, the lack of new resources within recent years and a reduction in the availability of social support all predicted how much N would increase during the study period. E was reduced when major illness was present and when the need for new resources was increasingly ignored (ibid).

The items on the N scale measure facets such as fear, depression, anger and vulnerability among other things, so these changes are hardly surprising. However, it is a problem that the available data does not make it possible to decide whether we should see these changes as an expression of a temporary state due to stress and adversity in life, or whether we should see them as permanent changes and therefore changes in personality traits. The same problem applies with regard to changes in E: facets such as energy, activity and positive emotions are (not surprisingly) affected by poor health and a life situation characterised by insufficient resources. Consequently, it is important that as far as possible a distinction should be drawn between reversible and irreversible changes. This is a general issue facing studies whose aim is to illustrate the degree of stability of personality traits, since to some extent scores in personality tests may be influenced by the current situation of the individuals being tested (Maiden et al., 2003). However, it is possible that in some extreme cases environmentally conditioned changes may result in permanent changes in E and N, such as changes caused by stress-related hormonal changes causing changes in the neural basis of the personality. For instance, high levels of stress hormones such as cortisol may cause irreversible brain damage in the long term. Hormones can be influenced by environmental factors; and owing to the fact that hormones can activate or deactivate genes (McEwen, 1988; Larsen, 2003), and because genes presumably lie behind personality, it is probable that the environment can influence the biological basis of the personality in this way. And indeed connections have been found between personality traits and hormone levels (Larsen, 2003).

Another perspective from which the stability of personality traits can be explained takes its point of departure in the idea that we interact with the world around us on an ongoing basis, and that in this dynamic interaction we influence our surroundings – as they influence us. Viewed from this perspective it has been pointed out that stable relations with and factors related to the world around us (marriage, roles, work relationships and friends) support stable personality traits (Caspi & Roberts, 2001; Roberts & DelVecchio, 2000). The aspects emphasised in this connection include the fact that the demands and reactions of the world around us do not change significantly, including the potential provided by your context for pursuing your own goals and interests (Caspi & Roberts, 2001). The social-cognitive tradition, which has been particularly critical with regard to trait psychology, also emphasises the relative stability that can be found in the cognitive system, including behavioural competences and self-regulating systems, values and goals as well as convictions about options for action and energy in specific situations (Cervone, 1997; Mischel & Shoda, 1995). One of the explanations of increasing stability in personality traits is that over time (from childhood to adulthood) there is an increasing degree of concord between the characteristics of a person (interests, goals, competences) and the surrounding world (Roberts & DelVecchio, 2000). One of the reasons for this is that each individual increasingly develops a range of competences, including skills in pursuing and achieving their own goals; and that each person tries to find contexts and situations which match his/her personal characteristics. Finally, these characteristics are also influenced by the world around us (Mischel & Shoda, 1995; Roberts & DelVecchio, 2000; Lazarus, 1991). Consequently, new situations or rather significant changes in one or more context, resulting in irreversible changes both in relations with the world around us and in the concord existing between personal characteristics and context, will influence the processes that promote stability and thereby lead to changes in personality traits. In addition, new situations mean that individuals need to develop new competences, including abandoning old goals and values and possibly focusing on new ones. According to Roberts (1997), this can be observed in business life, for instance, where employment in prestigious positions leads to changes in E and C. The study mentioned above, which probably showed changes of personality traits owing to negative life changes (Maiden et al., 2003) can also be understood from this perspective: it is changes in stability-promoting relations with the world around us that lead to changes in personality traits. However, this perspective is not without its problems. For instance, neither Roberts (1997) nor Maiden et al. (2003) tried to assess the duration of the changes they found; and nor did they prove that the changes apply no matter what the situation in question – making it difficult to assess whether trait changes have really occurred. In addition, it is necessary to define the interaction between individuals and the world around them in greater detail in order to assess the extent to which life changes or problematic events can be regarded as one single process of events, with the consequences this may imply (Lazarus, 1991; Folkman & Moskowitz, 2004; Somerfield & McCrae, 2000). Failure to do this leads to the risk of confusing reactions that seek to handle problems with the actual consequences of such problems for wellbeing, self-understanding or even personality traits. In this connection it is worth mentioning that signs of reduced wellbeing or crisis (+N) may be due to passive resignation caused by the feeling that you are unable to change your situation, leading to a sense of helplessness (Munk, 1999; Seligman, 1975). Even though the state may be long-lasting, leading to negative consequences such as depression, it can of course also be changed both by supplying compensatory resources and by administering psycho-pharmaceutical treatment or psychotherapeutic intervention. So there is good reason to study changes in relations with the world around us in detail with a view to distinguishing between permanent and temporary consequences or reactions. Finally, it should be mentioned that there may be big differences in the degree to which situations allow personality to be expressed (Carver & Scheier, 2000). For instance, a Sunday picnic in the woods allows considerable freedom for the expression of personality, while participation in a military exercise only allows very limited freedom. The significance of a situation for the personality must be expected to be greatest at action level, growing less as we move up through various personality criteria from action to habits, traits and dimensions respectively (Larsen & Winsløv, 2005, p. 25).

Pathological changes

We will now briefly discuss a range of factors which may lead to personality changes despite the overall picture of stability.

Moderate somatic complaints do not seem to affect personality traits significantly (Costa, Metter & McCrae, 1994), which matches the fact that personality traits are generally stable in the elderly even though somatic complaints grow increasingly frequent with age (Schaie & Willis, 2002). However, complaints such as urinary tract infections, dehydration, certain forms of vitamin deficiency and hormonal imbalances will result in significant but reversible changes in behaviour and personality (Gulmann, 2001, chapter 4).

The same does not apply to substance abuse (Gulmann, 2001, p. 8), the influences of pharmaceuticals (Kramer, 1997; Kunik, Yudofsky, Silver & Hales, 1994), mental illness (Hirschfeld, Klerman, Clayton et al., 1983; Kramer, 1997), neuro-pathology (Chatterjee, Strauss, Smyth & Whitehouse, 1992; Hawkins & Trobst, 2000) and brain trauma (Costa & McCrae, 2000; Golden & Golden,

2003), all of which may cause significant personality changes. Particularly significant changes occur in connection with dementia and brain damage in the frontal regions (Hawkins & Trobst, 2000; Neary & Snowden, 1996; Lebert, Pasquier & Petit, 1995). These changes will typically involve a major increase in N and reduced E, O, A and C. The frequency of personality changes in elderly people suffering from dementia is extremely high (Finkel, 1997). In great age the symptoms of dementia are common (Schaie & Willis, 2002), so personality changes must be expected to occur more frequently at this stage of life.

As mentioned above, traumatic experiences and extreme stress are also related to personality changes. However, it is less clear whether such changes are temporary or permanent. It has been proved that long-term stress and associated adrenergic dysfunction can cause structural changes in the limbic system (McEwen, Gould & Sakai, 1992). Unless very long-term stress is involved, such changes are reversible. However, the question of causality in connection with traumatic experiences is not easy to resolve. It has been proved that individuals with pre-morbid trait constellations resembling those observed in traumatised individuals (high N in particular) seem to be liable to a higher trauma risk (Lauterbach & Vrana, 2001).

Significant changes in personality seem largely to be linked to pathological changes in the brain. The typical changes are higher N and lower E, O, A and C. So pathological changes, particularly in the form of higher N and lower A and C, will be clearly different than the minor age-related changes seen in normal ageing.

Practical perspectives

In conclusion we will outline the potential practical implications of the knowledge that has been gained. The psychological treatment of cognitively well-preserved elderly people, the early identification of dementia, and care for infirm elderly people with reduced mental functions are some of the areas in which this knowledge might be applied.

It has been shown that people of a certain personality type experience the greatest wellbeing in early adulthood (Type A), while others experience greater wellbeing when they are elderly (people with a Type B personality). Strube et al. found that Type A individuals, who were energetic, impatient and aggressive, felt best when they had a hectic career – but found it difficult to adjust to a quieter life when they became elderly. By contrast, Type B individuals, who were more phlegmatic by nature, functioned better when they became elderly (Strube, 1985). Consequently, the advice of psychologists when it comes to planning your old age and retirement will vary depending on which type of personality you have. Type A individuals should perhaps postpone their retirement for as long as possible and then try to find work-like recreational pursuits for themselves; while Type B individuals might be well advised to stop work early and leave themselves plenty of time to enjoy their retirement.

Viewed from the perspective of the clinical psychologist, assessing the personality traits of clients may be one way in which psychologists can systematically explore the strengths of their clients and use these strengths in their therapeutic work (Costa, Yang & McCrae, 1998). For instance, it is assumed that a high A score has a positive role with regard to the formation of the therapeutic alliance (Miller, 1991); that a high O score means a high degree of personal flexibility and therefore willingness to accept change; and that a high C score may mean that clients work consistently and hard towards therapeutic goals.

The stability of personality traits might lead the clinical psychologist to focus less on changing the client's "negative" traits (high N, for instance) and instead direct their efforts towards teaching the client new strategies for use in handling the interaction between their personality and a variety of contexts.

The psychological treatment of the elderly often contains psycho-educative elements: clients can learn strategies that are adapted to their personality and their current age-related problems. Apart from interventions targeting (for instance) a pessimistic attribution style, extremely extrovert elderly people may need strategies designed to maintain their social network as far as possible; while very nervous elderly people may need strategies designed to avoid highly stimulating social contexts.

It is also important to remember that different forms of personality may require different forms of treatment. Therapy consisting of a great deal of talking and sharing your experiences and feelings in a group-therapy context will probably appeal to clients who are highly extrovert; while highly introvert clients may benefit more from written tasks and psycho-pharmacological treatment (Costa, Yang & McCrae, 1988).

One of the main themes in processes of therapy involving old people who have already lived the major part of their lives involves reconciling yourself with the life you have lived (Butler, 1963). Retrospectively there will always be a number of things that old people wish had been different, and in such circumstances the therapist may be able to help identify characteristic tendencies to act that (for better or worse) would have been very difficult to change – thereby helping the client to reconcile themselves with the life they have lived.

Knowledge of the stability of personality can also be used to detect early signs of neuro-pathology. As outlined above, significant personality changes leading to higher N and lower E, O, A and C are connected with serious pathology. In the case of early dementia, the family and friends often notice changes in behaviour and personality before they recognise cognitive debilities. Information about the connection between personality and dementia will equip the people caring for the elderly (both personal and professional carers) to detect early signs of dementia and thereby provide early medical and psychological treatment.

Knowledge of personality traits can also be used by carers looking after infirm elderly people with a reduced functional level. In Denmark more than half of all the residents of care homes suffer from some degree of dementia (Sørensen, 2001). As their illness progresses, most of these elderly people suffering from dementia will be affected by personality changes. One important element in individual care for elderly people suffering from dementia involves organising everyday activities to comply with the personality of the person concerned (Kitwood, 1999). Unless the context matches the personality, the result will often be suffering and problematic behaviour. Consequently, it is also necessary to adjust the context and communication on an ongoing basis to match the changes occurring as the illness progresses. These are large demands to make on carers, many of whom have relatively short training courses behind them. And this is why the care sector must be regarded as a central area of focus for geropsychology in future.

REFERENCES

Bazana, P.G. & Stelmack, R.M. (2004). Stability of Personality Across the Life Span: A Meta-analysis. In: Stelmack, R.M. (Ed.), *On the psychobiology of personality – Essays in Honor of Marvin Zuckerman*. Oxford: Elsevier Ltd.

Baltes, P.B., Reese, H.W., & Nesselroade, J.R. (1977). *Life-span developmental psychology: Introduction to research methods*. Monterey, CA: Brooks/Cole.

Bond, M.H. (2000). Localizing the imperial outreach: The Big Five and more in Chinese culture. *American Behavioral Scientist, 44,* 63-72.

Bruner, J. (1990). Culture and Human-Development – A New Look. *Human Development, 33,* 344-355.

Borgatta, E.F. (1964). The structure of personality characteristics. *Behavioral Science, 12,* 8-17.

Butcher, J.N., Levenson, M.R., Spiro, A., Aldwin, C.M., BenPorath, Y.S., & Bosse, R. (1991). Personality and Aging – A Study of the Mmpi-2 Among Older Men. *Psychology and Aging, 6,* 361-370.

Butler, R.N. (1963). Life Review – An Interpretation of Reminiscence in Aged. *Psychiatry, 26,* 65-76.

Carver, C.S. & Scheier, M.F. (2000). *Perspectives on Personality* (4 ed., 56-89). Needham Heights: Allyn and Bacon.

Caspi, A. & Roberts, B.W. (1999). Personality Continuity and Change across the Life Course. In: L.A. Pervin & O.P. John (Eds.), *Handbook of Personality: Theory and research.* 2. ed., 300-326. New York: The Guilford Press.

Caspi, A. & Roberts, B.W. (2001). Personality development across the life course: The argument for change and continuity. *Psychological Inquiry, 12,* 49-66.

Cervone, D. (1997). Social-cognitive mechanisms and personality coherence: Self-knowledge, situational beliefs, and cross-situational coherence in perceived self-efficacy. *Psychological Science, 8,* 43-50.

Chatterjee, A., Strauss, M.E., Smyth, K.A., & Whitehouse, P.J. (1992). Personality Changes in Alzheimers-Disease. *Archives of Neurology, 49,* 486-491.

Costa, P.T., Herbst, J.H., McCrae, R.R., & Siegler, I.C. (2000). Personality at midlife: Stability, intrinsic maturation, and response to life events. *Journal of Personality Assessment, 7,* 365-378.

Costa, P.T. & McCrae, R.R. (1976). Age-Differences in Personality Structure – Cluster Analytic Approach. *Journals of Gerontology, 31,* 564-570.

Costa, P.T. & McCrae, R.R. (1988). Personality in Adulthood – A 6-Year Longitudinal-Study of Self-Reports and Spouse Ratings on the Neo Personality-Inventory. *Journal of Personality and Social Psychology, 54,* 853-863.

Costa, P.T. & McCrae, R.R. (1992). *Revised NEO Personality Inventory (NEO-PI-R) and NEO Five-Factor Inventory (NEO-FFI) Professional Manual.* Odessa, FL: Psychological Assessment Resources.

Costa, P.T. & McCrae, R.R. (2000). Comtemporary personality psychology. In: C.E. Coffey & J.L. Cummings (Eds.), *Textbook of geriatric psychiatry.* 2., ed., 453-462. Washington, D.C.: American Psychiatric Press.

Costa, P.T. & McCrae, R.R. (2004). *NEO PI-R Manual – klinisk.* København: Dansk psykologisk Forlag.

Costa, P.T., Metter, E.J., & McCrae, R.R. (1994). Personality Stability and Its Contribution to Successful Aging. *Journal of Geriatric Psychiatry, 27,* 41-59.

Costa, P.T., Yang, J. & McCrae, R.R. (1998). Aging and Personality Traits: Generalizations and clinical Implications. In Nordhus, VandenBos, Berg & Fromholt (Eds.). *Clinical Geropsychology.* Washington, DC: American Psychological Association.

Cummings, W.H. (1995). Age Group-Differences and Estimated Frequencies of the Myers-Briggs Type Indicator Preferences. *Measurement and Evaluation in Counseling and Development, 28,* 69-77.

Cushman, P. (1996). *Constructing the self, constructing America: A cultural history of psychotherapy.* Addison-Wesley/Addison Wesley Longman, Inc.

De Fruyt, F. & Mervielde, I. (1996). Personality and interests as predictors of educational streaming and achievement. *European Journal of Personality, 10,* 405-425.

Douglas, K. & Arenberg, D. (1978). Age-Changes, Cohort Differences, and Cultural-Change on Guilford-Zimmerman Temperament Survey. *Journals of Gerontology, 33,* 737-747.

Eisdorfer, C. (1963). Rorschach Performance and Intellectual-Functioning in the Aged. *Journals of Gerontology, 18,* 358-363.

Erikson, E.H. (1998). *The Life Cycle Completed.* New York: W.W. Norton & Company.

Eysenck, H.J. & Eysenck, M.W. (1985). *Personality and Individual Differences – A Natural Science Approach*. New York: Plenum Press.

Eysenck, H.J. & Eysenck, S.B.G. (1991). *Eysenck Personality Scales (EPS Adult)*. London: Hodder & Stoughton.

Folkman, S. & Moskowitz, J.T. (2004). Coping: Pitfalls and promise. *Annual Review of Psychology, 55*, 745-774.

Finkel, S. (1997). Behavioural and psychological signs and symptoms of dementia. *International Journal of Geriatric Psychiatry, 12*, 1060-1061.

Fiske, D.W. (1949). Consistency of the factorial structures of personality ratings from different sources. *Journal of Abnormal and Social Psychology, 44*, 329-44.

Gergen, K.J. (2001). Psychological science in a postmodern context. *American Psychologist, 56*, 803-813.

Golden, Z. & Golden, C. (2003). Impact of Brain Injury Severity on Personlaity Dysfunction. *International Journal of Neuroscience, 113*, 733-745.

Greene, R.L. (1990). Stability of MMPI Scale Scores Within 4 Codetypes Across 40 Years. *Journal of Personality Assessment, 55*, 1-6.

Gulmann, N.C. (2001). *Praktisk gerontopsykiatri*. 3 ed., København: Hans Reitzels Forlag.

Hartmann, P. (2006). The Five-Factor Model: Psychometric, biological and practical perspectives. *Nordisk Psykologi, 58*, 150-170.

Haugen, P.K. & Krüger, R.E. (1999). *Din tanke er din skæbne – Sol Seim og hennes forskning*. Tore Mårds: Akribe.

Hawkins, K.A. & Trobst, K.K. (2000). Frontal lobe dysfunction and aggression: Conceptual issues and research findings. *Aggression and Violent Behavior, 5*, 147-157.

Helson, R., Jones, C., & Kwan, V.S.Y. (2002). Personality change over 40 years of adulthood: Hierarchical linear modeling analyses of two longitudinal samples. *Journal of Personality and Social Psychology, 83*, 752-766.

Hirschfeld, R.M.A., Klerman, G.L., Clayton, P.J., Keller, MacDonald-Scott, P. & Larkin, B.H. (1983). Assessing Personality: Effects of depressive states on trait measurement. *American Journal of Psychiatry, 140*, 695-699.

John, O.P., Angleitner, A., & Ostendorf, F. (1988). The Lexical Approach to Personality: A Historical Review of Trait Taxonomic Research. *European Journal of Personality, 2*, 171-203.

John, O.P. & Srivastava, S. (1999): The big five trait taxonomy: History, Measurement and Theoretical Perspectives. In: Pervin, L.A. & John, O.P. (Eds.), *Handbook of Personality: Theory and Research*. 2. ed., 102-138, New York: The Guilford Press.

Joireman, J. & Kuhlman, D.M. (2004). The Zuckerman-Kuhlman Personality Questionnaire: Origin, Development, and Validity of a Measure to Assess an Alternative Five-Factor Model of Personality. In: R.M. Stelmack (Ed.), *On the Psychobiology of Personality* 49-64. Oxford: UK: Elsevier.

Jones, C.J., Livson, N., & Peskin, H. (2003). Longitudinal hierarchical linear modeling analyses of California psychological inventory data from age 33 to 75: An examination of stability and change in adult personality. *Journal of Personality Assessment, 80*, 294-308.

Kitwood, T. (1999). *En revurdering af demens*. 1 ed., Frederikshavn: Dafolo Forlag.

Kramer, A.M. (1997). Rehabilitation care and outcomes from the patient's perspective. *Medical Care, 35*, 48-57.

Kunik, M.E., Yudofsky, S.C., Silver, J. M., & Hales, R.E. (1994). Pharmacological Approach to Management of Agitation Associated with Dementia. *Journal of Clinical Psychiatry, 55*, 13-17.

Larsen, L. (2003). *Testosterone as a factor in psychological and behavioral traits.* Psykologisk Instituts Ph.d.-skriftserie. Aarhus: Psykologisk Institut, Aarhus Universitet.

Larsen, L. & Winsløv, J-H. (2005). Stadig mig selv efter alle disse år – om den aldrende personlighed. In: Larsen, L. & Winsløv, J.H. (eds.), Tema: Gerontopsykologi. *Nordisk Psykologi, 57 (1)*, 21-46.

Lauterbach, D. & Vrana, S. (2001). The Relationship Among Personality Variables, Exposure to Traumatic Events, and Severity of Posttraumatic Stress Symptoms. *Journal of Traumatic Stress, 14*, 29-45.

Lazarus, R.S. (1991). *Emotion and adaptation.* New York: Oxford University Press.

Lebert, F., Pasquier, F., & Petit, H. (1995). Personality traits and frontal lobe dementia. *International Journal of Geriatric Psychiatry, 10*, 1047-1049.

Leon, G.R., Gillum, B., Gillum, R. & Gooze, M. (1979). Personality stability and change over a 30-year period-middle age to old age. *Journal of Consulting and Clinical Psychology, 47*, 517-524.

Lewis-Beck, M.S. (1994). *Factor analysis and related techniques.* London: Sage.

Loehlin, J.C. & Martin, N.G. (2001). Age changes in personality traits and their heritabilities during the adult years: evidence from Australian Twin Registry samples. *Personality and Individual Differences, 30*, 1147-1160.

Maiden, R.J., Peterson, S.A., Caya, M. & Hayslip, B. (2003). Personality Changes in the Old-Old: A Longitudinal Study. *Journal of Adult Development, 10 (1)*, 31-39.

McCrae, R.R. & Costa, P.T. (1990). *Personality in Adulthood.* New York: The Guildford Press.

McCrae, R.R. & Costa, P.T. (2003). *Personality in Adulthood – A Five-Factor Theory Perspective.* 2 ed., New York: The Guilford Press.

McCrae, R.R., Costa, P.T., de Lima, M.P., Simoes, A., Ostendorf, F., Angleitner, A. et al. (1999). Age Differences in Personality Across the Adult Life Span: Parallels in Five Cultures. *Developmental Psychology, 35*, 466-477.

McCrae, R.R. & John, O.P. (1992). An Introduction to the Five-Factor Model and its Applications. *Journal of Personality, 60*, 175-215.

McDougall, W. (1932). Of the words character and personality. *Character and Personality; A Quarterly for Psychodiagnostics & Allied Studies, 1*, 3-16.

McEwen, B.S. (1988). Steroid-Hormones and the Brain – Linking Nature and Nurture. *Neurochemical Research, 13*, 663-669.

McEwen, B.S., Gould, E.A., & Sakai, R.R. (1992). The Vulnerability of the Hippocampus to Protective and Destructive Effects of Glucocorticoids in Relation to Stress. *British Journal of Psychiatry, 160*, 18-24.

McGue, M., Bacon, S., & Lykken, D.T. (1993). Personality Stability and Change in Early Adulthood – A Behavioral Genetic-Analysis. *Developmental Psychology, 29*, 96-109.

Miller, T. (1991). The psychotherapeutic utility of the five-factor model of personlity: A clinician's experience. *Journal of Personality Assessment, 57*, 415-433.

Mischel, W. & Shoda, Y. (1995). A Cognitive-Affective System-Theory of Personality – Reconceptualizing Situations, Dispositions, Dynamics, and Invariance in Personality Structure. *Psychological Review, 102*, 246-268.

Munk, K.P. (1999). *Belastninger i Alderdommen*. Aarhus, Denmark: Institut for Filosofi, Aarhus Universitet.

Neary, D. & Snowden, J. (1996). Fronto-temporal dementia: Nosology, neuropsychology, and neuropathology. *Brain and Cognition, 31*, 176-187.

Neugarten, B.L. (1977). Personality and Aging. In: J.E. Birren & K.W. Schaie (Eds.), *Handbook of the psychology of aging* 1 ed., 626-649. New York: Van Nostrand Reinhold.

Norman, W.T. (1963). Toward an adequate taxonomy of personality attributes: replicated factor structure in peer nomination personality ratings. *Journal of Abnormal and Social Psychology, 66*, 574-83.

Pancoast, D.L. & Archer, R.P. (1989). Original Adult MMPI Norms in Normal Samples – A Review with Implications for Future-Developments. *Journal of Personality Assessment, 53*, 376-395.

Pedersen, N.L. & Reynolds, C.A. (1998). Stability and change in adult personality: Genetic and environmental components. *European Journal of Personality, 12*, 365-386.

Popper, K.R. (1935). *Logik der Forschung*. Wien: Springer.

Roberts, B.W. (1997). Plaster or plasticity: Are adult work experiences associated with personality change in women? *Journal of Personality, 65*, 205-232.

Roberts, B.W. & DelVecchio, W.F. (2000). The rank-order consistency of personality traits from childhood to old age: A quantitative review of longitudinal studies. *Psychological Bulletin, 126*, 3-25.

Ryff, C.D., Kwan, C.M.L. & Singer, B.H. (2001). Personality and Aging. In: J.E. Birren & K. Warner Schaie (Eds.), *Handbook of the psychology of aging*. 5. ed. 477-499, San Diego: Academic Press.

Saucier, G. & Goldberg, L.R. (1996). The Language of Personality: Lexical Perspectives on the Five-Factor Model. In: J.S. Wiggins (Ed.), *The Five-Factor Model of Personality: Theoretical Perspectives*, 21-50, New York: The Guildford Press.

Schaie, K.W. (1977). Quasi-experimental research designs in the psychology of aging. In: J.E. Birren & K.W. Schaie (Eds.). *Handbook of the psychology of aging*, 36-69. New York: Van Nostrand Reinhold.

Schaie, K.W. (1996). *Intellectual development in adulthood: the Seattle longitudinal study*. New York: Cambridge University Press.

Schaie, K.W. (2005). *Developmental influences on adult intelligence: The Seattle Longitudinal Study*. New York: Oxford University Press.

Schaie, W.K. & Willis, S.L. (2002). Research Methodology in Adult Development and Aging. In: K.W. Schaie & S.L. Willis (Eds.). *Adult Development and Aging*, 109-129. New Jersey: Prentice Hall.

Seim, S. (1997). *Tenåringen blir pensjonist, Rep. No. 23/97*. Oslo: Norsk institutt for forskning om opvekst, velferd og aldring.

Seligman, M.E.P. (1975). *Helplessness. On depression, development and Death*. San Francisco: Freeman

Siegler, I.C., George, L.K., & Okun, M.A. (1979). Cross-Sequential Analysis of Adult Personality. *Developmental Psychology, 15*, 350-351.

Smith, J. & Baltes, P.B. (1999). Changes in profiles of functioning in the old and oldest old. *Zeitschrift fur Gerontologie und Geriatrie, 32,* 42.

Somerfield, M.R. & McCrae, R.R. (2000). Stress and coping research: Methodological challenges, theoretical advances, and clinical applications. *American Psychologist 55 (6):* 620-625.

Strube, M.J., Berry, J.M., Goza, B.K., & Fennimore, D. (1985). Type-A Behavior, Age, and Psychological Well-Being. *Journal of Personality and Social Psychology, 49,* 203-218.

Sørensen, L.U. (2001). *Psychiatric morbidity and the use of psychotropics in Danish nursing homes, (Rep. No. 31).* Institut for Epidemiologi og Socialmedicin.

Thurstone, L.L. (1934). Primary Mental Abilities. *Psychometric Monographs, 1.*

Trull, T. J., Useda, J. D., Costa, P.T., & McCrae, R.R. (1995). Comparison of the MMPI-2 personality psychopathology five (PSY-5), the NEO-PI, and the NEO-PI-R. *Psychological Assessment, 7,* 508-516.

Tupes, E.C. & Christal, R.E. (1992). Recurrent Personality Factors Based on Trait Rating. *Journal of Personality, 60 (2),* 225-251.

Warr, P., Miles, A., & Platts, C. (2001). Age and personality in the British population between 16 and 64 years. *Journal of Occupational and Organizational Psychology, 74,* 165-199.

THE AGEING INTELLECT

Erik Lykke Mortensen

Summary

In this chapter the focus is on observational studies of ageing and intellectual functions. A detailed account is given of studies of the Glostrup 1914 cohort, which was followed using Wechsler's intelligence test over a 40-year period from the age of 50 to the age of 90. It is shown that in longitudinal studies with sufficiently long follow-up periods at a high age there is substantial decline in intellectual function and that in general the Danish results are fully in accordance with the results of Schaie's Seattle Longitudinal Study, which is based on a complex cohort-sequential design with participants from seven birth cohorts. This means that age-related changes in intellectual functions are not a myth but a reality, even though significant changes were not observed in the 1914 cohort until the age of 70. There are substantial individual differences with regard to age-related changes in intellectual functions, but in the 1914 cohort it has been difficult to identify consistent predictors of individual differences.

Introduction

A wide range of literature is now available on ageing and intellectual functioning. Briefly, this literature can be divided into two categories describing experimental and observational research respectively. Experimental research into age and intellectual functions seeks to illuminate cognitive processes in young and elderly individuals to identify age-related changes in for example attention and memory processes (e.g. Craik & Salthouse, 1992). Experimental studies often focus on very specific issues concerning cognitive processes, and the large amount of detailed observations means that these studies contribute only little to a general picture of age-related changes in intellectual functions.

Observational research based on psychometric tests supplemented by questionnaires and interviews focuses instead on a general description of age-related changes in intellectual functions. A survey of both empirical data and theory in this area can be found in Salthouse (1991). It is characteristic that such studies seek both to achieve general descriptions of age-related changes in cognitive functions, and to describe and understand individual differences with regard to age-related changes in intellectual functions (Mortensen, 2000).

A survey of much of the literature on ageing and cognition was published in Danish about 10 years ago (Stuart-Hamilton, 2001) and can of course be found in international text and handbooks on the subject (Birren & Schaie, 2001). It should be added that the literature on age-related changes in cognitive functions has largely focused on changes in the average level of performance in psychometric and experimental cognitive tests, while there has been less focus on individual differences and the development of the individual through the life course. The literature typically deals with changes in performance level in studies focusing on the mean performance of groups of individuals or population samples, while changes and stability in the performance of single individuals compared to age peers are normally illustrated by using correlation coefficients. Naturally, both of these aspects are important, and an increasing number of studies are now being published aiming to identify predictors of individual differences in age-related changes in cognitive functions (cf. Waldstein & Elias, 2001).

Historical background

Already with the testing of American recruits during the First World War, a negative correlation became apparent between age and test results: recruits in their 20s achieved better test results than older age groups (Salthouse, 1991). The association between age and test scores was found not only on the American draft board intelligence test, but also in the normative data collected by Wechsler for the Wechsler Bellevue in 1939 and the WAIS in 1955. However, recruitment and standardisation data are naturally based on a cross-sectional population sample at a specific point in time, and at an early stage various sources of error appeared in comparisons of test performance of different age groups (e.g. generation differences in education or differences in the selection of age groups). Wechsler (1958) did not believe that these sources of error in cross-sectional studies could explain the relatively low test performances of older age groups. Among other things, he compared the age-related decline in intellectual functions with a corresponding age-related decline in the weight of the brain (cf. Wechsler, 1958, p. 206). However, he also pointed out that only few longitudinal studies had followed the same individuals over long time periods, a study design which would make it possible to analyse changes in intellectual functions in the same individual.

During the following decades the results of a number of longitudinal studies were published. In general these studies showed no age-related decline in test performance – or much less decline than observed in cross-sectional studies; and for a while the "myth" of age-related decline was discussed (cf. Baltes & Schaie, 1974; Lambrechtsen, 1976). At first it was often forgotten that longitudinal studies also contain sources of error (e.g. retest effects and selective drop-out) and that naturally most of the first available studies reported results based on relatively short follow-up periods in individuals who had not yet reached high age. One of the main objectives of this chapter is to describe the age-related changes found in studies which assess intelligence in individuals at high age and can compare these results with the participants' cognitive performance at an entirely different stage of their life span. Thus, a relatively detailed account will be given of the results obtained in Denmark by following a single cohort (the Glostrup 1914 cohort) over a very long time period using Wechsler's intelligence test. The Danish results will be compared with the results of other longitudinal studies of ageing and intellectual function, but no attempt will be made to present a thorough review of the vast amount of literature on this subject.

Schaie's studies

The apparent effects of age in cross-sectional studies may be mistaken for generation differences. This is important in the study of ageing and intellectual function, since in most Western countries a trend towards improved performance in intelligence tests has been observed (Neisser, 1998). In Denmark Tom Teasdale has convincingly demonstrated generation differences in performance in the draft board intelligence (e.g. Teasdale & Owen, 1989). The tendency for younger generations to perform better than older generations means that the observed differences between age groups in cross-sectional studies reflect not only age differences but also generation differences. In this perspective one of the major advantages of longitudinal studies is that they make it possible to monitor directly changes in intellectual functions as the individual grows older. However, longitudinal studies may be influenced by factors such as retest effects and changes in social and living conditions which directly or indirectly influence test performance and thereby cause associations between testing time (time period) and test performance. It is sometimes difficult to assess the importance of such factors because the effects of age and testing time cannot be separated in longitudinal studies in which a single cohort is tested at several points in time. In attention and memory tests testing time would not be expected to have a substantial impact on the results, but this cannot be excluded in verbal WAIS subtests such as Information, Vocabulary and Arithmetic since testing time may influence how many people know that Rome is the capital of Italy, how many people can explain the meaning of the word "energy", and how many people are used to doing mental arithmetic instead of using a calculator.

In an attempt to avoid the problems of "pure" cross-sectional and longitudinal studies, Schaie in particular has emphasised the advantage of combining the two study designs, making it possible to analyze longitudinal changes in intellectual performance for several cohorts in a so-called cohort-sequential design (Schaie 1977, 1996, for instance). Schaie implemented the technique in the Seattle Longitudinal Study which is described in Schaie (1996, 2005). This study started in 1956 with the assessment of 500 individuals selected from cohorts born in 1889, 1896, 1903, 1910, 1917, 1924 and 1931. Further studies were carried out in 1963, 1970, 1977, 1984, 1991 and 1998. Each study was conducted partly as a follow-up study of birth cohorts who had already been studied once or more times, and partly as a new cross-sectional study of selected age cohorts. As an example in 1956 the 1889 cohort was 67 years old and the results for this cohort could be compared with the 1896 and 1903 cohorts because these cohorts were 67 in 1963 and 1970 respectively. This makes it possible to analyze differences between birth cohorts or generations as well as to compare the results of participants who had taken part in previous studies with the results of new participants being tested for the first time, thereby making it possible to assess retest effects. Finally, this technique makes it possible to carry out analyses controlling cohort and retest effects and evaluating any systematic effects associated with the testing time or test period.

The Glostrup 1914 cohort

Compared with Schaie's systematic but also complex sequential study design, the design of the Danish studies of the Glostrup 1914 cohort is relatively simple, comprising a number of follow-up studies of a single cohort born in 1914 (for a summary, see Avlund et al., 2004). Since this is a longitudinal study following the same individuals, generation differences have no impact on internal validity, whereas retest effects and the effects of testing time may influence the results. In addition, the focus on a single cohort is an obvious limitation with regard to estimating the extent to which the results can be generalized to earlier or later generations. Consequently, the external validity of the results for the 1914 cohort must be assessed by comparing the results with other longitudinal studies, and here the main emphasis will be on comparisons with the Seattle Longitudinal Study.

In 1964 a total of 698 individuals (391 men and 307 women) participated in the first psychological study of the 1914 cohort, and this 50 year baseline study was followed up by 60, 70, 75, 80, 85 and 90 year studies. Even though the natural drop-out rate was high, 121 and 78 of the original participants participated in the 85 and 90 year studies – which, with a 35-40 year follow-up period, must be regarded as unique. However, like other longitudinal studies, the 1914 cohort study was also affected by selective attrition (Siegler & Botwinick, 1979). Hess (1983) reported that the 101 non-participants in the 60 year follow-up performed significantly poorer on the WAIS at the age of 50 than the 528 participants in the 60 year follow-up and the group who had died in the intervening period. Similarly, Mortensen & Kleven (1993) reported that the 141 participants in the 50, 60 and 70 year studies achieved significantly better WAIS results than the remaining 154 participants tested by Kleven at the 50 year baseline study.

Since only a small proportion of the original 698 men and women participated in the most recent studies, it is important to distinguish between attrition as a result of mortality and drop-out due to other reasons. At the age of 50 no significant differences in WAIS scores were found between the 329 individuals who were still alive for the 80 year follow-up and the 367 individuals who had died in the intervening period (Mortensen & Høgh, 2001). However, this obviously does not answer the question of how well the 367 deceased individuals would have performed at the age of 80, had they been alive. This question may seem highly hypothetical and theoretical, but it is extremely relevant at a time when life expectancy is increasing and more people reach an age at which dementia is a serious problem.

Of the 329 original participants who were still alive, 189 participated in the 80 year follow-up and this group had performed much better on the WAIS at the 50 year baseline than the 140 participants who were still alive but who did not participate in the 80 year follow-up (Mortensen & Høgh, 2001). This result raises the question of how representative the participants in the 80 year follow-up were of the original 1914 cohort, but also compared to 80 year old Danes in general. When studying cognitive function at a high age in particular, it must be assumed that the individuals who participate generally tend to be cognitively well functioning – which means that most longitudinal studies underestimate age-related changes in intellectual functions. This is presumably also the case for the 1914 cohort, but both the 85 and 90-year follow-ups took place in the homes of the participants, which is like to reduce bias of this type.

General and specific cognitive functions

It is important to distinguish between descriptions of the cognitive processes or functions which are activated when an individual performs a specific task (attention, information processing and memory), and models describing the structure of the intellect based on studies of individual differences in cognitive functions (Mortensen, 2000). Most of the models describing individual differences adopt a hierarchical approach in which a distinction is drawn between cognitive skills at different levels. At the lowest level so-called primary factors are described, which are closely linked to groups of cognitive tests with high intercorrelations. At the next level secondary factors are derived from groups of primary factors correlating with each other, and finally, many models operate with a third level corresponding to a general cognitive factor, derived from correlations between the secondary factors and usually referred to as general intelligence or the *g* factor (see Cooper, 1998, for instance). The foundation of the hierarchical model is the fact that cognitive test scores almost always show positive intercorrelations, and that usually higher correlations are observed among related cognitive tests than between less closely related tests. Similar correlation patterns are observed between examination grades at school: all correlations are positive, and usually higher intercorrelations are observed among language subjects than between language subjects and science subjects, such as biology and physics (Mortensen, 2000).

Research on age-related changes in cognitive functions includes a wide range of literature focusing on specific cognitive functions such as reaction time, attention and memory (Stuart-Hamilton, 2001). A source of inspiration for such studies is neuro-psychology which focuses on specific cognitive functions and their neural basis. However, another line of research has primarily used psychometric test batteries, developed from studies of individual differences in cognitive skills. For instance, in the Seattle Longitudinal Study Schaie used Thurstone's (1938) battery of tests measuring primary mental abilities (Schaie, 1996): Spatial Orientation, Verbal Ability, Word Fluency, Number Skills, Perceptual Speed, Verbal Memory, and Inductive Reasoning (a total index of cognitive function was also calculated, corresponding to a traditional index of intelligence or IQ).

Ageing and various forms of intelligence

In the history of psychology there are of course many different conceptions of intelligence and of alternative forms of intelligence. One distinction which is particularly relevant to the study of age-related changes in intellectual functioning is the distinction between intellectual functions reflecting language and experience, and functions reflecting basic intellectual processes and thinking. For instance, Hebb (1949) distinguished between the original hereditary potential for intellectual development (intelligence A) and the intelligence actually developed in an individual (intelligence B). More familiar in geropsychology is the distinction between "fluid" and "crystallised" intelligence (Horn & Cattell, 1966), which focuses on the difference between tasks which require the ability to combine and understand logical relations and tasks which reflect knowledge and skills that have already been acquired. Studies typically reveal a considerable age-related decline in the first type of test, and minor changes or even improvement at relatively high age in the second type of test.

The distinction between fluid and crystallised intelligence has inspired a great deal of research, but it has also been criticised and modifed. For instance, Baltes et al. (1999) developed a two-component model distinguishing between "cognitive mechanics" (fluid intelligence) and "cognitive pragmatics" (crystallised intelligence). When interpreting age-related changes in intellectual functions, it is important that such distinctions point to the difference between two types of cognitive tests: 1) Tests of general knowledge and vocabulary which reflect the experience of a long life and the acquisition of knowledge, thereby largely reflecting the function of the brain through a substantial part of the life span (and to a lesser extent the current function and state of the brain); 2) Tests of reaction times and the ability to understand logical relations (e.g. Raven's matrices) which require current information processing and problem-solving, and primarily reflect the current state and function of the brain (and to a lesser extent the function of the brain during the course of life). Naturally, longitudinal studies show the greatest age-related decline in the cognitive tests that more or less directly reflect the state of the brain in elderly people, and in studies of the neural basis of individual differences in cognitive function, the strongest correlations are usually observed in this type of test (e.g. studies of patients suffering from brain damage). However, it is important to remember that it is misleading to distinguish sharply between the two types of intelligence and the various types of cognitive tasks, which most realistically should be regarded as the extreme poles on a dimension.

Wechsler's intelligence test

When the baseline study of the Glostrup 1914 cohort was initiated in 1964, Wechsler's intelligence test had just been translated into Danish, and there were only few other cognitive tests available in Danish. Consequently, the psychologists responsible for the study – Grethe Hess and Mogens Kleven – chose to administer the complete WAIS. In order to assess age-related changes in cognitive functions, the full WAIS was subsequently repeated at the 60, 70, 80 and

85 follow-ups (only some of the WAIS subtests were administered at the 75 and 90 follow-ups). This means that the strengths and weaknesses of the WAIS are an important aspect of the studies: on the one hand it is the most widely used clinical intelligence test and on the other hand the 11 subtests included in the WAIS do not constitute a complete cognitive or neuro-psychological test battery. The 11 subtests assess a range of different cognitive functions, but tests of learning and memory are not included. Many will consider this a major weakness in any study of age-related changes in intellectual functions since the WAIS cannot be used to assess age-related changes in learning and memory (see for example Stuart-Hamilton, 2001).

It is well-known that the WAIS test consists of six verbal subtests and five performance (non-verbal) subtests: Information, Comprehension, Similarities, Arithmetic, Digit Span, Vocabulary, Digit-Symbol, Picture Completion, Block Design, Picture Arrangement and Object Assembly (Wechsler, 1958). The verbal subtests assess general knowledge, comprehension, verbal abstraction, elementary arithmetic, vocabulary and immediate reproduction of series of digits. Four of the performance subtests require skills in analyzing and structuring visual impressions: one task involves detecting logical errors and things missing in pictures; another involves arranging "cartoon pictures" in a logical sequence; a third task involves positioning red and white squares to produce specific patterns; and a fourth is a simple jigsaw puzzle. The fifth task is a concentration and speed test, involving connecting numbers and specific symbols as quickly as possible. Verbal factors obviously influence the ability of any individual to analyse and structure visual impressions, and consequently the term "non-verbal tests" must not be taken too literally. In studies of age-related changes in cognitive functions it is important to remember that verbal subtests largely assess knowledge, while performance subtests make greater demands on active problem-solving and incorporate time limits, meaning that concentration and working speed influence test scores.

Roughly speaking the difference between verbal and performance IQ corresponds to the difference between "fluid" and "crystallised" intelligence, and virtually all studies of age-related changes using the WAIS have found larger decline in performance subtests than in verbal subtests. However, it should be pointed out that Wechsler's (1958) classic distinction between "hold" and "don't hold" subtests does not correspond to the distinction between verbal and performance subtests, because the "hold" subtests include Vocabulary, Information, Object Assembly and Picture Completion, while the "don't hold" subtests include Digit Span, Similarities, Digit-Symbol and Block Design. Thus, the "don't hold" subtests require some degree of here and now information processing and problem-solving, and this is the reason why age-related changes and impaired

scores as a result of brain damage are primarily observed on these subtests. However, it is now known that the "hold" subtests also show age-related changes and
to some degree are affected by brain damage. As a result, other techniques are
now used to estimate intellectual function in young adulthood before a patient
was affected by any brain damage. Instead of testing the meaning of words, as
done with the Vocabulary subtest, the pronunciation of loan words is tested
because this ability seems to be affected very little by age-related changes and
brain damage.

Based on the WAIS, scores are normally calculated on three levels corresponding to a hierarchical model of intelligence. The subtest level is the lowest
level, the Verbal and Performance IQ can be regarded as the intermediate level
corresponding to secondary cognitive factors, and the Total IQ may be considered a measure of the general intelligence factor. Over the years factor analysis has often been applied to the WAIS subtests, and the primary alternative
to traditional scoring is a three-factor model in which a distinction is drawn
between a verbal factor, a perceptual-organisational factor and an attention-
concentration factor (Hill et al., 1985). The traditional scoring of the WAIS
will be the basis of this presentation. All the WAIS subtests correlate with each
other; the Total IQ is an index of the average performance on all subtests, while
the Verbal and Performance IQ are indexes of the average performance on the
verbal and performance subtests respectively. All three IQ values are normally
derived by comparing the average performance levels to a representative sample
of similar age as the tested individual, since IQ is constructed to remain relatively
constant throughout the life course. This means that for traditionally derived
IQs it is not possible to monitor age-related changes in intellectual function.
To avoid this problem for the 1914 cohort, IQ is always derived using the test
performance at the 50 year baseline as standard. The WAIS results for the 698
participants at the 50 year baseline are described in detail in Hess (1974), while
the norms based on this sample are described in Kyng (1978).

The significance of intelligence over the life span

IQs are normally calculated by setting the mean IQ of the population at 100,
with an IQ above 100 representing above average performance and an IQ below
100 representing below average performance (Mortensen, 1998). The standard
deviation in the population is set at 15. Partly because the results of subtests
are transformed into a normal distribution (Mortensen & Gade, 1992), the
distribution of IQ corresponds roughly to a normal distribution in most large
population samples. As a result, roughly half of the population will have an IQ
in the normal range between 90 and 109. If well functioning normal individuals

(with an IQ of 110-119) and poorly functioning normal individuals (with an IQ of 80-89) are included, the normal range comprises about 80 per cent of the population. Poorly functioning individuals make up a relatively small proportion of the population, with about 7 per cent traditionally being categorised as backward (with an IQ of 70-79) and only about 2 per cent of the population being categorized as mentally retarded (with an IQ below 70).

In studies of large population samples IQ is usually observed to be associated with indicators of success in life such as occupation and education (Mortensen, 1998). The association between intelligence and education probably reflects one of the highest correlations between a mental ability and a demographic factor. However, these correlations are often no larger than about 0.50-0.75 (Mortensen et al., 1989; Mortensen, 1999; Mortensen & Gade, 1993), and the associations between intelligence and other criteria of success in life are often much lower (approximately 0.30). In other words, high scores in intelligence tests by no means guarantee that an individual will have success in life. It is rather that a low IQ limits the potential of an individual – for instance with regard to education. For individuals of about the same IQ (e.g. normal intelligence), personality and social factors usually determine success in life.

Seen in this light, it is surprising that the concept of intelligence and intelligence tests is so controversial. This may be related to the fact that even though the correlations are not high, scores on intelligence tests correlate with virtually all psychological and social factors which are considered positive in modern society (Bouchard, 1997; Gottfredson, 2002; Jensen, 1998). For example, there are positive associations between intelligence and virtually all types of indexes of social stratification. In recent years associations have also been found between intelligence and both somatic (Batty et al., 2005a; Whalley & Deary, 2001) and mental health (Batty et al., 2005b; Mortensen et al., 2005b), and it is possible that inter-individual differences in intelligence explain a substantial part of the social health gradients that have been observed in most societies (Gottfredson, 2004).

In this context the significance of intelligence or the global level of cognitive functioning at various stages of life should be considered. Intelligence tests are historically based on the need to differentiate between school pupils (Thorpe, 1970) and as stated above there is a strong statistical association between intelligence and level of education. However, intelligence is not only important for education: a great number of studies have demonstrated that intelligence or global cognitive function is the single factor that has the greatest impact on a person's occupational career (Gottfredson, 2002; Schmidt & Hunter, 1998). As the complexity of jobs increases with increasing demands for flexibility and supplementary education, it must be assumed that the general importance of intelligence in occupational contexts will also increase. Thus, preserving intellectual abilities will be a critical prerequisite if people are to remain on the labour market as they grow older. A successful transition to a life as retired presumably also requires flexibility and the ability to adapt, which are associated with intelligence. An increasing number of people are reaching a high age, and preserving adequate intellectual function may be a vital factor in ensuring the quality of their lives and their ability to remain independent.

The development of intelligence at the early stages of life

Complex mental characteristics such as personality traits and intelligence are not inborn – they develop as we grow up. Both hereditary factors (Sternberg & Grigorenko, 1997; Teasdale & Owen, 1984) and prenatal environmental factors (Mortensen et al., 2005a; Reinisch et al., 1995) influence cognitive development. Children are born with various potentials for intellectual development. Stable individual differences with regard to cognitive function develop gradually as a result of the interaction between hereditary potential and physical, mental and social environmental influences (e.g. Mortensen et al., 2002; Sternberg & Grigorenko, 2001). Stable individual differences cannot be measured with reasonable precision until a child's language has developed, but there is some association between intellectual functions at the age of 3-4 and adult performance on intelligence tests. Furthermore, most studies have observed substantial associations between school age and adult test scores (Mortensen et al., 2003; Schuerger & Witt, 1989). The variance between individuals increases during childhood and youth, and one of the most striking aspects of human cognition is the subtantial individual differences in performance on cognitive tests in young adults. These differences are reflected in average test scores and thus in intelligence quotients, which are the basis for classifications of intelligence. One of the facts demonstrated by studies of the 1914 cohort is that individual differences in average cognitive function are extremely stable throughout most of the adult life span (Mortensen & Kleven, 1993). The correlations between IQs at the ages of 50 and 80 were 0.84, 0.74 and 0.84 for Verbal, Performance and Total IQ respectively. Despite age-related changes in cognitive function and the occurrence of age-related neurological disorders, individual differences in intellectual function remain stable until very high age.

Development between ages 20 and 50

The 1914 cohort was not assessed before the age of 50, and so there is a need to consider cognitive development from early adulthood until this age. Cross-sectional studies often reveal signs of non-linear associations between age and test scores, with young individuals often performing slightly better than middle-aged individuals, who in turn perform much better than people above the age of 60 (e.g. Mortensen & Gade, 1993). Age-related changes in test performance demonstrate a characteristic pattern, with the largest decline occurring in tests in which working speed plays a major role, and associations between age and slower reaction time and psycho-motor speed have been demonstrated in a large number of experimental studies (Madden, 2001). As described above, age and generation differences cannot be separated clearly in cross-sectional studies, and consequently it is important that the Seattle Longitudinal Study and other longitudinal studies indicate only minor changes in intellectual functions between the ages of 20 and 50. Thus, Schaie believes that substantial decline before the age of 60 is almost always pathological. However, he also points out that different cognitive functions show different ageing patterns: Reasoning and Verbal Ability reach their peak at the age of 40-60, while Number Skills and Word Fluency peak earlier and show a modest decline as early as the 50s (Schaie, 2005).

Development between ages 50 and 60

528 individuals from the 1914 cohort participated in the both the 50 and 60 year studies, and 518 of these participants were tested by the same tester at both assessments (298 by Hess and 220 by Kleven). This material is probably the largest WAIS sample with a ten-year follow-up, and for this large sample the results indicate small and unimportant changes in intellectual function during the age period in question. The subsample tested by Hess scored higher in verbal tests at the age of 60 than at the age of 50, while the subsample tested by Kleven showed a decline at the age of 60. In other words, with regard to verbal intellectual functions the typical changes between the ages of 50 and 60 were so small that the WAIS was not precise enough to measure decline, independent of tester effects. For the total sample the Verbal IQ was virtually identical at the ages of 50 and 60, while a more consistent and tester independent decline was observed between 50 and 60 on the performance subtests. However, the changes in test performance were still very moderate, corresponding to about 2.5 IQ points in Performance IQ and about one IQ point in Total IQ. These results clearly corroborate the findings of the Seattle Longitudinal Study and Schaie's (2005) conclusion that there are no substantial changes in intellectual functions before the age of 60. The small changes observed do not significantly influence working capacity which is important because most of the people in this age group are still on the labour market. Consequently, it is a very impor-

tant conclusion that the studies of the 1914 cohort prove that in most respects 50-60 year-olds function intellectually at the same level as they did when they were young adults. It means that most 50-60 year olds are able to use their life and work experience and that they are able to learn new work procedures and to function in new working areas on an equal footing with their younger colleagues (Mortensen, 1997).

Not only the sample means, but also the individual test results were stable at the ages of 50 and 60 for most of the participants. For the two testers the ten-year retest correlation was 0.96 and 0.95 respectively, which means that the IQ of more than 25 per cent of the participants changed by no more than one point between the two assessments. Even on the performance subtests only slightly more than 10 per cent showed a decline in IQ of more than 10 IQ points, and the fact that so few participants showed substantial decline in test performance may explain why it has not been possible to identify convincing predictors of intellectual decline between the ages of 50 and 60.

The fact that intellectual functions seem to be extremely stable between the ages of 50 and 60 makes it possible to evaluate whether there were any changes in the relative difficulty of the individual items between the 50 and 60 year studies. Hess (1983) carried out this kind of analysis and provided examples of items which had become easier at the 60 year follow-up in 1974-75: On the Information subtest many more participants knew how many MPs are in the Danish Parliament (the increase was attributed to a greater general interest in politics) and on the Similarities test more participants replied "energy" when asked about the similarity between wood and petrol (this was attributed to the recent energy crisis). However, in general there were very few signs that the WAIS subtests worked differently at the two assessments, and it may be concluded that in interpreting the results of the repeated tests of the 1914 cohort it is possible to ignore secular trends and timing of testing – since this was not a significant determinant of WAIS results.

Development between ages 60 and 70

When the 70 year follow-up was conducted in 1984-85 psychologist Grethe Hess had died, and only 141 participants were administered all the WAIS subtests by Mogens Kleven (for the other participants the data collection only included four of the Wechsler subtests, which were administered by Kirsten Avlund). The 141 participants had also been tested by Kleven at the 50 and 60 year studies, and this group showed a moderate decline in Verbal IQ (about 1.6 IQ points) between 50 and 60 – corresponding to the result for all participants (a total of 220) tested by Kleven at the 60 follow-up. The decline in the verbal subtests was about the same between 60 and 70, whereas the decline in the performance subtests was much larger between 60 and 70 (about 5.2 IQ points) than between 50 and 60 (about 1.9 IQ points). Thus, for the performance subtests there were signs of a non-linear association between age and test performance, and closer analysis revealed that this could not be explained by the importance of working speed for the results of the performance subtests (Kleven scored the results of three of these subtests both with and without time limits). In other words, the age-related changes were not due solely to changes in tempo and working speed (cf. Mortensen & Kleven, 1993).

Over the 20-year period from 50 to 70 the decline was 3.2, 7.2 and 5.5 IQ points in Verbal, Performance and Total IQ. These changes correspond to 1/5, 1/2 and 1/3 standard deviation respectively and resemble the findings observed by Schaie at the ages of 67 and 74 with 21 and 28 year follow-up intervals (see Schaie, 1996, pp. 117-118). For the 1914 cohort a significant decline was found on all the WAIS subtests apart from Information and Comprehension (suggesting no significant changes in general knowledge). In three subtests there was a significantly larger decline in men than in women, and with regard to Performance IQ larger decline was also observed in men (5.5 and 8.7 IQ points for women and men respectively). However, no gender differences in age-related decline in intellectual function were detected at the ages of 80 and 85, which may be a consequence of the fact that men aged 80 comprise a highly selected group.

Both cross-sectional and longitudinal studies have suggested that individuals with high education show less decline in intellectual functions compared to individuals with low education. At IQ level there was no interaction between education and age in the 1914 cohort, but this was the case for the Digit-Symbol and Block Design subtests. Closer analysis revealed that the level of education only played a role for decline in men between the 60 and 70 year follow-ups. However, the decline between these ages was not smaller, but larger, in well educated men, and it is possible that for this group of men retirement leads to slower speed on the Digit-Symbol task.

In July 1991, 27 of the 141 participants had died. Statistical analysis revealed that the group of deceased individuals had displayed a substantial decline in intellectual functions at the age of 70, whereas there was only a slight decline in the 114 individuals who were still alive (the decline in Performance IQ was 11.2 and 3.8 IQ points in the two groups). The same tendency was apparent in an analysis of all the 336 participants in the 70 year follow-up. There were 74 deceased individuals, and the decline in test performance was larger in the 38 individuals who died in the first three years after the 70 year follow-up than in the 36 individuals who died 4-6 years after this follow-up.

There seems to be a time gradient with the largest decline being observed in individuals who died shortly after the 70 year follow-up. This so-called "terminal decline" phenomenon has been observed in a number of other studies, and the most important observation on the 1914 cohort may be the clear demonstration of the significance of the time factor – both with regard to the time between testing and death and with regard to the time interval prior to the 70 year follow-up. Thus, no differences were observed between deceased individuals and survivors with respect to changes in test performance between the 50 and 60 studies – only between the 60 and 70 year follow-ups. These results were confirmed by a recent American study in which annual assessments of a group of elderly Catholic nuns and priests revealed that terminal decline starts 3-4 years before death (Wilson et al., 2003).

Even though there seems to be a subgroup displaying significant changes between the ages of 50 and 70, correlation analyses show that intelligence is a surprisingly stable mental characteristic in this age group. Thus, 20-year retest correlations were found to be 0.91, 0.82 and 0.90 for the Verbal, Performance and Total IQs respectively (Mortensen & Kleven, 1993). When evaluating these high correlations, it should be born in mind that the test scores of some of the participants at the 70 follow-up were probably influenced by noise from neurological disorders or other somatic disease, leading to lower correlations.

Development between ages 70 and 80

All the participants in the 80 year follow-up had of course lived for ten years after the 70 year follow-up, and therefore from a terminal decline point of view, significant decline in intellectual function compared with the 60 and 70 year results would not be expected. This proved in fact to be the case for a subsample of 54 individuals who participated in all four studies at the ages of 50, 60, 70 and 80. Between the 50 and 70 year studies this group displayed a total decline of 1.2 and 4.5 IQ points in Verbal and Performance IQ, while the decline in test scores between the 70 and 80 follow-ups was 5.7 and 11.1 IQ points. This decline parallels the familiar pattern, with much larger decline in scores on the performance subtests than on the verbal subtests. A new finding was that with a 30-year follow-up period clear signs were observed of a non-linear association with age for both the verbal and the performance subtests.

The 80 year follow-up included 189 of the 698 individuals who took part in the original 50 year baseline study (five psychologists administered the tests, but Kleven personally checked the scoring of all tests). Only 163 participants were able to complete the full WAIS at the age of 80, and relative to their results at the 50 year baseline this group showed a decline of 8.4, 18.4 and 14.1 IQ points in Verbal, Performance and Total IQ respectively (Mortensen & Høgh, 2001). Thus, the decline in Verbal IQ was close to 2/3 standard deviation, the decline in Total IQ was close to 1 standard deviation, and the decline in Performance IQ was more than 1 standard deviation. Schaie found a decline of about 8/10 and 9/10 standard deviation in 81 year olds with 21-year and 28-year follow-ups respectively (cf. Schaie, 1996, pp. 117-118). Both studies confirm that in longitudinal studies substantial decline is observed if the follow-up period is sufficiently long and testing is conducted at high age. For the 1914 cohort the presented results are for the 163 participants who were able to complete the full WAIS, and it is likely that the average decline was larger for the 26 individuals who were unable to carry out all the subtests.

Roughly 80 per cent of the 163 individuals who completed the full WAIS test had participated in the 50, 60 and 70 follow-ups, while the rest had taken part in one or two of the previous studies. Consequently, there is good reason to speculate whether test performance at the age of 80 was influenced by re-test effects. It is possible to gain an impression of the answer to this question, because 140 participants were WAIS tested for the first time at the 80 year follow-up. The group who had been tested previously performed better on all subtests. In four verbal subtests and one performance subtest the difference was significant which was also the case with regard to Verbal and Total IQ, where the difference was about 4-5 IQ points. This difference suggests retest effects, but it may also reflect background differences between the two groups as the difference between the two groups was somewhat reduced with statistical control for schooling and vocational training.

In the group who had been tested previously there were no significant differences between individuals who had taken part in all three previous tests and individuals who had only taken part in two, but the small subgroup who had only taken part in one of the previous tests scored much lower than the other two groups, and even lower than the group being tested for the first time at the 80 year follow-up. This suggests that the difference between the groups cannot be explained solely by retest effects, which is corroborated by the fact that the group who had only been tested once previously also performed poorly at the 50 year baseline. Consequently, there seems to be a tendency for individuals who performed poorly at the 50 year baseline to refrain from participating in the 60 and 70 follow-ups.

One striking feature is the substantial individual differences in decline in intellectual functions over the 30-year follow-up period. This is shown in figure 1, illustrating the mean test performance and the test performance for the 10 per cent displaying the smallest and largest decline in total IQ respectively.

Intelligence and age

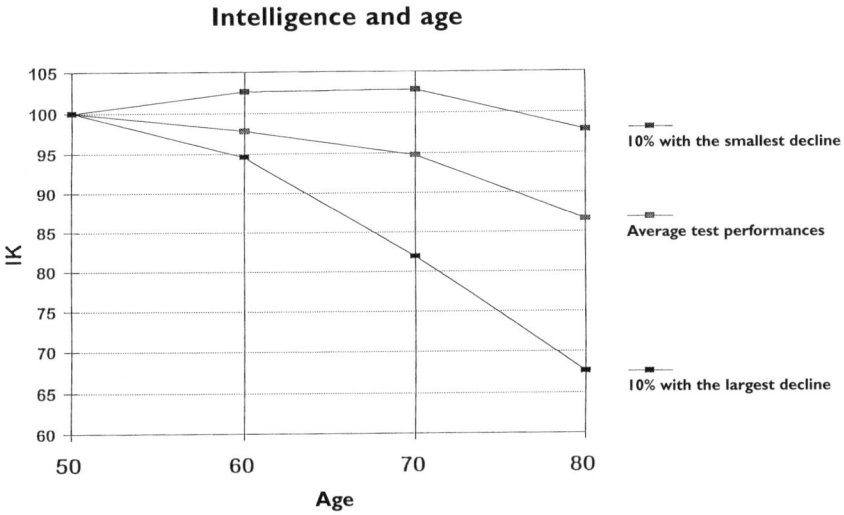

FIGURE I.

The data in this figure for the ages 60 and 70 is based on the 141 individuals described in Mortensen & Kleven (1993), and for the age of 80 on the 163 individuals described in Mortensen & Høgh (2001). The 50 year baseline mean is set at 100 for all groups, corresponding to the average IQ. The figure shows that the average decline in test performance only becomes substantial at the age of 80. It also shows that the group displaying the smallest decline at the age of 80 in general still functions at the same level as they did at the 50 year baseline. On the other hand, the group with the largest decline in test performance shows such substantial decline that intellectually these individuals function on entirely different levels at the ages of 50 and 80. With a decline in total IQ of more than 2 standard deviations, they will appear dramatically different at the age of 80 than they did at the age of 50, since the average person in this group declines from normal abilities according to WAIS standards at the age of 50 to below the level for mental retardation at the age of 80. It is of course likely that the test performance of a number of the participants in this group was influenced by incipient dementia.

The size of age-related changes in intellectual function should be evaluated on the background of the large individual differences observed in young and middle-aged adults. In this context, an important point is that there was a considerable overlap between the distributions of test scores of elderly and young individuals. This is particularly true for Verbal IQ, where the best 25 per cent of the 80 year-olds performed better than the poorest half of the 50 year-olds. However, it is also true for the Performance IQ, where the best 25 per cent of the 80 year-olds performed better than the poorest 25 per cent of the 50 year-olds.

Development between ages 80 and 85

A total of 172 individuals participated in the psychological 85-year follow-up, for which Hanne Karrebæk was responsible. Even though the studies were carried out in the homes of the participants and plenty of time was allowed, only 50 of the participants (less than one-third of the total) were able to complete all 11 WAIS subtests. About 20 per cent of the participants had to omit tests owing to impaired sight or hearing, while impaired motor function played a role in about 6 per cent of the participants. Tiredness was an important reason for omitting some WAIS subtests for about 20 per cent of the participants, while poor cooperation and unwillingness to be tested only played a role for about 8 per cent (Mortensen, 2004).

As part of the 85-year follow-up MMSE (Mini Mental State Examination) was also administered. This is a frequently used instrument to screen for dementia (Folstein et al., 1975). Almost one-quarter of the participants achieved an MMSE score suggesting dementia (an MMSE score of 23 or less), and only three of these individuals were able to complete all the WAIS subtests (achieving an IQ of 68, 74 and 75 respectively, based on norms for 50 year-olds). Statistically speaking there was a clear association between the MMSE score and the number of WAIS tests completed, and to avoid a situation in which IQ could only be calculated for intellectually well functioning individuals, IQ was calculated for all the individuals who were able to complete at least two verbal tests and two performance tests. IQs from the 50 and 80 studies were re-calculated using only the subtests which the participant was able to complete at the 85-year follow-up – this was done to ensure that changes in intellectual function were assessed on the basis of the same subtests at baseline and all follow-ups.

On this basis it was possible to calculate the full WAIS IQ for 82 individuals (36 men and 46 women), all of whom participated in the 50, 80 and 85-year follow-up. For the group as a whole the Total IQ mean fell by 5.6 between the 80 and 85 year follow-ups, and the total average decline since the 50 year baseline was 16.8 IQ points. This figure is not dramatically different from the 14.1 IQ points reported previously for a larger sample participating in the 50 and 80 year follow-ups (Mortensen & Høgh, 2001). This reflects the fact that the participants in the 85 year follow-up were an elite group who had declined less in WAIS performance at the age of 80 than the full sample participating in the 80 year follow-up (as a consequence it was not possible to extend the curves in figure 1 from the age of 80 to 85).

Over the 30-year period from the 50 year baseline to the 80 year follow-up there was a much larger decline on the performance WAIS subtests than on the verbal subtests, but between the 80 and 85 year follow-ups there were only small differences in the decline between the performance and verbal subtests. At the age of 85 the 36 men achieved an average IQ which was about 10 IQ points higher than that achieved by the 46 women. This gender difference in WAIS IQ was observed already at the age of 50, and no gender differences were observed with regard to the decline in test performance.

If the changes in the 1914 cohort are calculated for the entire 35-year period elapsing between the 50 and 85 year studies, the decline in Verbal IQ is about 11 points and the decline in Performance IQ is about 21 points, corresponding to 0.7 and 1.4 standard deviation respectively. A group of verbal subtests (Information, Comprehension and Similarities) display relatively small decline (about 1/2 standard deviation), while 4 out of 5 performance tests display decline corresponding to more than 1 standard deviation. The general pattern corresponds to Schaie's findings – between the ages of 25 and 88 he observed changes of about 0.75-2.00 standard deviation (Schaie, 1996, 2005). The smallest changes were observed for Verbal Ability and the largest for Spatial Orientation and Perceptual Speed.

Development between ages 85 and 90

A total of 123 individuals (41 men and 82 women) participated in the psychological 90 year follow-up, of whom 78 were from the original 1914 cohort. Ditte Dyrholm collected all data during a home visit, and it was decided to include only the Information and Digit-Symbol WAIS subtests. Of the participants 120 were able to complete the Information subtest, while only 92 were able to complete the Digit-Symbol test (the corresponding figures for the members of the original 1914 cohort were 75 and 59). The Digit-Symbol test had to be omitted for 21 participants owing to impaired vision, while unwillingness to do the test was decisive for 6-7 individuals (the test had to be abandoned for 2 participants owing to dementia). An MMSE was possible for 118 of the 123 participants, of whom 35 (about 30 per cent) achieved a score of 23 or less. However, it should be noted that maximum points were awarded for subtests that had to be omitted owing to impaired vision, so it is likely that the proportion of participants with suspected dementia according to the MMSE should be increased somewhat. Even so, it is striking that the majority of the 90-year-old participants did not show signs of dementia on the MMSE, and that the mean MMSE score did not decline dramatically between the ages of 85 and 90. It is true that there was a significant change, but it is more striking that the variance was much larger at the age of 90 (a small number of participants scored 10 or less).

A total of 54 participants completed the Information subtest at both the 85 and 90 year follow-ups, and for this group the same performance level was observed at the two assessments. This was also the case when Information scores at the 80 and 90 year follow-ups were compared, but it is perhaps more surprising that the 90-year-olds did not show significant decline on the Information subtest when compared with their 50 year baseline scores (although it is likely that the scoring criteria used were slightly more relaxed at the 90 year follow-up). However, the variance was much larger at the age of 90, reflecting the fact that more than 15 per cent were only able to achieve a few points on the subtest.

A different pattern is evident for the Digit-Symbol subtest: between the ages of 85 and 90 there was a decline of about 0.5 standard deviation, and between the ages of 50 and 90 the decline was about 1.7 standard deviation. There were no signs of gender differences in age-related decline between ages 85 and 90 (or with regard to total decline between the 50 and 90 studies) in either the Digit-Symbol test or the Information test.

The participants in the 90 year follow-up did not constitute an elite group when middle-aged since they achieved a Total IQ of about 100 at the 50 year baseline. Forty years later their performance in general knowledge was largely unchanged, while there was a dramatic decline in a test requiring concentration and speed such as the Digit-Symbol subtest. Roughly one-third of the participants scored below the MMSE cutoff for suspected dementia, and some participants in this group performed extremely poorly on both the MMSE and the Information subtest. On these tests there were dramatic differences between the best preserved and the most poorly functioning 90-year-olds.

Individual differences

The substantial individual differences in developmental patterns mean that one of the central research themes in geropsychology must be to identify predictors of differences in cognitive ageing patterns. Even though it is obvious that intellectual function primarily reflects the state of the brain, it is important that test performance and intellectual function at a high age may be influenced by sensory defects, reduced mobility, paralysis, etc. However, both with regard to the 1914 cohort (Mortensen & Kleven, 1993) and in other contexts (Salthouse, 1991) it has been demonstrated that changes in tempo and working speed do not provide a full explanation of age-related changes in test performance. Furthermore, in studies of age-related changes sensory and motor disabilities affecting the ability to complete one or more tests are usually identified.

To understand individual differences it is therefore natural to focus on the state of the brain and cerebral disease. In longitudinal studies it is possible to use epidemiological methods to assess the importance of potential risk factors for cerebral disorders and age-related decline in intellectual function. For the 1914 cohort interview and register data regarding the health of the participants have been collected beginning in 1964, including information about illnesses and traumas which may have influenced the brain and thus intellectual functions. During the 40-year follow-up period detailed information has also been collected regarding the lifestyle and social conditions of the participants, making it possible to identify both risk factors and the social and health consequences of age-related changes in intellectual functions.

There is now a considerable body of research demonstrating associations between cardiovascular risk factors and cognitive function (Waldstein & Elias, 2001). For instance, the associations between cognitive function and hypertension and between cognitive function and diabetes appear to have been reasonably well documented, and there is also a number of similar studies of cognitive function and lifestyle factors such as smoking and alcohol consumption (Elias et al., 2001). In the 1914 cohort it may be most efficient to conduct separate analyses for decline between the ages of 50 and 60 and between the ages of 60 and 80. This is because the number of participants is much larger at the ages of 50 and 60, and because significant changes in intellectual functions only occur after the age of 60.

When analysing predictors of age-related changes in intellectual function, a wide range of issues needs to be considered for the 1914 cohort:

1. The distinction between absolute test scores and changes in test scores. Naturally, correlations between potential predictors and WAIS results at the 50 year baseline reveal little about age-related changes, although they may be relevant in assessing the factors which influence the development of intelligence during the first half of the life course. Height and lung function are two examples of factors that correlate consistently with WAIS performance at the age of 50, and it is well known that in young adulthood there is also an association between height and intelligence (Teasdale et al., 1991) – possibly because both these variables reflect the extent to which conditions have been optimal during the growth and development period of the individual. For height there is a moderate association with changes in test performance between the ages of 60 and 80, even when the results are adjusted for social status and level of education.

2. Do the associations grow stronger or weaker when results are adjusted for background factors and potential confounders?

   If the variance associated with social factors and education can be regarded as "noise", associations between predictors and age-related changes should grow stronger when these and other background factors are controlled statistically. For most variables this is not the case with regard to associations with absolute test scores, but it does apply to height.

3. Stronger associations can be expected between causal predictors and decline between the ages of 60 and 80 than between the ages of 50 and 60. This expectation is due to the fact that decline on WAIS scores are much larger and more consistent between the ages of 60 and 80. This is not the case for an observed moderate association between diabetes and insulin measurements and changes in intellectual function between the ages of 50 and 60 since these health variables are not associated with changes in intellectual functions between the ages of 60 and 80.

4. Stronger associations can be expected between predictors and changes in performance subtests than between predictors and changes in verbal subtests.

   One example is diastolic blood pressure, which seems to be a stronger predictor of decline between the ages of 60 and 80 than between the ages of 50 and 60. However, the association is only apparent for Verbal IQ, which seems strange considering that performance subtests reflect the current state of the brain to a larger extent.

For the 1914 cohort it must be concluded that despite detailed information regarding life history, health, lifestyle and social conditions it has proved difficult to demonstrate convincing associations between such factors and age-related changes in intellectual function. To understand the background for this conclusion it is very important to distinguish between cross-sectional studies of elderly age groups and longitudinal studies incorporating cognitive baseline assessment at an early age where the risk factors in focus are unlikely to have affected the brain and thereby cognitive function to a significant extent. This is important because of the very large individual differences in intellectual function which can be observed in early adulthood, and because these individual differences may influence whether individuals are exposed to specific risk factors during their life course. For instance, there is evidence that alcohol consumption patterns are related to cognitive function (Mortensen et al., 2001; Mortensen et al., 2006), and that the risk of developing obesity and thereby hypertension is also associated with intelligence (Teasdale et al.,1992). Unless cognitive test scores are available from the early part of life, associations between risk factors and cognitive function at high age may be interpreted mistakenly as a reflection of causal mechanisms contributing to age-related decline – whereas in fact the observed associations between lifestyle and cognitive function may have been present during most of the earlier life periods.

Against these points, it can be argued that cross-sectional studies of elderly populations often incorporate statistical control of early cognitive function by adjusting for education and other demographic factors associated with cognitive function in early adulthood. However, such factors only have a moderate association with cognitive function corresponding to correlations of about 0.60-0.70 (cf. Mortensen & Gade, 1993; Mortensen et al., 1989), which means that adjusting completely for early cognitive function and intelligence is not possible. Consequently, there is a big risk of so-called residual confounding – associations between risk factors and cognitive function at a high age which do not reflect a causal relationship between the risk factors in question and age-related decline in intellectual functions. In contrast to cross-sectional studies, longitudinal studies do make it possible to examine associations between risk factors and directly observed changes in cognitive functions. Thus, the 1914 cohort makes it possible to analyse associations between risk factors and changes in cognitive function from the age of 50 and throughout a life period of 30-40 years. It is tempting to assume that the possibility of directly analyzing changes in cognitive function is one of the main reasons why far fewer associations have been identified in the 1914 cohort than in the literature in general. However, it should be added that other researchers – Schaie, for instance – in longitudinal studies have found associations between risk factors and age-related changes in intellectual function (Schaie, 2005). However, these associations are often very moderate, and in some cases they do not correspond to the associations observed in cross-sectional studies. Hypertension is one example: cross-sectional studies have often shown a negative association with cognitive function, but Schaie found that individuals in whom hypertension had not led to illness actually displayed less age-related decline (Schaie, 2005).

The studies of the 1914 cohort were originally planned to investigate the significance of cardio-vascular risk factors during the life course. Consequently, they should also provide possibilities for evaluating the importance of these risk factors and related lifestyle factors for age-related changes in intellectual functions. However, there is now a good deal of evidence that the importance of genetic factors for intellectual function does not decline but increases during the life course (Plomin et al., 2001). For instance, McGue et al. (1993) reported greater heritability of WAIS IQ for twins aged 60-88 than for twins tested in childhood or young adulthood. One of the most thoroughly documented hereditary factors is the so-called APOE-4 allele, which has also been analyzed in the 1914 cohort. In women an association was observed between APOE genotype and decline in intellectual functions between the 50 and 80 year follow-ups (Mortensen & Høgh, 2001). For men no association was found, and we do not know whether the association in women may be explained by the well-known increased risk of Alzheimer's associated with APOE-4 allele genotype or whether the finding reflects an association between the APOE-4 allele and normal age-related decline in intellectual functions.

With regard to studies of the state of the brain, at both 80 and 85 year follow-ups MR scans were conducted on 75 and 47 participants respectively. On MR scans so-called hyperintensities tend to increase in the white matter with age (Christiansen et al., 1994). At the age of 80 very moderate correlations were observed between these changes in the white matter and decline on the WAIS between the 50 and 80 year studies. The correlations were only significant for the Digit-Symbol, Block Design and Object Assembly subtests, and amounted to about 0.30-0.36, corresponding to 12-13 per cent explained variance (Garde et al., 2000). However, these results were based on expert ratings of the MR images and with a more accurate quantification of the number of hyperintensities, correlations of 0.65 were observed between changes in white matter and decline in Verbal IQ between the 80 and 85 year follow-ups (Garde et al., 2005). Incidentally, it is striking that the correlation was not reduced but increased when the results were adjusted for gender, education and WAIS results at the age of 50, thereby presumably reducing the variance in test results that was not associated with changes in the white matter. Thus, it seems that if sufficiently precise measurements are obtained of both changes in the brain and changes in intellectual function, extremely close associations can be observed.

In recent years there has been speculations regarding possible links between inflammatory conditions and cognitive function, and associations have actually been observed in both cross-sectional studies (Yaffe et al.,2003) and longitudinal studies (Wright et al., 2006). In the 1914 cohort blood samples were taken at both the 80 and 85 year follow-ups, and a collaborative project has now been initiated with Helle Brunsgaard and Karen Krabbe with focus on analysing associations between inflammatory conditions and cognitive function in the 1914 cohort.

Conclusions

The psychological studies of the 1914 cohort demonstrate that most of the participants experience no significant decline in intellectual function until they reach high age. However, in any population study there will always be a number of individuals who are not able or willing to participate for one reason or another.

Naturally, the number of individuals who are not tested increases with age, and consequently it is important to remember that the results obtained for the 1914 cohort only apply to the 70-, 80- and 85-year-olds who were able and willing to participate. Subject to this reservation, there are a number of conclusions that can be drawn regarding the development of intellectual functions during the second half of the life span:

1. Using a broad battery of intelligence tests such as the WAIS, significant decline is observed during the decade between the ages of 50 and 60. This decline was modest and only consistent for the performance subtests (with regard to Performance IQ the decline was less than 1/5 standard deviation). The results of the verbal subtests were tester-dependent, and during this period of life verbal ability seems to be largely unchanged. The results for the 1914 cohort show that in agreement with Schaie's conclusions (Schaie, 2005) the typical individual in the 50-60 age range is not significantly affected by age-related changes in cognitive functions.

2. Age-related changes become clearer at the 70 year follow-up. Compared with the results at the 50-year baseline, the decline amounts to about 1/4 standard deviation for Verbal IQ and up to 1/2 standard deviation for Performance IQ. This means that the results for the 1914 cohort match the results of Schaie (2005) who concludes that the first significant changes in intellectual function can be observed in many people at the end of the 60s and the beginning of the 70s.

3. At the 80 and 85 year follow-ups there is substantial decline in intellectual functions. All the WAIS subtests showed significant decline at the 80 year follow-up (0.6, 1.3 and 1.0 standard deviation for Verbal IQ, Performance IQ and Total IQ respectively). At the 85 year follow-up the retest interval was only five years, but even so there was a decline of about 5-7 IQ points (1/3 standard deviation or more) for the three WAIS IQs relative to the results at the 80 year follow-up. Thus, it must be concluded that with sufficiently long follow-up periods and testing at a sufficiently high age, the substantial age-related decline in intellectual functions observed in the typical individual must be taken into account in any realistic assessment of the situation of elderly people and their potential for living independently. It should be added that for the 1914 cohort the results may well be influenced by retest effects, making the results a conservative estimate of age-related decline.

4. In young adulthood substantial individual differences in intellectual functions can be observed, and compared with these differences age-related changes are of relatively little significance throughout most of the adult life span. This applies in particular to the well-learned skills that are tested in the verbal WAIS subtests, in which more than 35 per cent of the participants in the 1914 cohort at the age of 50 scored better than the poorest performing half of a large group of 20-26 year-olds (cf. Reinisch et al., 1993) – and this was still the case for more than 25 per cent of the participants at the age of 80. The situation is very different with regard to the Performance subtests, in which less than 10 per cent of the 50-year-old participants scored higher than the poorest half of the 20-26 year-olds – with the same being true of less than 1 per cent of the 80-year-old participants. However, there is reason to assume that generation differences play a relatively large role for the results of the performance subtests (Neisser, 1998) since the 20-26 year-olds were born in 1959-61.

5. There are substantial individual differences in absolute test performance in all age groups, and there are also very significant individual differences in age-related changes in intellectual functions. Based on the 1914 cohort, it has been difficult to identify consistent predictors of decline in cognitive function. However, as in other longitudinal studies (Schaie, 2005), both genetic and lifestyle factors seem involved. Cognitive function reflects the state of the brain, and using MR scans this has been demonstrated for age-related changes in intellectual functions for the long period between the 50 and 80 year studies and the relatively short period between the 80 and 85 year follow-ups.

6. In recent years there has been much interest in the significance of so-called "cognitive reserve" as a possible explanation of individual differences in cognitive changes caused by brain damage, normal ageing or dementia (Whalley et al., 2004). Scores in intelligence tests are often used as an index of cognitive reserves, and the question is whether total IQ at the 50 year baseline can be used as such an index, and whether associations can be observed in the 1914 cohort between test performance at the age of 50 and cognitive changes in the next 30-40 years. No consistent associations with the 50 year baseline performance were found in analyses of changes between the ages of 50 and 70 (Mortensen & Kleven, 1993) and in analyses of changes between the ages of 50 and 80 (Mortensen & Høgh, 2001). However the statistical models did not include other factors which might influence cognitive decline, and there is a need for further analysis of this issue.

One question which is often raised in relation to ageing and intellectual function is whether age-related decline can be delayed by using the brain or by systematic training. It must, however, be admitted that even though the detailed registration of lifestyle and social conditions should make it possible to contribute substantial knowledge to this important issue, such analyses have not yet been conducted for the 1914 cohort. This is regrettable, because many available studies focus on associations between recreational activities and the risk of dementia (Scarmeas & Stern, 2003), and because one obvious alternative possibility is that active elderly may be active because they are intellectually well preserved (Hultsch et al., 1999). Consequently, there is a need for analyses investigating prospective associations between activities and lifestyle and normal age-related changes in intellectual function.

Schaie and his coworkes have carried out intervention studies with training of cognitive skills and report long-term positive effects on test performance (Schaie, 2005). Even though it is unclear whether the effect of training can be generalised and applied to everyday functions, there are reasons for cautious optimism. An increasing number of people are reaching high age, and for most of our life span age-related decline in intellectual functions should perhaps be regarded not as an inevitable consequence of old age, but rather as something that can be counteracted by an active and healthy lifestyle.

Acknowledgements

I feel a deep sense of gratitude to Mogens Kleven because he with competence and kindness took the time to introduce me to a unique Danish psychological study. I am also grateful for a great number of rewarding discussions of the results and their theoretical implications, and because he critically evaluated the scoring of the WAIS from the 80 year follow-up despite suffering from serious illness. Finally, I thank Vibeke Munk for critical comments and help with the manuscript.

REFERENCES

Avlund, K.; Johannesen, A.; Mortensen, E.L.; Holm-Pedersen, P.; Pedersen, A.N. & Schroll, M. (Eds.). (2004). Livsforløbet fra 50 til 85 år. Data fra befolkningsundersøgelserne ved Forskningscenter for Forebyggelse og Sundhed. *Skriftserien fra Gerontologisk Institut 8*, 46. Gerontologisk Institut, København.

Baltes, P.B. & Schaie, K.W. (1974). Aging and IQ: The myth of the twilight years. *Psychology Today, 10*, 35-38.

Baltes, P. B.; Staudinger, U.M. & Lindenberger, U. (1999). LIFESPAN PSYCHOLOGY: Theory and Application to Intellectual Functioning. *Annual Review of Psychology, 50,* 471-507.

Batty, G.D.; Mortensen, E.L.; Andersen, A.N. & Osler, M. (2005a). Childhood intelligence in relation to adult coronary heart disease and stroke risk: evidence from a Danish birth cohort study. *Paediatric and Perinatal Epidemiology, 19,* 452-459.

Batty, G.D.; Mortensen, E.L. & Osler, M. (2005b). Childhood intelligence in relation to later psychiatric disorder: evidence from a Danish birth cohort study. *British Journal of Psychiatry, 187,* 180-181.

Birren, J.E. & Schaie, K.W. (2001). *Handbook of the Psychology of Aging.* New York: Academic Press.

Bouchard, T.J. (1997). IQ Similarity in Twins Reared Apart: Findings and Responses to Critics. Chapter 5, 126-160. In: R.J. Sternberg & E.L. Grigorenko (Eds.), *Intelligence, Heredity, and Environment.* Cambridge: Cambridge University Press.

Christiansen, P., Larsson, H.B.; Thomsen, C., Wieslander, S.B. & Henriksen, O. (1994). Age dependent white matter lesions and brain volume changes in healthy volunteers. *Acta Radiologica, 35,* 117-122.

Cooper, C. (1998). *Individual DiTherences.* London & New York: Arnold.

Craik, F.I.M. & Salthouse, T.A. (1992).)*e Handbook of Aging and Cognition.* Hillsdale, New Jersey: Lawrence Erlbaum Associates, Inc.

Elias, M.F.; Elias, P.K.; Robbins, M.A.; Wolf, P.A. & D'Agostino, R.B. (2001). Cardiovascular Risk Factors and Cognitive Functioning: An Epidemiological Perspective. Chapter 5, 83-104. In: S.R. Waldstein & M.F. Elias, M.F (Eds.), *Neuropsychology of Cardiovascular Disease.* Hillsdale, New Jersey: Lawrence Erlbaum Associates, Inc.

Folstein, M.F.; Folstein, S.E. & McHugh, P.R. (1975). "Mini-mental state". A practical method for grading the cognitive state of patients for the clinician. *Journal of Psychiatric Research, 12,*189-198.

Garde, E.; Mortensen, E.L.; Krabbe, K.; Rostrup, E. & Larsson, H.B.W. (2000). Relation between age-related decline in intelligence and cerebral white-matter hyper-intensities in healthy octogenarians: a longitudinal study. *Lancet, 356,* 628-634.

Garde, E.; Mortensen, E.L.; Rostrup, E. & Paulson, O. (2005). Decline in intelligence is associated with progression in white matter hyperintensity volume. *Journal of Neurology, Neurosurgery and Psychiatry: 76,* 1289-1291.

Gottfredson, L.S. (2002). *g:* Highly General and Highly practical. Chapter 13, 331-380. In: R.J. Sternberg & E.L. Grigorenko (Eds.), *General Factor of Intelligence. How General Is It?* Hillsdale, New Jersey: Lawrence Erlbaum Associates, Inc.

Gottfredson, L.S. (2004). Intelligence: Is It the Epidemiologists' Elusive "Fundamental Cause" of Social Class Inequalities in Health? *Journal of Personality and Social Psychology, 86,* 174-199.

Hebb, D.O. (1949). *The Organization of Behavior.* New York: John Wiley & Sons.

Hess, G. (1974). *WAIS anvendt på 698 50-årige.* København: Akademisk Forlag.

Hess, G. (1983). *WAIS anvendt på 528 60-årige.* København: Dansk psykologisk Forlag.

Hill, T.D.; Reddon, J.R. & Jackson, D.N. (1985). The factor structure of the Wechsler scales: a brief review. *Clinical Psychology Review, 5,* 287-306.

Horn, J.L. & Cattell, R.B. (1966). Age Differences in Primary Mental Ability Factors. *Journal of Gerontology, 21,* 210-220.

Hultsch, D.F., Hertzog, C., Small, B.J. & Dixon, R.A. (1999). Use it or lose it: engaged lifestyle as a buffer of cognitive decline in aging? *Psychology and Aging, 14,* 245-263.

Jensen, A.R. (1998). *The g Factor. The Science of Mental Ability.* Westport, CT & London: Praeger.

Kyng, M. (1978). *WAIS anvendt på 70-årige.* København: Dansk psykologisk Forlag.

Lambrechtsen, E. (1976). Myten om den normale, intellektuelle reduktion hos voksne og aldrende mennesker. *Skolepsykologi, 13,* 205-226.

Madden, D.J. (2001). Speed and Timing of Behavioral Processes. Chapter 12, 288-312 in J.E. Birren & K.W. Schaie (Eds.), *Handbook of the Psychology of Aging.* San Diego, CA: Academic Press.

McGue, M.; Bouchard, T.J. Jr.; Iacono, W.G. & Lykken, D.T. (1993). Behavioral Genetics of Cognitive Ability: A Life-Span Perspective. In: R. Plomin & G.E. McClearn (Eds.), *Nature, Nurture and Psychology,* 59-76. Washington, DC: American Psychological Association, 59-76.

Mortensen, E.L. (1997). Aldring og intelligens. *Gerontologi og Samfund, 13:* 76-78.

Mortensen, E.L. (1998). Intelligensforskning og intelligensprøver. In: J. Betak, C.S. Cogez & K.R. Jørgensen: *Din store Idiot,* 65-69. København: Rhodos.

Mortensen, E.L. (1999). *Social arv i Rigshospitalets Mor-Barn Kohorte.* Arbejdspapir, *11.* København: Socialforskningsinstituttet.

Mortensen, E.L. (2000). Psykiske egenskaber i neuropsykologien. *Nordisk Psykologi, 52,* 295-318.

Mortensen, E.L. (2004). Ændringer i intellektuelle funktioner med alderen. In: Avlund, K.; Johannesen, A.; Mortensen, E.L.; Holm-Pedersen, P.; Pedersen, A.N. & Schroll, M. (Eds.), Livsforløbet fra 50 til 85 år. Data fra befolkningsundersøgelserne ved Forskningscenter for Forebyggelse og Sundhed. *Skriftserien fra Gerontologisk Institut 8,* 17-23.

Mortensen, E.L.; Andresen, J.; Kruse, E.; Sanders, S.A. & Reinisch, J.M. (2003). IQ stability: The relation between child and young adult intelligence test scores in low birth weight samples. *Scandinavian Journal of Psychology, 44,* 393-396.

Mortensen, E.L. & Gade, A: (1992). Linear versus normalized T scores as standardized neuropsychological test scores. *Scandinavian Journal of Psychology, 33,* 230-237.

Mortensen, E.L & Gade, A. (1993). On the relation between demographic variables and neuropsychological test performance. *Scandinavian Journal of Psychology, 34,* 305-317.

Mortensen, E.L. & Høgh, P. (2001). A gender difference in the association between APOE genotype and age-related cognitive decline. *Neurology, 57,* 89-95.

Mortensen, E.L.; Jensen, H.H.; Sanders, S.A. & Reinisch, J.M. (2001). Better Psychological Functioning and Higher Social Status May Largely Explain the Apparent Health Benefits of Wine. A Study of Wine and Beer Drinking in Young Danish Adults. *Archives of Internal Medicine, 161,* 1844-48.

Mortensen, E.L.; Jensen, H.H., Sanders, S.A. & Reinisch, J.M. (2006). Associations between volume of alcohol consumption and social status, intelligence, and personality in a sample of young adult Danes. *Scandinavian Journal of Psychology,* 387-398.

Mortensen, E.L. & Kleven, M.(1993). A WAIS longitudinal study of cognitive development during the life span from ages 50 to 70. *Developmental Neuropsychology, 9,* 115-130.

Mortensen, E.L.; Michaelsen, K.F.; Sanders, S.A. & Reinisch, J.M. (2002). The association between duration of breastfeeding and adult intelligence. *Journal of the American Medical Association, 287,* 2365-2371.

Mortensen, E.L.; Michaelsen, K.F.; Sanders, S.A. & Reinisch, J.M. (2005a). A dose-response relationship between maternal smoking during late pregnancy and adult intelligence in male offspring. *Paediatric and Perinatal Epidemiology, 19,* 4-11.

Mortensen, E.L.; Reinisch, J.M. & Teasdale, T.W. (1989). Intelligence as measured by the WAIS and a military draft board group test. *Scandinavian Journal of Psychology, 31,* 315-318.

Mortensen, E.L., Sørensen, H.J., Jensen, H.H., Reinisch, J.M. & Mednick, S.A. (2005b). IQ and mental disorder in young men. *British Journal of Psychiatry, 187:* 407-415.

Neisser, U. (1998). *The Rising Curve.* Long-Term Gains in IQ and Related Measures. Washington, DC: American Psychological Association.

Plomin, R.; DeFries, J.C.; McClearn, G.E. & McGuffin, P. (2001). Behavioral Genetics. New York: Worth Publishers.

Reinisch, J.M.; Mortensen, E.L. & Sanders, S.A. (1993). Prenatal development project. *Acta Psychiatrica Scandinavica, 87,* Supplementum 370, 54-61.

Reinisch, J.M.; Sanders, S.A., Mortensen, E.L. & Rubin, D.B. (1995). In Utero Exposure to Phenobarbital and Intelligence Deficits in Adult Men. *Journal of the American Medical Association, 274,* 1518-1525.

Salthouse, T.A. (1991). *Theoretical Perspectives on Cognitive Aging.* Hillsdale, New Jersey: Lawrence Erlbaum Associates, Inc.

Scarmeas, N. & Stern, Y. (2003). Cognitive Reserve and Life Style. *Journal of Clinical and Experimental Neuropsychology, 25,* 625-633.

Schaie, K.W. (1977). Quasi-Experimental Designs in the Psychology of Aging. Chapter 2, 39-58 in: J.E. Birren & K.W. Schaie (Eds.), *Handbook of the Psychology of Aging.* New York: Van Nostrand Reinhold.

Schaie, K.W. (1996). *Intellectual Development in Adulthood. The Seattle Longitudinal Study.* New York: Cambridge University Press.

Schaie, K.W. (2005). *Developmental Influences on Adult Intelligence.* The Seattle Longitudinal Study. New York: Oxford University Press.

Schmidt, F.L. & Hunter, J.E. (1998). The validity and utility of selection methods in personnel psychology: Practical and theoretical implications of 85 years of research findings. *Psychological Bulletin, 124,* 262-274.

Schuerger, J.M. & Witt, A.C. (1989). The temporal stability of individually tested intelligence. *Journal of Clinical Psychology, 45,* 294-302.

Siegler, I.C. & Botwinick, J. (1979). A long-term longitudinal study of intellectual ability of older adults: the matter of selective attrition. *Journal of Gerontology, 34,* 242-245.

Sternberg, R.J. & Grigorenko, E. (Eds.) (1997). *Intelligence, heredity, and environment.* Cambridge University Press.

Sternberg, R.J. & Grigorenko, E. (Eds.) (2001). *Environmental Effects on Cognitive Abilities.* Mahwah, New Jersey & London: Lawrence Erlbaum Associates.

Stuart-Hamilton, I. (2001). *Aldringens psykologi.* Grundbog i gerontopsykologi. København. Gyldendalske Boghandel, Nordisk Forlag A/S.

Teasdale, T.W. & Owen, D.R. (1984). Heredity and familial environment in intelligence and educational level – a sibling study. *Nature, 309,* 620-622.

Teasdale, T.W. & Owen, D.R. (1989). Continuing secular increases in intelligence and a stable prevalence of high intelligence levels. *Intelligence, 13*, 255-262.

Teasdale, T.W., Owen, D.R. & Sørensen, T.I.A. (1991). Intelligence and educational level in adult males at the extremes of stature. *Human Biology, 63*, 19-30.

Teasdale, T.W., Sørensen, T.I.A. & Stunkard, A.J. (1992). Intelligence and educational level in relation to body mass index of adult males. *Human Biology, 64*, 99-106.

Thorpe, H. (1970). *Intelligensforskning og intelligensprøver.* København: J.H. Schultz Forlag.

Thurstone, L.L. (1938). *The Primary Mental Abilities.* Chicago: University of Chicago Press.

Waldstein, S.R. & Elias, M.F. (2001). *Neuropsychology of Cardiovascular Disease.* Hillsdale, New Jersey: Lawrence Erlbaum Associates, Inc.

Wechsler, D. (1958). *The Measurement and Appraisal of Adult Intelligence.* Baltimore, MD: The Williams & Wilkins Company.

Whalley, L.J. & Deary, I.J. (2001). Longitudinal cohort study of childhood IQ and survival up to age 76. *British Medical Journal, 322*, 819-822.

Whalley, L.J., Deary, I.J., Appleton, C.L. & Starr, J.M. (2004). Cognitive reserve and the neurobiology of cognitive aging. *Aging Research Reviews, 3*, 369-382.

Wilson, R.S., Beckett, L.A., Bienias, J.L., Evans, D.A. & Bennett, D.A. (2003). Terminal decline in cognitive function. *Neurology, 60*, 1782-1787.

Wright, C.B., Sacco, R.L., Rundek, T.R., Delman, J.B., Rabbani, L.E. & Elkind, M.S.V. (2006). Interleukin-6 is associated with cognitive function: the Northern Manhattan Study. *Journal of Stroke and Cerebrovascular Disease, 15*, 34-38.

Yaffe, K., Lindquist, M.S., Penninx, B.W., Simonsick, E.M., Pahor, M., Kritchevsky, S., Launer, L., Kuller, L., Rubin, S. & Harris, T. (2003). Inflammatory markers and cognition in well-functioning African-American and white elders. *Neurology, 61*, 76-80.

AGEING AND SOCIAL PARTICIPATION

Per Erik Solem

Summary

Based on the significance of social factors for the process of ageing, this chapter discusses changes in social participation at various levels. Age differences are clearest in the outer social circle, as reduced participation in working life and in politics. The elderly also participate less in clubs and other recreational activities – particularly after the age of 75-80.

For the close relations in the inner circle changes also occur as people grow older. Women lose their spouses earlier than men, and often live for many years as widows. Contact within the family, between old parents and their adult children, seems to be less influenced by age.

Roughly speaking there are two types of explanation as to why the elderly participate less, the first is based on individual changes as people grow older and the second on limitations in the environment, leading to restricted space for the social participation of the elderly. Dialectic models take both individual and contextual factors into account.

Attitudes to the elderly are complex and may reflect a certain degree of ageism. Negative stereotypes of the elderly may be influenced by cultural attitudes to ageing and death, and may lead to old people becoming more passive.

The influence of social conditions on ageing

Ageing is basically a biological process that takes place in varying material and social environments. The biological point of departure, material environment and social context are all prerequisites for the occurrence of the changes constituting ageing. For instance, if the biological process cannot take place in sufficiently favourable surroundings there can be no development or ageing. The individual dies. In other words, the social and material environment plays a vital role in the ageing process. Whereas the contribution of the environment can be summarised in the concept of secondary ageing, biological ageing is referred to as primary – it is biological ageing that ultimately sets the limit to life. The exact nature of the primary factors is not known, although the genes probably are involved (Viidik, 1998), yet these factors cause living organisms to age and die. However, the timing of death and the process leading to death are greatly influenced by environmental factors.

Combined with individual variations in genetic material, variations in environmental conditions lead to large individual variations in the process of ageing. This is apparent in the large differences in life expectancy between poor and rich countries, and between wealthy and poorer areas of major cities. In Oslo there is no less than 12 years' difference in the life expectancy of men in the inner, eastern part of the city compared to men living in the western outskirts of Oslo (Dybendal & Skiri, 2005). As people grow older individual differences in most characteristics also increase. Dannefer (2003) has called this "Cumulative Advantage/Disadvantage" (CAD), and it is also often referred to as the Matthew Effect (Merton, 1968). The term refers to the following quotation from the Gospel according to Matthew: "For the man who has will be given more, till he has enough and to spare; and the man who has not will forfeit even what he has" (Matthew 13:12). This generates accumulative environmental effects over the course of a lifetime. The size of these effects depends on the characteristics that are in focus, and they are not necessarily irreversible (Dannefer, 2003). Not least, contemporary environmental conditions will influence the behaviour and functional abilities of the elderly.

For instance, changes in the environment such as improved physical accessibility (Lawton, 1977) and more positive attitudes to the elderly (Levy, 2003) may lead to a considerable improvement in functional level. Fragile elderly people may become more competent and independent.

The relative strength of hereditary and environmental factors also varies depending on the ability or characteristic that is in focus. In general the genes have a greater influence on the physical changes associated with ageing such as increasing long-sightedness, reduced body height and greying hair. The environment has a greater influence on the psychological and social changes associated with ageing such as the development of wisdom and the end of working life. However, for all types of change associated with ageing there is an interaction between hereditary and environmental factors.

The relative influence of hereditary and environmental factors also changes with age. Developments in the embryo are largely genetically controlled and follow steps in a specific order. At various stages the embryo is particularly sensitive to various types of environmental influence – for instance, if an expectant mother contracts German measles during the first three months of pregnancy this may lead to serious deformities in her baby. Thus an optimum environment is extremely important even though the genetic factor is strong. The influence of the environment grows stronger during childhood and adulthood, yet, at the end of life the genetic influence grows stronger again. However, an interaction between hereditary and environmental factors is always involved.

The use of this simple hereditary/environmental model harbours a risk of overlooking a third important factor in the development and ageing process: the opportunities for individuals to influence their own situation (agency). For instance, in later life people can improve the functionality and accessibility of their housing situation, thereby removing potential causes of accidents. They can choose to mix with others, travel and meet new people, and attend clubs and meetings – or they can refrain from doing all these things. They may choose to move into a new social setting. However, the elderly prefer not to move other than by necessity. They feel at home in the place they live and are most comfortable with the people they know. In their "SPOT model" (Social-physical Place Over Time), Wahl & Lang (2003) postulate that the need for a social and physical sense of belonging grows stronger with age than the need for input from social and physical activities.

The significance of the immediate environment at a great age is also emphasised in Lawton's Environmental Docility Hypothesis (Lawton & Simon, 1968). The less skills possessed by ageing individuals, the more important environmental factors become to maintain wellbeing and adaptation. For instance, people suffering from dementia need to live in manageable surroundings so they can find their way around and avoid the unfortunate results of incontinence if they cannot remember where the toilet is. This is an example of the importance of the physical environment for the elderly to manage their everyday lives. The social environment also has a major influence owing to the available social roles, networks, expectations, attitudes and stereotypes encountered by the elderly in their surroundings (Levy, 2003).

In addition to the importance of the contemporary social context, the context during the biographical history also has an influence on the processes of biological, psychological and social changes that constitute ageing (Daatland & Solem, 2000). The social changes of ageing include changes in social participation, which we shall consider more closely in this chapter.

The social construction of age

Social ageing involves an automatic, progressive journey through various group affiliations or social categories which influence the creation of social identity (Giles & Reid, 2005). This journey runs from childhood to youth (with the transition occurring in the early teens); then to adulthood (with the transition in the early 20s); and then to middle age (with the transition in the mid-40s).

People become elderly in the mid-60s, and they become what we call "old" around the age of 80. This was the typical picture in the Norwegian population (aged 16-79) in 1993 (Daatland, 1994); and a later study in 2002/2003 (Daatland, Solem & Valset, 2006) confirms these divisions in general terms. However, in a previous study in 1969 (Helland, Solem & Trældal, 1973) there was a much shorter gap between "elderly" and "old" based on the number of years that divides the two categories. The averages were 70 and 73 years old respectively. In other words, the category known as "elderly" seems to have grown in both directions: down to about 65 years old, and up to almost 80 years old. "Elderly" now covers a wider time span both because people now retire earlier, but also because fragility and the need for help occur later than they once did. When people stop working and become pensioners they tend to be regarded as "elderly" – whereas the term "old" is probably associated with illness and fragility to a greater extent. So being "elderly" means being free from both work commitments and limitations in the form of health problems and fragility. It is therefore a period that provides the opportunity for a great deal of freedom and what Peter Laslett (1989) calls "personal fulfilment" – the best time of your life. Laslett (1989) describes this period as the third age. The first age involves growing up, dependence, socialisation and education. The second age comprises the years of adulthood with responsibility, maturity, independence and an income. The fourth age is the period of dependence, decline and death.

These four ages are not sharply distinguished by chronological age, and this may provide a basis for variation and flexibility. Similarly, Laslett (1989) points out that the unclear distinction between the third and fourth ages may mean that many elderly people who function well in the third age are contaminated by cultural attitudes to the fourth age and therefore may be excluded from various types of activity such as salaried employment. The same mechanism has been described by Anne Leonora Blaakilde in *Den Store Fortælling om Alderdommen* (The great narrative on old age). In our culture the main narrative about the elderly is primarily negative, stigmatising and patronising (Blaakilde, 1999), and people approaching the final stage of their lives are affected by this negative narrative even though they are still vigorous and active. In other people's eyes the elderly are very little valued. This means that attitudes to the elderly may serve as a barrier to activity in the third age. The behaviour and self-image of the elderly are influenced by negative images in society as a whole (Levy, 2003; Rothermund & Brandstädter, 2003). It is also possible to avoid this kind of negative influence by comparing oneself with negative stereotypes of the elderly. Exaggerating the general negative image of others may make oneself look quite good, after all (Pinquart, 2002).

There has been a greater focus on the positive aspects of ageing in gerontology as well as in the media and advertising in recent years. People talk about vital ageing, productive ageing or successful ageing (Rowe & Kahn, 1998). These concepts are used to describe the factors that promote ageing well: beneficial living conditions, healthy lifestyle and effective coping strategies. Some researchers have extended the concept of coping strategies to include what is described as "anti-ageing": the idea of counteracting ageing or simply disposing of it altogether (Vincent, 2003). Others propose the abandonment of social categories such as "elderly" and "old" (Bytheway, 1997, 2005).

This increased focus on the positive aspects of ageing can be seen as a form of resistance against the misery and mask of ageing (Featherstone & Hepworth, 1990). The contrast to the positive aspects would be the fragile ageing body, to which a distance can be created by underlining the positive sides of ageing. Underlining the idea of successful ageing can be an ambiguous project: on the one hand it may counteract the dominant perceptions of the elderly as fragile and in need of care, thereby creating the basis for increased activity and participation by the elderly. On the other hand, it may involve the cultural suppression of those who do not live up to the successful ideal: who is fragile or weak, or who looks old (Tulle-Winton, 1999), which may make life extremely difficult for those who are fragile, in need of care and "old".

Apart from the fact that negative perceptions and stereotypes have a negative effect on people who are healthy in the third age, the blurred borderlines between age categories may also make it easier to avoid identities such as "elderly" and "old" (Giles & Reid, 2005). In social terms it is hard to know how old one is (Andrews, 1999). The social construction of age is vague and makes it easier than it used to be to choose one's identity; and in such a situation we do not choose the less attractive identities such as "elderly" and "old". From about the age of 30-40 we feel younger than we are (Montepare & Lachman, 1989; Goldsmith & Heiens, 1992), and normally we want to be even younger than we feel. Daatland (2005) found that middle-aged and elderly Norwegians (aged 40-79) felt an average of 7.5 years younger than they were, and wanted to be 18 years younger than they were. A comparison between the US and Germany (Westerhof, Barrett & Steverink, 2003) shows significant cultural differences: Americans feel younger than Germans. And Daatland (1995) found that Americans felt younger than Norwegians too. In other words, American culture seems to have more youthful ideals than European culture, and also is more active in anti-ageing medicine (Vincent, 2003). As mentioned above, this may have a range of negative consequences such as making it harder to deal with infirmities, fragility and death. But it may also have a number of positive effects. Feeling younger than you are may lead to wellbeing and better quality of life (Gana, Alaphilippe & Bailly, 2004; Daatland, 2005), at least in a context where youthfulness, physical vitality and beauty are of the greatest value.

Social participation

Our knowledge about social participation by the elderly is largely based on surveys where people in the third age are over-represented compared to people in the fourth age. For one thing the upper age limit for these group studies is often 79; and for another, fragile elderly people – no matter what their age – are less available for interviews. This means that we may underestimate age-related changes in social participation. Putting it briefly, the elderly participate less in social contexts. The causes of this constitute one of the central questions in social gerontology.

If we imagine that the social relationships or participation of individuals are distributed in concentric circles around the individual, participation in working life and politics can be placed in the outermost circle. In this circle activities are formalised and located in society. At the next level there are various types of clubs and recreational activities with a varying degree of formal structure. The individual can take part at this level with varying degrees of commitment and effort (passive or active membership, participation in committees and so on). Their participation will vary in terms of how social it is, in the sense that it involves interaction with other people. At the innermost level of social contact we find more informal social relationships with family and friends. These are the closest relationships.

Age differences in social participation are clearest in the outermost circle. The elderly participate less in working life and politics. Middle-aged people up to the age of 60 are over-represented among politicians, while young people are over-represented among political activists. Political participation in terms of voting is more evenly distributed, at least from the age of 30 to the end of the 70s, while younger age groups tend to utilise their right to vote less frequently (Daatland, 1993; NOS, 2002a).

There are relatively few elderly people on the labour market. During recent decades the employment rates of elderly people have declined consistently in the industrialised world (Blöndal & Scarpetta, 1998). Several countries have taken steps to counteract this tendency and persuade the elderly to stay on the labour market for longer (Maltby, deVroom, Mirabile & Øverbye, 2004; Jørgensen, Larsen & Rosenstock, 2005). In some European countries less than 33 per cent of the 55-64 year-olds work (Austria, Slovakia, Poland, Belgium, Luxembourg, Italy, Hungary); while in other countries more than twice as many are still in employment (Norway 68 per cent, Sweden 69.5 per cent and

Iceland 82 per cent). Denmark is also in the top half, with 62 per cent of the 55-64 year-olds still in employment (OECD, 2005). This proves that there are large contextual variations in terms of social participation in working life by the elderly. This variation is particularly large among women, who have traditionally had a looser connection to the labour market than men.

Industrialisation led to the introduction of pension schemes marking a transition from the labour market to the later years of life. The elderly are no longer expected to be active on the labour market. The right to a pension implies accepting to lose the right to work, but some pensioners take on paid employment even so. Based on the available statistical information, in general less than 10 per cent of the population aged more than 65 is in paid employment (Maltby et al., 2004). For instance, 5-6 per cent of the 70-79 year-olds in Norway are in paid employment (Solem & Blekesaune, 2006). Few old people are employed, but in recent years the borderline between work and retirement has become less clear. The timing of retirement varies more than it did in the past: for one thing, the age at which people retire varies more; and for another, more elderly people combine their pensions with an income from employment.

Before industrialisation, when there were no pension schemes other than certain arrangements between old farmers and their descendants, the elderly took part in productive activities as long as their health permitted them to do so. But since industrialisation chronological age has become a far more important criterion than work ability. Pension schemes and age limits were introduced with the modernisation of society (Cowgill & Holmes, 1972); and in post-modern society these borderlines have become more fluid, leading to greater options for individual flexibility.

Participation in clubs and recreational activities is located in the second concentric circle. In general the elderly participate less in such activities, particularly when they are more than 75-80 years old. However, this does vary depending on what type of activity is involved. The elderly (especially elderly women) are more active in religious and humanitarian organisations but less active in sports clubs (Birkeland, Lunde, Otnes & Vigran, 1999). In general, elderly members are less active in organisations than younger members, and they are less likely to have posts as well. In their spare time they participate less in cultural activities such as going to concerts, the cinema, the theatre, art exhibitions and museums (Platz, 2000; NOS, 2002b). There is a clear decline in these cultural activities after the age of 67, and particularly after the age of 80. The elderly, including the over-80s, attend religious services or meetings more than younger people (Platz, 2000). They go to restaurants and cafes less often (particularly elderly men), and they go to sports matches less often as well (particularly elderly women). All in all the elderly spend more time at home, and both men and women spend more time on domestic tasks, cooking and meals – and on watching television.

There are also age-related changes affecting the close relations in the innermost circle. A greater number of older people have lost their spouses – this applies in particular to elderly women. While 75-80 per cent of the population of Norway aged 25-66 live with a partner, the same is true of only 20 per cent of all women above the age of 80. Contact between the generations within the family, between old parents and their adult children, seems to be good – a situation which has been stable for the past 30 years (Lingsom, 1997). The family does not seem to have grown any weaker as a social institution for the elderly. However, comparative studies in Europe indicate that contact between the generations is more frequent in Southern Europe than in Scandinavia. At the beginning of the 1990s 80-90 per cent of the elderly in Mediterranean countries had contact with their families at least once a week, while the same was true of 65-70 per cent of the elderly in Scandinavia (Walker, 1993). At the same time there has also been an international tendency over the past 30-40 years for fewer people to live in multi-generation households (Sundström, 1994). In general this development has been by mutual wish, illustrating the fact that people prefer what Rosenmayr & Köckeis (1963) called "intimacy at a distance".

The generations want close contact but they do not want to live together. Geographical distance can even help to improve emotional contact.

There are large cultural differences with regard to the occurrence of cross-generational communal living. A recent study of populations including a range of European towns showed that 7 per cent of all parents above the age of 75 in Norwegian towns lived with one of their children, while the corresponding figure for Spanish towns was 38 per cent (Daatland & Herlofson, 2004).

Social isolation and loneliness

The close relationships of the innermost circle have the greatest significance with regard to social isolation and loneliness. The lack or loss of close contacts has a particularly strong effect on the experience of loneliness (Thorsen, 1990). In a Norwegian study of level of living in 1995 "socially isolated" individuals were defined as people who did not have at least weekly contact with their family or friends. 10-15 per cent of the population aged above 25 was socially isolated, and the age differences were small. There are larger age-related differences when it comes to the feeling of loneliness – elderly women are particularly prone to feeling lonely. This is connected to the fact that a great number of elderly women live alone (Daatland & Solem, 2000). In many studies about 10 per cent of the elderly often feel lonely, and 20-30 per cent say that they feel lonely "occasionally" (Thorsen & Solem, 2005). In the study entitled Danskere med livserfaring

("Danes with Life Experience", Platz, 2000), it was found that 19 per cent of the elderly in their 70s were alone (when they did not want to be alone) either "often" or "occasionally". This was true for slightly fewer individuals in their 50s and 60s (15 per cent). A European study (Walker, 1993) showed surprisingly that the elderly in Southern Europe reported a greater degree of loneliness than the elderly in Northern Europe: 15-35 per cent in Southern Europe and 5-10 per cent in Northern Europe "often" felt lonely – despite closer family contact in Southern Europe. This illustrates that the connection between contact or social participation and loneliness is not a simple matter. There may be greater contrasts between the ideals of strong family norms in Southern Europe and the realities that the elderly actually encounter. However, close physical proximity is not the best foundation for emotional closeness (Rosenmayr & Köckeis,1963) as getting too close may create a need for psychological distance.

In general, close relationships with family and friends are maintained at high ages. Data from The Berlin Ageing Study, with a sample of persons aged 70-100, showed that the oldest respondents only had half as big a social network as the youngest respondents in this age group. However, the oldest respondents did not have fewer close emotional relationships than the youngest (Lang & Carstensen, 1994). Social participation was reduced primarily in the relationships that belong in the outermost circle. This was due to retirement, marking the transition to "the third age" (Laslett, 1989). In the third age active participation is maintained in the middle circle (clubs and recreational activities). Throughout the entire ageing process relationships are maintained in the close network. But reductions occur here as well – particularly when the spouse or same-age friends die. This means that contact with children and siblings becomes increasingly important when approaching the fourth age.

Theories of age differences in social participation

Roughly speaking there are two types of explanation as to why the elderly participate less in social contexts. One is linked to age-related changes in individuals, while the other is linked to the environment or to social structures that provide less room for participation by the elderly. The explanations are related to basic paradigms within developmental psychology called mechanistic and mentalistic models (Riegel, 1977) or mechanistic and organismic models (Lerner, 1997).

The mechanistic paradigm finds the determining forces of development in the environment. Individuals are more or less passive recipients of influences that shape them. Psychological and social changes that accompany ageing such as reduced social participation are perceived as a reflection of reduced opportunities for activity because the access to roles in social contexts has been reduced.

The so-called activity theory is a typical example of this conception: social participation decreases due to the expulsion of individuals from social contexts (the loss of a working role by retirement, for instance).

The mentalistic and organismic paradigm perceives development as being controlled from within – underlining either the individual's own intervention or choices (the mentalistic paradigm) or internal developmental forces in the organism (the organismic paradigm). The latter is often combined with stage models in which development unfolds according to predefined patterns (like the development of an embryo, for instance). Within the field of social gerontology, classical disengagement theory is an example of the way in which the reduction of social participation is regarded as being determined by inner forces. Disengagement is perceived as a natural feature of ageing: it is part of genetically controlled primary ageing.

Most scholars, including those who find the main explanation either in the individual or in the environment, would agree that development takes place in the form of an interaction between intrinsic and extrinsic factors. Individuals can influence their own development; however they depend on the opportunities or limitations provided by their environment and on the opportunities and limitations in their own genetic makeup. In ageing, genes unfold in processes which inevitably lead to death. The biological model, which describes the life course as consisting of development in the early stages leading to maturity, which is followed by decline in the final stages of life, tends to contaminate thinking about psychological and social ageing. However, psychological and social factors have a bigger impact on changes in thinking, emotions and social contact than on physical changes. Theories focusing on interaction between the ageing individual and the environment, which is subject to constant change, are often referred to as dialectic (Riegel, 1976) or contextual (Featherman & Lerner, 1985).

Intrinsic determinants
In the following I shall discuss some of the theories that focus on age-related changes in social participation. The first generation of social-gerontological theory, developed around 1960, focused directly on age-related changes in activity and participation (Marshall, 1999). This generation consists primarily of the disengagement theory (Cumming & Henry, 1961), which was presented by the sociologist Elanie Cumming and the psychologist William Henry, and was based on empirical data from The Kansas City Studies of Adult Life, carried out at the University of Chicago at the end of the 1950s.

This theory explains lower social participation by the concept that it calls intrinsic disengagement (Henry, 1964), a need which emerges at about the age of retirement. If the need for disengagement appears at about the same time as society needs older workers to retire, disengagement will lead to wellbeing. Old people will be happy to seek less contact and to spend more energy on their inner lives. Disengagement was also seen as a preparation for death; based on the idea that the less you live, the less you have to leave behind you when you die – making death less problematic. The idea of intrinsic disengagement was also based on projective tests showing that middle-aged individuals tended to direct more of their mental energy inwards. This energy was directed inwards before social disengagement was observed. It is tempting to believe that the aspects occurring first (mental aspects) are the cause of the aspects occurring later (social aspects). An alternative explanation involves anticipatory sociali-sation, which means that people start preparing themselves mentally for the changes they know will come (retirement, for instance).

The disengagement theory has never won much support – neither among researchers nor among practitioners – and the empirical data has largely sup-ported the activity theory. However, some scholars believe that important insight might be lost if the disengagement theory is completely rejected. The Swedish sociologist Lars Tornstam postulates in his theory of gerotranscendence (Torn-stam, 1989, 2003) an intrinsic drive to switch from a materialistic and rational life perspective to a cosmic and transcendent view of life. Also, he postulates an increasing age-related need for solitude, however without any direct link between gerotranscendence and a reduction in social participation. What this theory shares with the disengagement theory is an inner, organismic model of explanation: the idea that certain changes in interests and activities are con-nected to age-related changes in needs and to primary ageing. Such universal biological explanations of age-related changes in behaviour as part of human nature make great demands on empirical evidence. Even though many people claim that the available evidence does not lend sufficient support to this type of explanation (Blaakilde, 1994; Jönsson & Magnusson, 2001; Solem, 1995; Thorsen, 1998), the theory does remind us of the fact that many elderly people may need more time for reflection. Such reflection may be necessary in order to achieve ego-integrity (Erikson, Erikson & Kivnick, 1986), ego-transcendence (Peck, 1968) or selftranscendence (Levenson et al., 2005).

Socio-emotional selectivity
One recent theory on age changes in social participation is linked to the theory of "selective optimisation with compensation" (Baltes & Baltes, 1990). This is a more general theory about "successful ageing", which has inspired Laura Carstensen (1991, 1993; Carstensen, Isaacowitz & Charles, 1999) to present a theory of socio-emotional selectivity. She regards reduced social contact as a

result of the fact that the elderly seek to strengthen emotional ties and optimise their social environments. The background for this is that social interaction serves various purposes: on the one hand individuals need to collect information about the world and themselves; and on the other they also need to look for emotional support and self-affirmation. As young people need to collect information about the world and their own place in social contexts by finding new friends and new environments, older people need this less because their future perspectives are shorter. However, maintaining emotional support and also receiving confirmation on their identity becomes increasingly important. As a result older persons become less interested in superficial social contacts – they do not need them any more. Carstensen does not believe that this is primarily a defensive, reactive adjustment to reduced opportunities for contact – instead, she sees it as a proactive adaptation to changing needs and interests. The elderly deselect what interest them less (superficial contacts) and concentrate on the contacts that give them the most. Ageing individuals are active agents in inter-action with their environment. Individuals are, according to Laura Carstensen, not subjects to the degree of universal and biological determination that is implicit in the theory of gerotranscendence and in the disengagement theory.

Extrinsic determinants

The disengagement theory was developed through discussions by the group of researchers behind the Kansas City study. At that time the dominant activity paradigm claimed that older persons would take part in social activities and feel a greater sense of wellbeing if they were given opportunities to participate (Havighurst & Albrecht, 1953). Cumming & Henry (1961) argued against this; while other Kansas City researchers found empirical support for the activity theory in the same data set (Havighurst, Neugarten & Tobin, 1968). The activity views were not expressed in the form of an explicit theory until 1972. Lemon, Bengtson & Peterson (1972) proposed four postulates and six theorems which can be summarised as follows: the bigger the loss of role, the less the wish to engage in activities; and the bigger the loss of role, the lower the quality of life and wellbeing. In other words, the activity theory was expressed explicitly in the form of a role theory. Social disengagement is in an activity-theory perspec-tive seen as a reaction to low accessibility of social roles and thereby meagre opportunities for participation in old age. In other words, the explanation for decreased social activity is to be found in the environment, in social expulsion, and this expulsion results in reduced quality of life for the individual.

Roughly speaking, the consequences of the two theoretical perspectives are that we should either leave the elderly alone (disengagement theory) or give them opportunities for activities and participation (activity theory). In the practical care for the elderly most ideologies have been influenced by the activity perspective – sometimes in vulgar forms involving forcing the elderly to take part in activities in which they were not interested.

The roles available to ageing individuals are dependent on the core social values and also on the organisation of the society. One explanations at the macro-level is what is known as modernisation theory (Cowgill & Holmes, 1972), according to which the position of the elderly in society is determined by the basic way of production and on cultural changes. In societies where the majority of production is based on muscle power, the elderly will play a more active role than in industrialised societies where machines have taken over most of the production. There are several reasons why the elderly have a higher status in pre-modern societies. One reason is that pre-modern societies have fewer elderly people because life expectancy is low, thus the society does not need to make space for as many old people as modern societies do. In addition, pre-modern societies are heavily influenced by traditions and changes are slow. The elderly are familiar with the traditions and possess the knowledge which is important for everyone's survival. And as the written culture is less well de-veloped in this type of society, important knowledge is transferred by word of mouth by the old people themselves. The prevalence of stable settlements in which multi-generation families or village groups comprise the smallest social unit means that the elderly are better integrated and less dependent. Receiving help when old is perceived as a form of repayment for the help the old person has provided in the past. However, there is a limit as to how much illness and fragility this type of pre-modern society can tolerate. This limit is particularly clear in nomadic societies, where carrying a fragile individual when moving may threaten the survival of the whole group. There are descriptions of a number of rituals used in the past to dispose of old people who had become a burden on society (Gaunt, 1991). In Scandinavia the practice was known as "ættestup", although there is no evidence that such ritual killing of infirm older people has ever been particularly widespread.

The modernisation theory indicates that the social position of the elderly depends on their usefulness to society. In modern society this usefulness is lim-ited. The elderly are mostly regarded as a group creating problems simply due to their number, and are sometimes referred to as the "elderly wave". As long ago as the 1930s Alva and Gunnar Myrdal warned against what they called a wave of intellectual senility in social life which would sweep through Sweden within a couple of decades as a consequence of changes in the age distribution of the population, a wave which would seem intolerable for the generation at the peak of its powers (Myrdal & Myrdal, 1935: 128). Thus, elderly waves are not an unknown phenomenon – we have had them before. Despite the presence of elderly waves, our modern welfare state has managed to construct systems which take much better care of people in need of help than previous agricultural communities were able to. The welfare state guarantees a basic level of security for all elderly people, based on collective solutions including fixed age limits for the right (and obligation) to retire and receive an old-age pension. However, in order to receive this pension most workers have had to leave the labour market. Some feel that this amounts to expulsion from an important arena, but most old-age pensioners are in general pleased to be able to retire with a secure income from a pension scheme. According to Townsend (1981) social structures including pension schemes and welfare services involve a structurally created form of dependence, because the system of help and care contains elements that turn the elderly into passive recipients. Social security rates are too low to enable the elderly to participate as full members of society, and the services provided indicate that people who use them are a burden to society. Similar ideas can be found in critical gerontology (Phillipson, 1998) and feministic gerontology (Harper, 1997). Social structures at the macro-level limits the opportunities for the elderly to participate in society, and these limitations are different for women and men, poor and rich.

Interaction between intrinsic and extrinsic determinants
I have outlined various explanations and categorised them according to their focus on intrinsic and extrinsic factors respectively. More theories could have been mentioned, but the ones included here are representative examples of various types of explanatory models or theories. None of the theories are blind to the possibility that factors at other levels play a part, but they do not go as far as dialectic and contextual models in focusing directly on the interaction between intrinsic and extrinsic factors. An outline of an explicit dialectic theory of ageing can be found in Riegel (1976), who points to development as continuous conflicts between various levels of life phenomena: the inner biological, individual-psychological, immediate physical-environmental and socio-cultural levels. Permanent changes in the interaction between these levels lie behind development and ageing. This is a more general model of development and ageing than models which focus specifically on changes in social participation; still the model shows that such changes may take various directions and have varying degrees of importance in different contexts and for different individuals.

Lawton's (1980) ecological model focuses more directly on the interaction between the competences of individuals and the demands of their environment (particularly the material environment). Activity and participation are only possible if demands do not exceed the individual's resources. A perfect match is best for activity and wellbeing. But if the competences of individuals are to be developed, the demands should slightly exceed these competences. If the demands are too small this may lead to the development of dependence and passivity. The ecological model has been used in particular to arrange the physical environment in housing and institutions for the elderly to create preconditions for activity and participation and to counteract passivity and disengagement.

The resource model
Another model which aims to explain changes in activity and participation is the resource model (Solem, 1974; Daatland & Solem, 2000). The core of this model is its focus on the potential for individuals to influence their own situation. This potential gives a basis for active coping, and depends on the availability of individual, social and material resources (see table 1).

TABLE I

Individual resources	Social resources	Material resources
health, senses, physical strength, reaction time, knowledge, learning ability, self-image, personality etc.	network, social attachments, status, expectations and attitudes of other people etc.	financial situation, housing, transport, production equipment, climate, technical aids etc.

The individual resources include generalised expectations for internal versus external control which is part of personality. These expectations are shaped by people's previous experience when trying to influence their situation and by their access to resources in general. The experience of success strengthens people's expectations of having internal control.

According to the resource model, supply of resources will help the elderly to maintain influence over their own lives, thereby giving them opportunities for activity and participation. This might involve the provision of individual resources in the form of prophylactic and treatmentoriented health services, physical training and good learning situations; the provision of social resources in the form of positive and realistic expectations, the integration and inclusion of the elderly in social networks; or the provision of material resources in the form of adapting the physical environment to suit the abilities of the individual. Some competences are reduced with age, so it is important to be aware of the potential for taking steps in relation to an individual's environment. Another strategy to maintain internal control may involve avoiding (or withdrawing from) situations in which there is a risk of failure, a strategy that makes it possible to maintain activity and commitment by sticking to the situations that you master. This strategy can be called adaptive resignation (cf. Petersen, 1989), since it involves a form of resignation that serves adaptability as the individuals only reach for achievable goals. The positive effects of such a strategy are described by Brandstädter (1995; Brandstädter & Renner, 1990) as being less depression and a greater expectation of internal control. On the other hand, such adaptation may be maladaptive if the elderly become more resigned to the limitations imposed by their age than they need to be. At worst this may result in learned helplessness.

Autonomy
Maintaining a certain amount of influence over one's life may be particularly important when the resources are reduced and there is a need for a great deal of help to manage everyday activities. When an individual has a severely limited degree of autonomy owing to illness and infirmity, one of the vital factors in maintaining a certain level of activity and participation may be that the remaining basis for self-determination is supported and developed. Langer & Rodin's classic experiments at an American nursing home illustrate this point clearly.

The residents of one wing of a nursing home were summoned to an information meeting. The director of the home explained that the residents were responsible for their own lives at the home and mentioned a range of areas in which they could choose what they wanted to do (brightening up their own rooms, taking part in entertainments, choosing which residents they spent their time with etc.). In other words, the director presented the residents with a number of options enabling them to influence their own situation, and underlined that the responsibility for making the choices was theirs alone. The residents were also invited to choose a plant for their rooms which they would then have to look after, as well as being offered the chance to watch a film at a time of their choice (two possible times were offered). A similar meeting was held for similar residents of another wing of the same nursing home. However, at this meeting the director underlined that the staff was responsible for making the home as cosy as possible and that they would do everything they could to help the residents. The residents simply had to say how they would like things to be. Each resident was then given a plant and told that the staff would look after it and keep it watered. When the film was shown the residents were told which of the two showings they should attend.

One month later the residents in the first wing were more active than those in the second wing. They were more interested in contact and had a greater sense of wellbeing than the residents in the second wing. Follow-up 18 months later showed that the health of the residents in the first wing was also better. 15 per cent in the first wing had died in the intervening period, while 30 per cent had died in the second (Langer & Rodin, 1976; Rodin & Langer, 1977).

When people's resources are limited an apparently insignificant investment of resources and autonomy may have major consequences for the level of both activity and participation. It may be easy for the staff at nursing homes to forget this, however, it is possible for most residents to have some influence on i.e. if the window should be open or closed; if they should wear the yellow dress or the green one; and what kind of spread do they want in their sandwiches.

Attitudes to the elderly

The attitudes encountered by the elderly in society constitute part of the resources which can reinforce (or undermine) their social participation and level of social activity. People's perception of the elderly is often excessively negative, which means that the elderly become trapped in a vicious circle which limits their social participation. Most people think that the elderly are more fragile, forgetful and lonely than they really are, and that their financial situation is poorer than it is. (Daatland & Solem, 2000). Such negative stereotypes may be linked to the discomfort aroused by characteristics displayed by the elderly, or by uneasiness, fear and a need for keeping a distance to one's own ageing. When negative perceptions and emotions lead to discriminatory behaviour towards the elderly, we refer to it as age discrimination. These three components of attitudes: cognitive (perceptions of the elderly), affective (emotions regarding the elderly) and behavioural (actions towards the elderly) can be combined under the term "ageism" (Palmore, Branch & Harris, 2005). This term is used in various ways (Butler, 1969; Bytheway, 1997; Nelson, 2002, 2005) – and it is even used to describe discrimination against young people (Neugarten, 1969), or to describe both negative and positive discrimination (Palmore et al., 2005).

Ageism may become apparent in interaction between individuals; but it may also be incorporated in social and material structures – for instance in age limits, which can be regarded as a form of structural discrimination (Townsend, 1986). Ageism can be compared with racism and sexism, although there is one important difference: we are all gradually joining the group of "others" who are being discriminated against owing to old age. With regard to gender and race we are all placed in a single category and have very limited potential for inclusion in any other category. One type of discrimination which has certain similarities with ageism is the kind of discrimination that occurs in relation to people's sexual orientation. In this area the borderlines are more fluid, and the fear of being placed in the "wrong" category (homophobia) may explain some of the discrimination arising. Similar mechanisms are possible in relation to gerontophobia and age discrimination. Fear of the elderly, or fear of old age and death, may be part of the dynamics behind age discrimination. This is one way of understanding the phenomenon of ageism.

Another way of understanding it is what could be called sympathetic ageism (Binstock, 1983): we feel so strongly for "poor" old people that we overwhelm them with the kind of sympathy that turns them into passive recipients of excessive amounts of help. There may also be traces of excessively positive attitudes such as what Minchiello, Browne & Kendig (2000) call "sageism", reflecting the idea that "all" elderly people are wise. And finally there are systems in which positive and negative aspects are included in a kind of "bipolar ageism" (McHugh, 2003), involving the application of positive and negative stereotypes by turns, or positive chocolate-box images of ageing whose purpose is to cover up an underlying fear of infirmity and death. However, the negative images of old age seem to dominate the behaviour of many people. In working life most managers express both positive and negative perceptions of elderly employees; but in practice negative perceptions seem to dominate when hiring and firing people (Solem, 2001a).

Terror management theory

The "Terror management theory" (Solomon, Greenberg & Pyszczynski, 1991, 2004) is based on a thinking that is similar to the idea that ageism is caused by gerontophobia. It rests on the assumption that we need a defence against the fear of our own death, and that society has developed structures which help to reinforce this defence. It is not only religious institutions but also social order (the fact that we belong to a social system with joint opinions and cultural values) that ensure stability and continuity – with death representing a breach of this stability and continuity. According to this theory, we conform to social systems in order to gain a sense of belonging and an idea about the meaning of life which may protect us from the fear of death. Old people – who are closer to death statistically speaking – may remind us of our own mortality and death, which is why we want to keep a distance to them (Greenberg, Schimel & Martens, 2002). Even while they are still in employment, the elderly part of the workforce may suffer from discrimination owing to these dynamics. Our vulnerability to the fear of dying is weakened when our self-image is strong and positive. Thus support for a positive self-image may counteract the kind of discrimination against the elderly which is caused by terror management.

Research into ageism has been linked in particular to working life: discrimination when workers are appointed, promoted, trained and fired, for instance. A majority of the population in Western society (Walker, 1993; Solem, 2001b) believes that age discrimination does occur in working life. Far fewer people

(3-10 per cent) report that they have experienced this kind of discrimination themselves – a proportion which corresponds to the proportion who have experienced gender discrimination in working life. Two out of three people in a British study of both women and men above the age of 40 said that age was the greatest barrier preventing them from getting a better job (Ginn & Arber, 1996). Erdman Palmore (2004) has developed a questionnaire called the "Ageism Survey" which includes questions about a number of fairly innocent items (have you ever received a birthday card making fun of the 'elderly?) as well as more serious ones (have you ever suffered violence due to your age?). In a selection of readers of magazines for the elderly in the US and Canada, very few respondents had experienced the most serious forms of age discrimination; but 40-50 per cent of them said that they were treated with condescension owing to their age.

Internalised self-stereotypes

The idea of keeping thoughts of age, weakness and death at a distance may be a strategy used to maintain activities and participation without becoming paralysed by depression or dark thoughts about the future. However, there seem to be limits when it comes to keeping negative thoughts about ageing at a distance. Becca Levy (2003) argues that negative stereotypes about the elderly are internalised even in childhood, developing into self-stereotypes in the older years. Becca Levy has studied the effects of such self-stereotypes experimentally using subliminal presentation of negative and positive characteristics. Examples of negative subliminal stimulus terms were: Alzheimer's, confused, decrepit, illness, death, forgetfulness. The positive words included terms such as: advice, creative, well-informed, wise and insightful. A series of experiments enabled Levy and her staff to demonstrate a range of strong effects on memory functions, gait, balance and walking speed. The improvement of walking speed after introducing the positive words could be compared with the effect of a physical training programme lasting several weeks. Based on the handwriting of the participants, a panel judged the group who had "seen" the negative words as being much older than the group who had "seen" the positive words. The handwriting of the first group was judged to be shakier and "senile". The panel also found that the people exposed to the negative words had stronger physiological stress reactions in threatening situations as well as a lower will to live. These reactions all indicate that a negative self-image also has an indirect effect on processes which are important for activity and participation in society.

The attribution of the negative experiences to old age itself

If age is associated with primarily negative emotions, the result may be that the negative or undesirable phenomena occurring when we grow old are attributed to the ageing process; while positive events are perceived as occurring despite the ageing process. Age may be an easy scapegoat when things do not quite work out as we would wish. Rodin (1980) found that nursing-home residents who perceived their own difficulties and problems as being caused primarily by ageing were more active and enjoyed better health after they were given a range of environmental explanations of their problems. For instance, they were told that their difficulties in getting out of bed were caused by the fact that the bed was too low, that they were tired in the early evening because they had been woken up so early in the morning, and that it was difficult to walk round the home safely because the floors were so slippery and slanting that even young people could easily lose their footing too. The residents had mainly been sitting down because they felt old and dizzy and afraid of falling; but after being given an environmental explanation of their difficulties they started walking around more often. They had placed the cause of their problems outside themselves, outside their own ageing process, thereby avoiding maladaptive resignation.

Conclusion

Elderly people are shaped by their genetic composition and the social and material environment to which they are exposed during the course of life. Variations in environmental conditions lay the foundations for the increasing differences observed with increased age. The elderly do not constitute a social category of uniform individuals. On the contrary: they vary more than young people. Activity and participation in society and contact with other people also depend on the environmental conditions they encounter when in old age. To the extent that ageing leads to a weakening of abilities to master everyday life, the immediate environment will increase in importance as people grow older. Variations in environmental conditions, for instance to the extent to which they stimulate or limit activity, will therefore contribute to increasing differences between older persons. The social environment works through the social construction of age and the attitudes that individuals encounter, categorised as "elderly" or "old". Basic attitudes to the elderly in society are mainly negative and disparaging, and the behaviour of the elderly is influenced by this, making them more passive. In contrast to this negative picture, there is also a more positive perspective emphasising terms such as vital ageing, successful ageing and the anti-ageing movement, which ultimately seeks to abolish ageing entirely (or at least to postpone it significantly). A positive perspective may strengthen many elderly people and support their activity, participation and will to live; but it may also create a contrast to people who are fragile or who look old, making it difficult to accept the weakness that must be expected to occur if we grow old enough.

Negative attitudes to the elderly, internalised stereotypes and ageism may be barriers preventing the elderly from playing an active role in society. In line with the theory of terror management, visible elderly people in society will remind us of our mortality and future death – which we seem to need protection against. The industrialisation and globalisation of the economy have also made the elderly less useful because there is less room for their contribution, which is not regarded as 100 % effective in working life and elsewhere. These are examples of social explanations as to why the elderly participate less in social contexts than younger people. The importance of such explanations is underlined by the fact that in the outermost circles of society the differences between young and elderly people are larger. Politics and working life are arenas in which there are very few elderly players. However, the reduction of social participation must be seen in the light of both intrinsic and extrinsic factors and the interaction between ageing individuals and a changing society. Recent theories emphasise the importance of this interaction, of mutual adaptation to changes in the individual and the environment, and of autonomy.

Some elderly people are fragile and less able than others to manage their own affairs. For these individuals not the least, it is important to retain and elicit any remaining potential for autonomy.

REFERENCES

Andrews, M. (1999). The seductiveness of agelessness. *Ageing and Society, 19*, 301-318.

Baltes, P.B. & Baltes, M.M. (1990). Psychological perspectives on successful aging: The model of selective optimization with compensation. In: P.B. Baltes & M.M. Baltes (Eds.), *Successful aging. Perspectives from the behavioral sciences* (1-34). Cambridge: Cambridge University Press.

Binstock, R.H. (1983). The aged as scapegoat. *The Gerontologist, 23*, 136-143.

Birkeland, E., Lunde, E.S., Otnes, B. & Vigran, E. (1999). *Eldre i Norge*. Oslo: Statistisk sentralbyrå, SA 32.

Blaakilde, A.L. (1994). Som en fisk i vandet – kommentar til teorien om gerotranscendens. *Socialmedicinsk tidskrift, 71*, 281-283.

Blaakilde, A.L. (1999). *Den store fortælling om alderdommen*. København: Munksgaard.

Blöndal, S. & Scarpetta, S. (1998) The retirement decision in OECD countries. *OECD Economics Department Working Papers no 202*. Paris: OECD.

Brandstädter, J. & Renner, G. (1990). Tenacious goal pursuit and flexible goal adjustment: Explication and age-related analysis of assimilative and accommodative strategies of coping. *Psychology and Aging, 5*, 58-67.

Brandstädter, J. (1995). The resiliency of the aging self: Strategies and mechanisms of adaptation. Paper presented at the III European Congress of Gerontology, Amsterdam.

Butler, R.N. (1969). Ageism: Another form of bigotry. *The Gerontologist, 9*, 243-246.

Bytheway, B. (1997). *Alderisme. Fordomme omkring alder og diskrimination mod ældre.* Frederikshavn: Dafolo forlag.

Bytheway, B. (2005). Ageism and age categorization. *Journal of Social Issues, 61*, 361-374.

Carstensen, L. (1991). Socioemotional selectivity theory: Social activity in life-span context. *Annual Review of Gerontology and Geriatrics, 11*, 195-217.

Carstensen, L. (1993). Motivation for social contact across the life span: A theory of socioemotional selectivity'. In: J. Jacobs (Ed.), Nebraska symposium of motivation 1992. *Developmental perspectives on motivation, 40* (209-254). Lincoln: University of Nebraska Press.

Carstensen, L.L., Isaacowitz, D.M. & Charles, S.T. (1999). Taking time seriously. A theory of socioemotional selectivity. *American Psychologist, 54*, 165-181.

Cowgill, D.O. & Holmes, L.D. (1972). *Aging and modernization.* New York: Appleton-CenturyCrofts.

Cumming, E. & Henry, W. (1961). *Growing old.* New York: Basic Books.

Dannefer, D. (2003). Cumulative advantage/disadvantage and the life course: Cross-fertilizing age and social science theory. *Journal of Gerontology: Social Sciences, 58B*, 327-337.

Daatland, S.O. & Herlofson, K. (2004). *Familie, velferdsstat og aldring. Familiesolidaritet i et europeisk perspektiv.* NOVA rapport 7 (04). Oslo: Norsk institutt for forskning om oppvekst, velferd og aldring.

Daatland, S.O. & Solem, P.E. (2000). *Aldring og samfunn. En innføring i sosialgerontologi.* Bergen: Fagbokforlaget.

Daatland, S.O., Solem, P.E. & Valset, K. (2006). Subjektiv alder og aldring. In: B. Slagsvold & S.O. Daatland, (Eds.), *Lokal variasjon i livsløp, aldring og generasjon.* NOVA-rapport.

Daatland, S.O. (1993). Aldring og politikk. *Aldring & Eldre, 10* (2), 14-19.

Daatland, S.O. (1994). En ny fase av livet. *Aldring & Eldre, 11* (1), 21.

Daatland, S.O. (2005). Hvor gammel vil du være? Om aldersidentiteter og subjektiv alder. *Aldring og livsløp, 22* (2), 2-7.

Dybendal, K.E. & Skiri, H. (2005), Klare geografiske forskjeller i levealder mellom bydeler i Oslo. *Samfunnsspeilet, 19*, 18-27.

Erikson, E.H., Erikson, J.M. & Kivnick, H.Q. (1986). *Vital involvement in old age: The experience of old age in our time.* New York: Norton.

Featherman, D.L. & Lerner, R.M. (1985). Ontogenesis and sociogenesis: Problematics for theory and research about development and socialization across the life span. *American Sociological Review, 50*, 659-676.

Featherstone, M. & Hepworth, M. (1990). Images of ageing. In: J. Bond & P. Coleman (Eds.), *Ageing in society. An introduction to social gerontology,* 250-275. London: Sage.

Gana, K., Alaphilippe, D. & Bailly, N. (2004). Positive illusions and mental and physical health in later life. *Aging and Mental Health, 8*, 58-64.

Gaunt, D. (1991). Det förlorade paradiset eller paradisets förlorare – gamlingars status i olika kulturer. *Socialmedicinsk tidskrift, 68*, 78-83.

Giles, H. & Reid, S.A. (2005). Ageism across the lifespan: towards a self-categorization model of ageing. *Journal of Social Issues, 61*, 389-404.

Ginn, J. & Arber, S. (1996). Gender, age and attitudes to retirement in mid-life. *Ageing and Society, 16*, 27-55.

Goldsmith, R.E. & Heiens, R.A. (1992). Subjective age: a test of five hypotheses. *The Gerontologist, 32*, 312-317.

Greenberg, J., Schimel, J. & Martens, A. (2002). Ageism: Denying the face of the future. In: T.D. Nelson (Ed.), *Ageism. Stereotyping and prejudice against older persons*, 27-48. Cambridge, Massachusetts: The MIT Press.

Harper, S. (1997). Constructing later life/constructing the body: some thoughts from feminist theory. In: A. Jamieson, S. Harper & C. Victor (Eds.), *Critical approaches to ageing and later life* (160-172). Buckingham: Open University Press.

Havighurst, R.J. & Albrecht, R. (1953). *Older people*. New York: Longmans Green.

Havighurst, R.J., Neugarten, B.L. & Tobin, S.S. (1968). Disengagement and patterns of aging. In: B.L. Neugarten (Ed.), *Middle age and aging: A reader in social psychology* (161-172). Chicago: University of Chicago Press.

Helland, H., Solem, P.E. & Trældal, A. (1973). *Eldres integrasjon*. Oslo: Sosialdepartementet/Universitetsforlaget, NOU 1973: 60.

Henry, W.E. (1964). The theory of intrinsic disengagement. In: P.F. Hansen (Ed.), *Age with a future* (415-418). København: Munksgaard.

Jönson, H. & Magnusson, J.A. (2001). A new age of old age? Gerotranscendence and the re-enchantment of aging. *Journal of Aging Studies, 15*, 317-331.

Jørgensen, M.S., Larsen, M. & Rosenstock, M. (2005). *Et længere arbejdsliv. Tilbagetrækningsordninger og arbejdspladsens muligheder*. København: Socialforskningsinstituttet (05:03).

Lang, F.R. & Carstensen, L. (1994). Close emotional relationships in later life: further support for proactive aging in the social domain. *Psychology and Aging, 9*, 315-324.

Langer, E.J. & Rodin, J. (1976). The effects of choice and enhanced personal responsibility for the aged: A field experiment in an institutional setting. *Journal of Personality and Social Psychology, 34*, 191-198.

Laslett, P. (1989). *A fresh map of life. The emergence of the third age*. London: Weidenfeld and Nicolson.

Lawton, M.P. & Simon, B.B. (1968). The ecology of social relationships in housing for the elderly. *The Gerontologist, 8*, 108-115.

Lawton, M.P. (1977). The impact of the environment on ageing and behavior. In: J.E. Birren & K.W. Schaie (Eds.), *Handbook of the Psychology of Ageing* (276-301). New York: Van Nostrand.

Lawton, M.P. (1980). *Environment and aging*. Monterey: Brooks/Cole.

Lemon, B.W. & Bengtson, V.L. & Peterson, J.A. (1972). An exploration of the activity theory of aging: Activity types and life satisfaction among in-movers to a retirement community. *Journal of Gerontology, 27*, 511-523.

Lerner, R.M. (1997). *Concepts and theories of human development.* Second Edition. Mahwah, New Jersey: Lawrence Erlbaum.

Levenson, M.R., Jennings, P.A., Aldwin, C.M., & Shiraishi, R.E. (2005). Self-transcendence: Conceptualization and measurement. *International Journal of Aging and Human Development, 60,* 127-143.

Levy, B.R. (2003). Mind matters: Cognitive and physical effects of aging self-stereotypes. *Journal of Gerontology: Psychological Sciences, 58B,* 203-211.

Lingsom, S. (1997). *The substitution issue. Care policies and their consequences for family care.* NOVA rapport 6-1997 Oslo: Norsk Institutt for forskning om oppvekst, velferd og aldring.

Maltby, T., deVroom, B., Mirabile, M.L. & Øverbye, E. (Eds.), (2004). *Ageing and the transition to retirement. A comparative analysis of European welfare states.* Aldershot: Ashgate.

Marshall, V.W. (1999). Analyzing social theories of aging. In: V.L. Bengtson & K.W. Schaie (Eds.), *Handbook of theories of aging,* 434-455. New York: Springer.

McHugh, K.E. (2003). Three faces of ageism: Society, image and place. *Ageing & Society, 23,* 165-185.

Merton, R.K. (1968). The Matthew effect in science. *Science, 159,* 56-63.

Minchiello, V., Browne, J. & Kendig, H. (2000). Perceptions and consequences of ageism: Views of older people. *Ageing and Society, 20,* 253-278.

Montepare, J.M. & Lachman, M.E. (1989). 'You're only as old as you feel': self-perceptions of age, fears of aging, and life satisfaction from adolescence to old age. *Psychology and Aging, 4,* 73-78.

Myrdal, A. & Myrdal, G. (1935). *Kris i befolkningsfrågan.* Stockholm: Bonniers.

Nelson, T.D. (Ed.) (2002). *Ageism. Stereotyping and prejudice against older persons.* Cambridge, Massachusetts: The MIT Press.

Nelson, T.M. (2005). Ageism: Prejudice against our feared future self. *Journal of Social Issues, 61,* 207-221.

Neugarten, B.L. (1969). *The old and the young in advanced industrial societies.* In: Proceedings from the 8th International Congress of Gerontology Washington, D.C., Vol I, 448-450.

NOS (2002a). *Stortingsvalget 2001. NOS C 710.* Oslo: Statistisk sentralbyrå.

NOS (2002b). *Levekårsundersøkinga 1996-1998. NOS C 704.* Oslo: Statistisk sentralbyrå.

OECD (2005). *Employment outlook 2004.* Paris: OECD.

Palmore, E. (2004). Research note: Ageism in Canada and the United States. *Journal of CrossCultural Gerontology, 19,* 41-46.

Palmore, E.B., Branch, L. & Harris, D.K. (Eds.) (2005). *Encyclopedia of ageism.* New York: Haworth.

Peck, R. (1968). Psychological development in the second half of life. In: B.L. Neugarten (Ed.), *Middle age and aging: A reader in social psychology,* 88-92. Chicago: University of Chicago Press.

Petersen, E. (1989). Life conditions and quality of life in Denmark during the period 1976-1986, and how Danes coped with the 1980-1982 crisis. In: R. Veenhoven & A. Hagenaars (Eds.), *Did the crisis really hurt? Effects of the 1980-1982 economic recession on satisfaction, mental health and mortality,* 64-93. Rotterdam, The Netherlands: Universitaire Pers.

Phillipson, C. (1998). *Reconstructing old age. New agendas in social theory and practice.* London: Sage.

Pinquart, M. (2002). Good news about the effects of bad old-age stereotypes. *Experimental Aging Research, 28,* 317-336.

Platz, M. (2000). *Danskere med livserfaring – portræt i tal: Aspekter af levekår i fødselsårgangerne 1920, 1925, 1930, 1935, 1940 og 1945.* København: Socialforskningsinstituttet 00 (8).

Riegel, K. (1977). Past and future trends in gerontology. *The Gerontologist, 17,* 105-113.

Riegel, K.F. (1976). The dialectics of human development. *American Psychologist, 31,* 689-700.

Rodin, J. & Langer, E.J. (1977). Long-term effects of a control-relevant intervention with the institutionalized aged. *Journal of Personality and Social Psychology, 35,* 897-903.

Rodin, J. (1980). Managing the stress of aging: The role of control and coping. In: S. Levine & H. Ursin (Eds.), *Coping and Health,* 71-202. New York: Plenum Press.

Rosenmayr, L. & Köckeis, E. (1963). Propositions for a sociological theory of aging and the family. *International Social Science Journal, 15,* 410-426.

Rothermund, K. & Brandtstädter, J. (2003). Age stereotypes and self-views in later life: evaluating rival assumptions. *International Journal of Behavioral Development, 27,* 549-554.

Rowe, J.W. & Kahn, R.L. (1998). *Successful Aging.* New York: Pantheon.

Solem, P.E. & Blekesaune, M. (2006). Pensjonering og tilknytning til arbeid – lokale variasjoner. In: B. Slagsvold & S.O. Daatland (Eds.), *Eldre år, lokale variasjoner,* 161-175. NOVA-rapport 15/06. Oslo: Norsk institutt for forskning om oppvekst, velferd og aldring.

Solem, P.E. (1974). Tilgang til ressurser og sosial deltagelse blant eldre. *Nordisk Psykologi, 26,* 137-144.

Solem, P.E. (1995). Aktivitet eller gerotranscendens? Et kritisk lys på sosialgerontologisk teori. In: S.O. Daatland & P.E. Solem (Eds.), *Aldersforskning i kritisk lys* 7-23, Oslo: Norsk gerontologisk institutt, rapport 2-1995.

Solem, P.E. (2001a). *For gammel? Kunnskapsstatus om aldring, arbeid og pensjonering.* NOVA rapport 4/01. Oslo: Norsk institutt for forskning om oppvekst, velferd og aldring.

Solem, P.E. (2001b). Diskriminering av eldre i arbeidslivet. *Søkelys på arbeidsmarkedet, 18,* 93-99.

Solomon, S., Greenberg, J. & Pyszczynski, T. (1991). Terror management theory of self-esteem. In: C.R. Snyder & D.R. Forsyth (Eds.), *Handbook of social and clinical psychology. The health perspective* (21-40). New York: Pergamon.

Solomon, S., Greenberg, J. & Pyszczynski, T. (2004). The cultural animal. Twenty years of terror management theory and research. In: J. Greenberg, S.L. Koole, & T. Pyszcxynski (Eds.), *Handbook of Experimental Existential Psychology,* 13-34. New York: Guildford.

Sundström, G. (1994). Care by families: An overview of trends. In: OECD, *Caring for frail elderly people: New directions in care.* Paris: OECD, Social policy studies no. 14.

Thorsen, K. (1990). *Alene og ensom, sammen og lykkelig? Ensomhet i ulike aldersgrupper.* Oslo: Norsk gerontologisk institutt, rapport 2-1990.

Thorsen, K. (1998). The paradoxes of gerotranscendence: The theory of gerotranscendence in a cultural gerontological and post-modernist perspective. *Norwegian Journal of Epidemiology, 8,* 165-176.

Thorsen, K. & Solem, P.E. (2005). Vil ensomheten øke i årene fremover? In: B. Slagsvold & P.E. Solem (Eds.), *Morgendagens eldre. En sammenlikning av verdier, holdninger og atferd blant dagens middelaldrende og eldre* (125-130). NOVA-rapport 11/05. Oslo: Norsk institutt for forskning om oppvekst, velferd og aldring.

Tornstam, L. (1989). Gero-transcendence: A meta-theoretical reformulation of the disengagement theory. *Aging, 1,* 55-63.

Tornstam, L. (2003). *Gerotranscendence from young old age to old old age.* Online publication from The Social Gerontolgy Group, Uppsala. www.soc.uu.se

Townsend, P. (1981). The structured dependency of the elderly: A creation of social policy in the twentieth century. *Ageing and Society, 1,* 5-28.

Townsend, P. (1986). Ageism and social policy. In: C. Phillipson & A. Walker (Eds.), *Ageing and social policy. A critical assessment,* 15-44. Aldershot: Gower.

Tulle-Winton, E. (1999). Growing old and resistance: toward a new cultural economy of old age? *Ageing and Society, 19,* 281-299.

Viidik, A. (1998). Den biologiske aldringsmodell. In: H. Kirk & M. Schroll (Eds.), *Viden om aldring – veje til handling,* 33-51. København: Munksgaard.

Vincent, J. (2003). Review article: What is at stake in the 'war on anti-ageing medicine'? *Ageing & Society, 23,* 675-684.

Wahl, H.-W. & Lang, F.R. (2003). Aging in context across the adult life course: integrating physical and social environmental research perspectives. In: H.-W. Wahl, R.J. Scheidt & P.G. Windley (Eds.), *Annual Review of Gerontology and Geriatrics, 23,* 1-33. New York: Springer.

Walker, A. (1993). *Age and attitudes. Main results from a Eurobarometer study.* Bruxelles: Commission of the European Communities.

Westerhof, G., Barrett, A. & Steverink, N. (2003). Forever young? A comparison of age identities in the United States and Germany. *Research on Aging, 25,* 366-383.

LIFE SATISFACTION IN OLD AGE

Mimi Y. Mehlsen

Summary

The aim of this chapter is to explore how it is possible from a psychological point of view to maintain life satisfaction in old age despite losses and limitations. Life satisfaction in old age may be linked to what is known as successful ageing, which occurs when the process of ageing results in a minimum of physical, mental or social losses of function in ageing individuals – or no such losses at all. But successful ageing is a relatively rare phenomenon, and normal ageing is connected with losses and some reductions of function. Despite this fact, most people are satisfied with their lives in old age. To find out whether there is a life-long development in psychological processes helping individuals to maintain life satisfaction in limited circumstances, general life-span theories are presented in this chapter regarding the psychological processes of selection, optimisation, compensation and primary and secondary control. This is followed by a description of the way in which cognitive processes are used not only in adapting to loss and adversity in life but also in evaluating how satisfactory life is. The acceptance of loss and adaptation to the conditions of old age are derived from a general process of development throughout adulthood leading to an increased use of value-adjusting and compensatory control strategies that enable people to handle loss adaptively.

Background

In old age most people consider the years in which they married and had children, completed an education and had a career as the best period of their lives (Field, 1997; Mehlsen, Platz & Fromholt, 2003; Mehlsen, Thomsen, Viidik, Olesen & Zachariae, 2005). The past might seem brighter because old age often means loss – for instance, loss of social relations or physical capabilities, and ultimately loss of the ability to lead the life you want to lead. However, the vast majority of elderly people are satisfied with their lives in old age and actually say that they are just as satisfied with their lives here and now as they were when they were younger (Diener, Suh, Lucas & Smith, 1999). How can this be so? This is an interesting question which has not only theoretical relevance in the form of increased understanding of adaptive psychological processes in old age, but also potential clinical relevance for elderly people suffering from depression and other conditions characterised by reduced life satisfaction.

This chapter starts by defining life satisfaction and successful ageing, and then focuses on the way in which cognitive processes are used not only to adapt to loss and adversity in life, but also to evaluate how satisfactory life is. In this way general life-span theories regarding psychological processes that determine adaptation to life in old age are combined with a cognitive approach to the concept of life satisfaction.

What is life satisfaction?

As life satisfaction is the basic concept of this chapter, we shall start by defining what we mean by this concept. If you ask someone "How satisfied are you with your life?" the answer will normally be in the form of a general, overall evaluation. Life satisfaction is the result of this kind of overall evaluation of how satisfactory people feel their lives are (Andrews & Withey, 1976). Evaluations of life satisfaction are subjective because they are based solely on the personal feelings of the individual in question; and they are global because they comprise a general evaluation of all aspects of life. The emotional aspect of the concept of life satisfaction, the presence of positive and the absence of negative feelings, is connected with the cognitively evaluative aspect because people are more likely to regard their lives as satisfactory if they have many positive feelings and few negative ones. However, a surplus of positive feelings is not always sufficient to make people feel that their lives are satisfactory. Sometimes people's current emotional state may even run counter to their evaluation of life satisfaction: their emotional state may be a brief reaction to a passing event; whereas life satisfaction depends on the result of an overall summary of the lives they have led (Pavot & Diener, 1993).

Life satisfaction can be defined as a global, cognitive evaluation of your life. This evaluation may be influenced by feelings, but it is not in itself a direct measurement of feelings (Diener, 1984). So life satisfaction in old age concerns the extent to which elderly people regard their lives as satisfactory. We may assume that any such evaluation is greatly influenced by the way life has turned out. In some cases old age is a period of illness, loneliness and a lack of resources; while in other cases old age can be a rich, active but unstressful period of life with the freedom to focus on the activities and people of your choice. Such cases can be referred to as examples of successful ageing.

Successful ageing

In the population as a whole and in large sections of the field of psychology, ageing is typically connected with the loss of functions and resources. Everyone above a certain chronological age is lumped together without regard to the considerable variations in both functional abilities and resources that actually apply within the group of elderly. Some 80-year-olds are mentally infirm and cannot look after themselves; while others are disabled or have to live with painful, chronic illnesses making them dependent on the help of others. But many people aged 80 are still able to lead an active life and to maintain their previous activities despite age-related ailments and minor health issues. And finally, a few 80-year-olds seem to be largely unmarked by age, leading a life similar to that of 30-40 year-olds in terms of content and activity level. To maintain awareness of this large variation in ageing, it has been proposed within the field of gerontology that the ageing process should be regarded as constituting three different but typical variations: pathological ageing, normal ageing and successful ageing. Successful ageing is the optimum result of the ageing process, so if we use our observations of normal or even pathological ageing as a point of departure for the understanding of ageing, we risk underestimating the true potential of the ageing individual.

Successful ageing occurs when the ageing process only causes a minimum of functional loss (or no loss at all) in ageing individuals (Schulz & Heckhausen, 1996). Successful ageing implies a positive result of the ageing process within areas such as health (the absence of illness), cognitive function (the absence of cognitive reduction) and everyday function (the absence of reduction in functional abilities). One common denominator of all these criteria is that they focus on broad, measurable areas of function which can be used at all stages of life – areas in which there is broad cultural agreement that the higher the functional level the more positive the situation becomes for the individual concerned (Schulz et al., 1996). In other words, in different cultures there is general agreement that people who score highly in terms of all these criteria – no matter what their age – are actually more successful than people who do not. Factors such as a healthy diet, further or higher education, sufficient exercise and social support are regarded as the prerequisites of successful ageing. In other words, successful ageing depends on optimum conditions in the areas on which physical, mental and social wellbeing depend.

Schulz and Heckhausen (1996) have the following to say about the criteria for successful ageing:

...it is important to focus on criteria of success that are externally measurable and include domains of functioning that have been and continue to be valued by cultures throughout time. These include physical functioning; cognitive, intellectual, affective, and creative functioning; and social relations. We recognize and acknowledge that trade-offs have to be made in attempting to maximize functioning in individual or multiple domains and that performance can be evaluated comparatively, as specified above. In this context, subjective evaluations such as satisfaction with ageing can be viewed as one of many components of affective and intellectual functioning, but they are not treated as major criteria of successful development.

Schulz & Heckhausen, 1996, p. 704-705

So successful ageing is defined based on objective criteria. It is possible that people who are satisfied with their lives in old age are satisfied because their lives largely live up to these criteria. But if this is the case, differences in the life satisfaction of elderly people must be assumed to be due to differences in the extent to which they have experienced loss and age-related reduction. Are the people who are most satisfied with life in old age the people who are least influenced by the negative consequences of old age? Perhaps, but it is still important to remember that successful ageing with no loss of functional abilities (or very little such loss) does not represent the typical ageing process. Normal ageing is associated with loss and a certain amount of reduction, but even so most people are satisfied with their lives in old age. Even though many elderly people experience reductions of function and losses which would be devastating for younger people, the elderly are in general just as satisfied with their lives as young people are (Diener et al., 1999). The elderly seem to be better than young people at maintaining a sense of satisfaction despite the limitations of their lives, and this may be due to the fact that during the course of life there is a development in the psychological processes helping individuals to maintain life satisfaction despite loss and reduction.

Selection – optimisation – compensation.
Adapting to changes in old age

The theoretical model designed by Baltes and Baltes relating to Selective Optimisation with Compensation (SOC) is one of the most widespread and recognised general theory of developmental adjustment over the course of life (Baltes & Baltes, 1990). The SOC model was designed as a general framework for the understanding of developmental changes and powers of resistance during the course of life. As a result, psychological processes that help to maintain life satisfaction in old age despite age-related losses belong within the explanatory field of this model.

The central components of the model are the psychological processes known as selection, optimisation and compensation. These processes can be described as follows:

Selection involves choosing areas of focus. People select such focus areas all the time, and basically it is this selection that determines the interaction between individuals and their environment. Selection determines both diversity and focus in the areas chosen by each individual. Selection is necessary because our resources (including time and energy) are limited – so we are forced to focus on certain areas and goals. There are two types of selection: *elective selection*, comprising the adjustment processes used to choose between a number of alternative development paths; and *loss-based selection*, which is a reaction to loss of resources or loss of the tools which were formerly available in order to achieve goals. Elective selection is carried out in a broad life perspective when we choose which education, partner, accommodation or recreational activities we wish to focus on. But elective selection also takes place in an everyday perspective on an ongoing basis: deciding whether to spend your weekend doing overtime, or to spend it with your family or on recreational activities; or choosing to buy gifts for your grandchildren instead of buying new clothes for yourself. Loss-based selection comprises processes such as the reconstruction of goal hierarchies and the establishment of new goals: for instance, when you choose on retirement (loss of career) to spend more of your energy on family life (giving higher priority to the values of family life); or when you decide to start studying for exams again at a mature age once the children have left home (establishment of new goals). Selection determines the way in which we handle the world, so loss-based selection processes like the ability to find new goals and reconstruct previous goal hierarchies are important when a loss of any kind deprives the individual of previous goals. Because without the ability to find new goals, people will lack the tools needed to control their actions and take their lives in new directions.

Optimisation involves marshalling and refining inner and outer resources with a view to achieving a higher functional level within selected areas or in relation to specific goals. For instance, people might optimise their resources if they feel that they risk being fired or being deserted by their partners – they might invest extra energy in the area that is threatened. But they may also choose to spend time on taking a course of supplementary education with a view to gaining extra qualifications and finding a new job at some point. The fewer resources individuals possess, the more necessary it becomes for them to optimise their use of these resources. Consequently, people who are good at marshalling and refining their resources will be better equipped to handle loss.

Compensation occurs when people's interaction with their environment does not lead to the desired result: in other words, when we do not succeed in what we set out to do. In such circumstances, compensation mechanisms are required in order to retain the potential for handling the situation despite losses and apparent defeats. Compensation refers to the processes of substitution that are necessary to maintain a given functional level when we experience a decline in resources or lose the tools needed to achieve our goals. We perform compensatory processes every day: if we have run out of coffee when visitors turn up unexpectedly, we decide that another drink such as tea can replace coffee. Compensatory strategies are also involved if we cannot find the recipe for a cake we wish to bake: we call a friend to ask them for help. And we write the next appointment with the dentist in our diaries to make sure we do not forget it. Compensation is simply our way of handling all the situations that do not progress as we would wish and as we have planned. The more a situation differs from what we would have wished and what we planned, the more necessary compensation strategies become. So like loss-based selection and optimisation, effective compensation processes are necessary in order to handle the losses that occur during a lifetime.

The SOC model has been presented here as a general model for lifelong development; but it can be assumed that the dynamics of the SOC processes grow stronger in old age. This is because ageing is often related to losses in the form of health-related limitations, the loss of functional capacity and the limitation of resources, leading to a greater need for compensatory measures in elderly people (Freund & Baltes, 1998).

For instance, it has been shown that elderly people with plenty of resources employ SOC processes to a larger extent than elderly people with a poorer level of physical, social and cognitive function (Lang, Rieckmann & Baltes, 2002). In daily life selection mechanisms occurred in the form of increased contact with family members and a reduction in the number of recreational activities by elderly people with plenty of resources – but the same did not apply to elderly people with reduced physical and mental powers. Compensation strategies (taking more rest during the day) and optimisation (flexibility in the time allocated to various daily activities) were also observed in elderly people with strong resources but not in elderly people with weak resources. In other words, prioritising your energy and using SOC processes in an appropriate manner seem to require a certain level of resources.

It may seem like the irony of fate that the people who have most resources are the people who are best at utilising selection, optimisation and compensation strategies in old age to ensure the best possible daily life. Because the fewer the resources you have, the greater the need to optimise them. On the other hand, it is important to remember that resources in old age are largely a result of priorities, choices and actions occurring at much earlier stages of life. To some extent good health in old age is connected with lifelong habits in terms of diet, exercise and other health-related issues. Family life, friendships and social integration in general are also built up during the course of an entire life (Antonucci & Akiyama, 1987). Even mental energy and intellectual function are influenced by the extent to which you have used your brain, allowed yourself to be stimulated intellectually, and seized the mental challenges with which you have been presented (Bosma et al., 2003; Christensen et al., 1996). So it is possible that elderly people with many resources have used SOC processes in a relevant manner throughout their entire lives, thereby developing a reserve of resources for use in old age as well.

This may indicate the presence of a connection between SOC processes and successful ageing. The connection between SOC processes and successful ageing was studied in a large group of elderly people in the Berlin Aging Study: questionnaires were used to measure SOC processes and a selection of indicators of successful ageing, including life satisfaction, loneliness, and positive and negative emotions. The results showed that the major use of SOC processes was connected in general with successful ageing but not with life satisfaction (Freund et al., 1998). So to the extent that SOC processes are significant for life satisfaction in old age, the connection is probably indirect with SOC processes influencing the sources of life satisfaction. This connection can also be seen as a logical consequence of the fact that life satisfaction is the result of people's evaluation of their own lives, and the SOC model is a general description of processes that people use to shape their lives in the most satisfactory manner. This is done by selecting relevant goals, optimising resources, and compensating as well as possible for losses.

The next question we will explore is whether it is possible to use the SOC model as a point of departure to gain insight into specific development processes that are related directly to the subjective evaluation of life which determines a person's level of life satisfaction.

A life-span theory of control

Baltes & Baltes' (1990) SOC model is a general model for adapting and optimising resources throughout life. Schulz & Heckhausen (1995) have expanded this model to include a life-span theory of control which provides an explanation for this kind of ongoing adaptation and optimisation. This theory proposes that the concept of control is the central theme during life course development. The assumption is that it is a basic human need to exercise control of our surrounding environment by our actions. It is this need to control and handle your surroundings that provides people with a source of motivation for adapting and optimising their resources on an ongoing basis.

The theory divides control into primary and secondary control. *Primary control* is directed at the outside world and reflects the individual's attempts to control what happens in the world around them by taking action. *Secondary control* targets the individual and the adjustment of the inner world. Both primary and secondary control may involve both thoughts and actions, although primary control is almost always exercised in the form of behaviour in relation to the outside world and secondary control is mainly exercised in the form of processes inside the individual (Heckhausen & Schulz, 1995; Schulz et al., 1996). You could also say that whereas primary control seeks to control life with a view to ensuring that you obtain the conditions you require, secondary control controls the very nature of the conditions that you require.

The life-span theory of control comprises four control-related processes:

Selective primary control is the focused investment in resources such as effort, time and abilities, which is necessary in relation to a chosen goal. The conscious development of skills and abilities is an example of selective primary control: e.g. when a 75-year-old woman decides to learn how to use a computer and spends time and money on doing so. The effect of selective primary control strategies depends on whether one has the resources that are relevant in order to achieve the goal one has set for oneself. In the example above, the woman will probably not learn much about actually using a computer if she just borrows a few leaflets on computer programmes and tries to learn how to use these programmes by merely reading the leaflets, or, if she cannot afford to buy a computer. However, people also need to feel that they have the necessary resources before even trying to use selective primary control strategies. In other words, unless the woman basically believes that she will be able to work out how to use a computer, she will never even make the attempt to learn this new skill.

Selective secondary control comprises the inner representation of the motivational value attributed to a selected goal. In other words, selective secondary control determines the value allocated to any given thing. For instance, the woman who wants to learn how to use a computer gives this considerable value because she regards access to a computer as a way of being part of the development of the society around her, thereby maintaining her identity as an active, well informed citizen. Whereas her husband may regard the opportunities provided by a computer as irrelevant to his daily life and does not allocate any motivational value to the ability to use a computer. Motivational force may be the value allocated to the goal itself, but it may also be the value allocated to alternative goals – the expected potential to achieve the goal and the expected consequences of achieving it. The woman allocates higher value to the use of a computer than the alternative goals she could have created for the use of her time – for instance, it is more important for her to understand and take part in the computer-based aspects of the information society than to spend her time growing vegetables. Her husband, on the other hand, regards working on his allotment as being of greater value than using a computer because he does not believe that the expected reward will justify the effort required to learn how to use a computer. In other words, selective secondary control processes regulate the values we attribute to selected goals.

Compensatory primary control is developed when people's physical and cognitive abilities are not sufficient to achieve a selected goal. In other words, when you cannot perform a task or manage the work required to achieve a goal, alternative strategies are required in order to achieve the goal anyway. Compensatory primary control involves the use of external resources such as assistance from other people and technical aids such as hearing aids, nappies, Zimmer frames etc. with a view to increasing your functional ability. For instance, the husband who wishes to keep his allotment but finds this difficult because his back hurts could buy electrically powered gardening tools enabling him to continue to do some of the tasks himself, as well as asking other people to help him with the more physically demanding tasks.

The aim of *compensatory secondary control* is to compensate for the negative consequences of defeat and loss with regard to the individual's motivation for exercising primary control. In other words, when you fail to achieve a specific goal you need to implement compensatory secondary control strategies in the form of mental processing of the situation to prevent yourself from losing your belief that in general you are capable of achieving the goal in question. Compensatory secondary control comprises processes such as abandoning previous goals, getting involved in alternative goals, self-protective patterns of causality allocation, and the strategic use of social and intra-individual (temporal) comparisons. For instance, if the woman in the example above never really learns to use her computer she may decide to give up and let her grandchild have it (*abandoning goals*), deciding instead to get involved in the voluntary work of the Red Cross by visiting people in need (*involvement in alternative goals*). She may later feel that the reason why she failed to learn how to use a computer was that her teacher at evening school had been no good at teaching as well as being prejudiced against her, and that the computer she had bought was too cheap and never worked properly anyway (*self-protective causality allocation*). She may also compare herself with her more passive friends and neighbours (or even with her husband), who have never shown any interest in keeping up with the world around them (*strategic social comparison*). And finally, she may think back over her life and compare her current level of activity and social involvement favourably with the memory that when she was young she was only interested in her appearance and what other people thought of her (*strategic temporal comparison*).

In terms of development it is normally assumed that selective primary control increases during childhood and youth but decreases in old age. By contrast, it is assumed that secondary control increases throughout the course of life. With the occurrence of age-related loss of primary control (limitation of the potential for living your life in the most satisfactory way), the importance of adaptive secondary control strategies increases with age. Consequently, secondary control strategies are vital with regard to fulfilling the needs of the individual to exercise control in old age. One result of age-related losses of function and reduced resources is that the potential for exercising selective control is also reduced, so a repertoire of compensatory control strategies becomes increasingly important.

It is possible that the maintenance of life satisfaction in old age despite losses can be attributed to the lifelong development of compensatory strategies. Primary compensatory strategies can compensate for limitations arising owing to the loss of functional capacity. In other words, when people lose the ability to perform their usual activities in old age, they find new ways of doing things or acquire aids that make their daily lives feasible. Secondary compensatory strategies can compensate for the experience of defeat in connection with the lack of ability to achieve desired goals, because they make it possible to view things in a more acceptable manner by adjusting the value allocated to the goal in question.

Life satisfaction depends on a cognitive evaluation of life. In other words, the value allocated to your life is significant in terms of how satisfying it seems to you. Secondary control strategies can determine life satisfaction by adjusting the value allocated to various aspects of life. If the greatest value is allocated to areas associated with loss and reduction, people will tend to be more dissatisfied; whereas greater life satisfaction will be experienced if greatest value is allocated to areas which continue to function effectively.

Secondary compensatory control strategies are part of the cognitive assessment of life satisfaction because they regulate the goals in relation to which life is evaluated. How this occurs is not described in detail in Schulz & Heckhausen's life-span theory of control. Specific insight into the process that determines life satisfaction in old age requires a more detailed description of the cognitive evaluation of life satisfaction and the possible goals that may constitute the standards of evaluation.

The cognitive evaluation of life satisfaction

As mentioned by way of introduction, life satisfaction is defined as the outcome of a general evaluation of life as a whole. The central term here is *evaluation*, which is regarded as a cognitive process. As a result, Schwarz and Strack (1991) use cognitive psychology research in their model of the evaluation process that determines life satisfaction. This model is based on a general principle of cognitive accessibility. The principle states that the information included in evaluating satisfaction is the information that is most easily accessible – the information you think of first. The model claims that people tend to report satisfaction with their lives based on their current emotional state because emotional states are sources of immediate and easily accessible information. However, the informative value of a current emotional state may be irrelevant or insufficient in relation to any overall evaluation of how satisfied people are with their lives. Also, comparative strategies can be used to determine your current level of satisfaction by comparing your life with other standards (Schwarz & Strack, 1991). For instance, people could compare their current life situation with previous periods of life – this is known as *temporal comparison* (for instance when an 80-year-old evaluates his health by comparing it with his health 30 years previously). People may also compare their current life situation with that of others – this is known as *social comparison* (for instance when our 80-year-old compares his health with that of his peers). In both cases people's current life situation can be compared with a better or a worse standard. These are also known as *upward* and *downward* comparisons (Wilson & Ross, 2000).

The principle of cognitive accessibility also applies in connection with processes of comparison – in other words, both information about your own life and the selection of comparative standards are determined by the information that is most easily accessible in the current situation (Schwarz et al., 1991). This means that the outcome of an evaluation of life satisfaction is influenced by the current context in which the evaluation occurs, so people's evaluation of their lives as being more or less satisfactory can be influenced by adjusting the standards with which they compare themselves. This kind of conscious selection of specific, advantageous comparison standards is a secondary control strategy because in choosing the basis of comparison people are adjusting the way in which they wish to perceive themselves and their own performance.

Factors of significance for life satisfaction

The evaluation of life satisfaction is a conscious process in which people evaluate the achievement of personal goals and their own success criteria; and life satisfaction can only be achieved if the gap between daily life and such inner goals and success criteria is not too large (Pavot et al., 1993). In other words, people become dissatisfied with their lives if they do not feel that their lives fulfil their expectations (Cummins & Nistico, 2002). The evaluation of life satisfaction takes place within the areas that people regard as important, areas in which they have particular expectations.

An advanced level of education, previous employment as a self-employed person or skilled workman, the opportunity to continue previous activities, not feeling lonely and feeling that your health is good – these were all found to be factors connected with life satisfaction in a study of a large group of elderly Danes. A low level of education, unskilled work, inactivity, poor social relations, a poor financial situation and a poor perception of health were all connected with seeing old age as the worst period of your life (Mehlsen et al., 2003). In other words, factors such as education, previous employment, financial situation, level of activity, social relations and health may constitute some of the criteria used by individuals to evaluate their satisfaction with life in old age.

However, at this point it is important to point out that the criteria for a good life are rarely concrete goals which you have (or do not have). Instead, they are abstract values by which people evaluate their lives on an ongoing basis (for instance values such as "being loved", "creating something meaningful", or "being financially independent"). So there is not necessarily any connection between having more of anything (money, friends or power) and being more satisfied. The most general form of abstract value by which people evaluate themselves is themselves. If you are satisfied with yourself, perceive yourself as generally good, valuable and competent, you will in general be satisfied with your life. Satisfaction with yourself can be divided into three aspects, each of which is connected with life satisfaction: *self-worth*, *the feeling of control* over the world around you, and *optimism* (Cummins et al., 2002). In order to fulfil these requirements for self-worth, the feeling of control and optimism, people need to be able to think positively about themselves. It has been demonstrated that there is a set of positive feelings in most people which tends to exaggerate positive aspects to some extent (Taylor & Brown, 1988). Such ideas may lead people to feel that they are responsible for their successes but not for their failures, that they allocate a greater value to qualities that they possess than to qualities that they do not possess, and that they regard themselves as more fortunate, intelligent and responsible than the general population. One core characteristic of these positive ideas is that they are unspecific, and that in principle they are therefore difficult to disprove. You cannot deny that a person is kinder, wiser or more popular than most people if you have not specified who "most people" are. In this connection it is interesting that elderly people seem to accept a more realistic picture of themselves than younger people: the gap between their self-image and their ideal self is less than that of young people (Ryff, 1991). All else being equal, this kind of greater acceptance of yourself will lead to greater life satisfaction because there will be fewer discrepancies between people's experience of themselves and their inner standards and expectations. Greater psychological maturity in the elderly, reflected in a closer match between their self-image and their ideal selves, may contribute to greater life satisfaction in old age. However, a big difference between what you expect of yourself and what you are actually able to achieve will be just as great a problem in old age as it is for young people. In addition, the loss of functions in old age often means that you can achieve less than you could in the past, and (all else being equal) without greater self-acceptance this will lead to a reduction in life satisfaction. This is why secondary control strategies in the form of a reduction of the value allocated to "perfection" or similar requirements in the previous ideal self are necessary in order to maintain a positive self-evaluation and thereby life satisfaction in old age.

Positive images are important for life satisfaction, so maintaining these images is also relevant with regard to life satisfaction. Cummins & Nistico (2002) state that people's positive image of themselves is challenged when a generally positive view of the world is threatened by negative events. People will normally start a process of cognitive adjustment to the events concerned. For instance, this can be done by trying to find out what the events mean, thereby regaining the feeling of control in relation to what has happened. People can also compare themselves with others who are in a worse situation in order to maintain a sense of self-worth, or they may create unrealistic expectations about the future development of the situation in order to remain optimistic.

In order to determine their life satisfaction in old age, people can evaluate their lives here and now based on the criteria that they have for a good life. Some factors will be generally associated with greater life satisfaction, such as good health, a good financial situation or gratifying social relations. Most people would agree that these factors are important in any satisfying life. But in old age the evaluation of life satisfaction may also extend beyond the immediate situation and cover the evaluation of an entire life span, leading to the more wide-ranging question "All in all, am I satisfied with the life I have lived?" Negative events at a previous stage of life presumably play a role in this connection, because there is evidence to indicate that people regard the worst periods of their lives as the periods in which specific negative events occurred (Mehlsen et al., 2005). But in fact the influence of specific events on people's wellbeing seems to decline after a relatively short period of time (Headey & Wearing,

1989; Suh, Diener & Fujita, 1996). So it is possible that it is the subjective impact of an event on a person's self-perception and self-worth that influences life satisfaction in the long term. In this connection, the way in which events are incorporated into people's life histories is significant: for instance, is a divorce 30 years ago perceived as a traumatic event leading to all the subsequent disasters in a life? Or was it a trial that was necessary in order to finally find Mr. (or Mrs.) Right?

Another criterion that individuals may use in evaluating their lives covers normatively given, culture-dependent ideas concerning what people should experience in the course of a normal life and the time at which certain experiences or events "should" occur. These cultural ideas about life are known as a *life script*, a term reflecting the implicit (but not always expressed) common understanding of a "normal" life course which is shared by people of the same culture (Berntsen & Rubin, 2002). In middle-class Danish culture in the year 2005 an overall life script for an individual would look like this: school, education, job, marriage, children, retirement, loss of spouse. But in reality a life could just as easily look like this: school, unskilled labour, child, unemployment, compulsory re-employment, marriage, unskilled labour, unemployment, divorce, early retirement on the grounds of ill health. Such people can at any point compare their lives with the cultural life script, and will often evaluate their lives as being less than satisfactory because the life script colours their expectations of life with regard to the future and influences their evaluation of their success in the past.

Apart from a culturally determined life script relating to the order of events in a "normal" person's life, there will also be other cultural ideas about the content and values of a successful life: ideal images of what could be called "the good life". These cultural ideas will often appear in stereotypical images of the lives of successful role models in the media and advertising. Interestingly enough, in recent years there have been a number of advertisements featuring elderly role models portrayed as greatly loved, respected grandparents or (more innovatively) as energetic, smiling, grey-haired individuals who are physically, culturally, socially and sexually active. There are images of elderly people going for a brisk walk by the sea, visiting cultural destinations, enjoying the company of happy friends and a loving family, with a healthy-looking partner, enjoying good food, playing golf, and not least benefiting from a good financial situation and good health. This development might indicate the incipient cultural formulation of an explicitly positive ideal picture of old age in a society containing an increasing number of self-aware, articulate elderly people capable of making an impact in terms of politics and the formation of attitudes. The risk is that as these culturally defined, positive images of old age become more explicit and idealised, the elderly will evaluate their life satisfaction as being increasingly poor because the gap between their daily lives and these ideal images will become increasingly large. But positive images of ageing showing opportunities instead of limitations in old age may also be sources of inspiration and role models capable of motivating the individual. In addition, a more positive cultural image of the elderly may influence the social identity of the elderly in relation to their reference group based on the following rationale: "Elderly people are active and have lives full of meaningful content. I'm an elderly person. I can be active and have a life full of meaningful content". When a positive image of ageing adds new value to the process of growing old, it becomes apparent once again that secondary control strategies can be used effectively with regard to maintaining satisfaction in old age.

Cognitive evaluations – a summary

The inner standards such as private goals and success criteria, and the culturally defined standards such as life script and prototypical presentations of the good life, constitute standards in relation to which individuals can evaluate their current lives. There are also comparative standards in the form of social and temporal comparisons. Social comparisons with people who are worse off than you can help to increase your life satisfaction; but comparisons with people who are more successful than you may also promote life satisfaction owing to the motivational aspect of such upward comparisons (Heidrich & Ryff, 1993). In temporal comparison people use their memories of themselves at an earlier stage of life by way of comparison with their current situation. In this connection it is important to remember that memories are subjective. What is involved here is memory as a (re)construction. So the remembered reconstruction of previous performances, competences and life conditions will be influenced by the self-image and normative ideas about personal development of the person concerned. Owing to the subjective nature of memory, temporal comparisons are useful in reinforcing satisfaction with your current life because people often tend to evaluate their previous selves as poorer than their current selves (Wilson & Ross, 2001). So even though we might expect comparisons with performances and competences at an earlier stage of life to constitute a threat to life satisfaction in old age, it has actually been discovered that temporal comparisons are connected with increased satisfaction in old age (Mehlsen et al., 2005), which can presumably be attributed to the tendency to strategically underestimate the past.

According to Fleeson and Heckhausen, 1997, p. 125:

...individuals identify themselves not just by their current personality but also by their personality in the past and their personality in the future, and that such 'perceived life-time personalities' might play a central role in actual development. That is, development and the self-concept share a reciprocal relationship: Development is a fundamental part of the self-concept, and the self-concept may be critical to understanding the course of development.

Self-image and life are not phenomena isolated from time and history, and nor can life satisfaction be determined outside the context of life history. When people evaluate how satisfied they are with their lives, included in this evaluation is their lives here and now and in the past, as well as their expectations with regard to the future – reflecting the importance of life-history evaluation criteria such as life script and temporal comparisons. So life satisfaction in old age should be seen against the background of the life span that ageing individuals have already experienced.

Conclusion

Life satisfaction in old age is the norm rather than the exception. From a psychological point of view, the acceptance of loss and adaptation to the conditions of old age are derived from a standard process of development throughout adulthood leading to the increasing use of value-adjusting and compensatory control strategies enabling people to handle loss adaptively. The development of these control strategies makes it possible to reduce the demands people make on themselves (leading to a greater degree of self-acceptance), and to select evaluation standards that ensure that the results of comparisons are favourable.

The use of such control strategies requires mental flexibility. The more flexible you are, the greater the likelihood that you will regard your life as satisfactory. In other words, the ability to maintain life satisfaction despite losses requires people to have the mental capacity to regard their situation from new angles and find emotionally compensatory alternatives. Greater self-acceptance and the acknowledgement of any age-related limitations that might occur can lead to a reduction in people's expectations with regard to their own performance, thereby helping to ensure greater satisfaction with the performance achieved.

This combination of general life-span theories about the psychological processes that control adaptation to life in old age and the cognitive approach to the concept of life satisfaction provides us with insight into the way in which psychological mechanisms in the form of compensatory, value-adjusting strategies are developed throughout the course of life. This makes it easier to understand why the vast majority of elderly people are satisfied with their lives despite the losses that they suffer. At the same time, greater knowledge of the formation of (and training in the use of) compensatory and value-adjusting strategies may constitute the potential foundations for the development of therapeutic tools to help elderly people who have been unable to maintain life satisfaction in old age.

REFERENCES

Andrews, F.M. & Withey, S.B. (1976). *Social indicators of well-being. Americans' perceptions of life quality.* New York: Plenum Press.

Antonucci, T.C. & Akiyama, H. (1987). Social networks in adult life and a preliminary examination of the convoy model. *Journals of Gerontology, 42,* 519-527.

Baltes, P.B. & Baltes, M.M. (1990). Psychological perspectives on successful aging: The model of selective optimization with compensation. In: P.B. Baltes & M.M. Baltes (Eds.), *Successful aging: Perspectives from the behavioral sciences,* 1-34. New York: Cambridge University Press.

Berntsen, D. & Rubin, D.C. (2002). Emotionally charged autobiographical memories across the life span: The recall of happy, sad, traumatic, and involuntary memories. *Psychology and Aging, 17,* 636-652.

Bosma, H., van Boxtel, M.P.J., Ponds, R.W.H.M., Houx, P.J., Burdorf, A., & Jolles, J. (2003). Mental work demands protect against cognitive impairment: MAAS prospective cohort study. *Experimental Aging Research, 29,* 33-45.

Christensen, H., Korten, A., Jorm, A.F., Henderson, A.S., Scott, R., & Mackinnon, A.J. (1996). Activity levels and cognitive functioning in an elderly community sample. *Age and Ageing, 25,* 72-80.

Cummins, R.A. & Nistico, H. (2002). Maintaning life satisfaction: The role of positive cognitive bias. *Journal of Happiness Studies, 3,* 37-69.

Diener, E. (1984). Subjective well-being. *Psychological Bulletin, 95,* 542-575.

Diener, E., Suh, E.M., Lucas, R.E., & Smith, H.L. (1999). Subjective well-being: Three decades of progress. *Psychological Bulletin, 125,* 276-302.

Field, D. (1997). Looking back, what period of your life brought you the most satisfaction. *International Journal of Aging & Human Development, 45,* 169-194.

Fleeson, W. & Heckhausen, J. (1997). More or less "me" in past, present, and future: Perceived lifetime personality during adulthood. *Psychology and Aging, 12,* 125-136.

Freund, A.M. & Baltes, P.B. (1998). Selection, optimization, and compensation as strategies of life management: Correlations with subjective indicators of successful aging. *Psychology and Aging, 13,* 531-543.

Headey, B. & Wearing, A. (1989). Personality, life events, and subjective well-being – towards dynamic equilibrium-model. *Journal of Personality and Social Psychology, 57,* 731-739.

Heckhausen, J. & Schulz, R. (1995). A life-span theory of control. *Psychological Review, 102,* 284-304.

Heidrich, S.M. & Ryff, C.D. (1993). The role of social comparisons processes in the psychological adaptation of elderly adults. *Journals of Gerontology, 48,* 127-136.

Lang, F.R., Rieckmann, N., & Baltes, M.M. (2002). Adapting to aging losses: Do resources facilitate strategies of selection, compensation, and optimization in everyday functioning? *Journals of Gerontology Series B-Psychological Sciences and Social Sciences, 57,* 501-509.

Mehlsen, M., Platz, M., & Fromholt, P. (2003). Life satisfaction across the life course: Evaluations of the most and least satisfying decades of life. *International Journal of Aging & Human Development, 57,* 217-236.

Mehlsen, M., Thomsen, D.K., Viidik, A., Olesen, F., & Zachariae, R. (2005). Cognitive processes involved in the evaluation of life satisfaction: Implications for well-being. *Aging & Mental Health, 9,* 281-290.

Pavot, W. & Diener, E. (1993). Review of the Satisfaction With Life Scale. *Psychological Assessment, 5,* 164-172.

Ryff, C.D. (1991). Possible selves in adulthood and old-Age – A tale of shifting horizons. *Psychology and Aging, 6,* 286-295.

Schulz, R. & Heckhausen, J. (1996). A life span model of successful aging. *American Psychologist, 51 (7),* 702-714.

Schwarz, N. & Strack, F. (1991). Evaluating one's life: a judgment model of subjective well-being 26. In: F. Strack, M. Argyle, & N. Schwarz (Eds.), *Subjective Well-Being. An Interdisciplinary Perspective,* 27-47. Oxford: Pergamon Press.

Suh, E., Diener, E., & Fujita, F. (1996). Events and subjective well-being: Only recent events matter. *Journal of Personality and Social Psychology, 70,* 1091-1102.

Taylor, S.E. & Brown, J.D. (1988). Illusion and well-being – A social psychological perspective on mental-health. *Psychological Bulletin, 103,* 193-210.

Wilson, A.E. & Ross, M. (2000). The frequency of temporal-self and social comparisons in people's personal appraisals. *Journal of Personality and Social Psychology, 78,* 928-942.

Wilson, A.E. & Ross, M. (2001). From chump to champ: People's appraisals of their earlier and present selves. *Journal of Personality and Social Psychology, 80,* 572-584.

PATHOLOGICAL AGEING

Mental illness

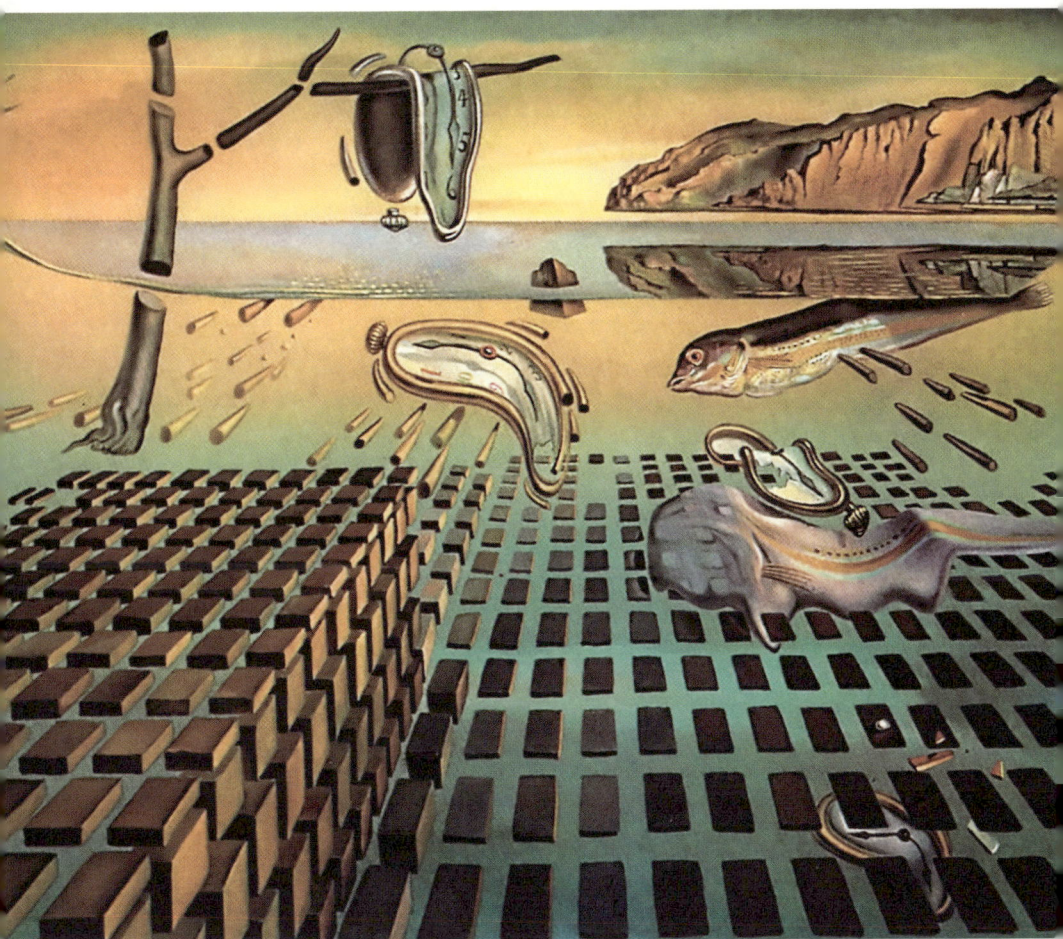

DIAGNOSING THE PSYCHOPATHOLOGY OF THE ELDERLY

Uffe Seilman

Summary

The elderly constitute a highly inhomogeneous group not only socially but also psychologically and in terms of health. So diagnosing the psychopathology of elderly people requires good knowledge both of normal ageing and of the special circumstances that can influence the often widely varying symptoms encountered in clinical practice. Any such diagnosis requires individual identification of the background and personality of elderly people, their current social situation and any somatic illnesses from which they may suffer. The initial occurrence and development of symptoms over time is vital with a view to providing a diagnosis and proposing interventions, so information from the families of elderly people or care staff who know them well may be extremely valuable. However, such information can never replace clinical interviews, which sometimes have to be supplemented by more formal study methods. A range of somatic, psychological and ethical issues apply to elderly people which are important with regard to the choice of test method used and the interpretation of the test results obtained. It is important to remember that the purpose of testing is to identify the maximum capacity of elderly people in a way that makes it possible to gain an idea of their strengths and weaknesses without pulling the ground from beneath the feet of the individuals being tested. Test results can never stand alone, but must be understood in relation to the background and personality of the elderly people concerned and the development of symptoms over time. One of the aspects of great practical value involves ensuring that the results of studies are communicated to elderly people and their surroundings in such a way that these results can benefit elderly people as far as possible in the form of rehabilitation, psychotherapy or social measures.

The mosaic of diagnosis

As life expectancy increases in the Western world, an increasing number of people can look forward to a long life of old age. But this extra life comes at a cost. For one thing, the frequency of suicide is higher among the elderly than among younger people (Segal et al., 1998, p. 237 f). And for another, the risk of suffering from a range of mental illnesses such as depression and above all dementia increases with age. Dementia has been a familiar problem for thousands of years – the Icelandic sagas had a word for it (*gammeltullet*), and in ancient India people used their word for "above 60" to describe the phenomenon. Today we know that dementia occurs when the ageing process goes out of control – it is an illness and not a direct consequence of age, even though the risk of dementia increases with age.

Apart from dementia, mental illness in the elderly largely resembles mental illness in young people: after all, the elderly are people too. Even so, there are a number of special circumstances applying to the diagnosis and understanding of mental illness in the elderly. Firstly, somatic illness can cause symptoms that resemble mental illness. For instance, urinary tract infections sometimes cause symptoms resembling dementia, but these symptoms disappear once the infection has been treated. Another example is Parkinson's disease, which may lead to introverted, detached behaviour resembling depression. Secondly, existential tiredness with life (also known as "depletion") may cause symptoms that resemble depression but which do not prove the presence of depression – and somatic symptoms seem to be more widespread in elderly people suffering from depression too (Kasl-Godley et al., 1998, p. 211). Thirdly, the social situation and existential conditions of elderly people are often very different from those of young people. This may influence not only the reactions of elderly people but also the way in which other people interpret the nature of their problems. And finally, generational differences may apply with regard to the interpretation of problems by elderly people and their way of tackling them (for a discussion of the concept of coping, see Lazarus, 1998, for instance).

The elderly constitute the most inhomogeneous age group of all, both physically and mentally (Fromholt, 1992, p. 22). For instance, some people seem old and infirm at the age of 70 while others are still leading an independent life at the age of 90. Similarly, there are major differences between what elderly people can manage and deal with in a purely physical sense. A great deal depends on how you have lived your life, whether you have had a difficult life in which you have depended on very few coping strategies – or whether you have developed a great number of flexible strategies during your life (see Lazarus, 1998 ibid, for instance).

These differences become apparent in the ability of elderly people to handle the challenges of old age – challenges which include physical and mental illness. They are also revealed by the performance of elderly people in tests used by psychologists in the diagnosis of psychopathology. In other words, all in all it is important to include not only biological but also social and personality-related factors when working with the diagnosis of elderly people.

The mosaic of diagnosis is also complicated by the fact that the illnesses encountered in real life are often far less clear-cut than the theoretical medical books may indicate. This is because several different illnesses may be present at the same time (co-morbidity), or because some symptoms may correspond to several different mental illnesses with very different prognoses and treatment requirements. Depression and early dementia are examples of such differential diagnosis problems. It is often in connection with this kind of issue that mental tests become relevant with a view to resolving any doubts that may be present. Owing to the complexity of the area and the serious nature of the dementia diagnosis, this particular diagnosis requires great caution and an ethically sound approach.

All in all the diagnosis of psychopathology in the elderly requires the inclusion of many different factors before finalising a diagnosis and treatment plan. Figure 1 shows an example of the check lists used in connection with the diagnosis of psychopathology in geropsychiatry and among neuropsychologists. Some of these points are explained in greater detail below:

- Reason for referral
- Current symptoms
- Medical history
- Education and previous occupation
- Social conditions
- Substance abuse issues
- Patient's own complaints
- Information from family
- Previous level of mental function
- Clinical impression
- Previous mental illnesses
- Previous and current somatic illnesses
- Current medical status
- Tendency towards mental illness in family
- Previous main traumas
- Other examinations

FIGURE 1. *An all-round picture*

Medical information

As mentioned above, the symptoms of psychopathology may be caused by somatic illness. This is true of all age groups, but the elderly are more liable to suffer from somatic illness than other groups. In addition, the reserve capacity of elderly people (see Fromholt, 1992, p. 24) may be limited, which is why current or recent physical illnesses may influence the mental functions of the elderly significantly for a period of time. As a result, it is always important to ensure that there is a thorough and up-to-date medical diagnosis of elderly people who show symptoms of mental illness. This is why people involved in the field of psychiatry sometimes refer to dementia as a diagnosis of exclusion. Detailed guidelines regarding the forms of medical diagnosis that are required in connection with the diagnosis of psychopathology in elderly people can be found in Gulmann (1992).

It should be mentioned at this point that the concept called "diagnosis of exclusion" may be misleading because efforts must of course always be made to find positive evidence of any given disorder. So efforts are always made to render the diagnosis of dementia probable based on brain scans, clinical assessment, medical history and (when in doubt) neuropsychological examinations. Similarly, it is inadvisable to categorise given symptoms such as pain as being functionally based (based on mental issues) simply because it is impossible to identify a biological cause (for a discussion of the concept of psychosomatic complaints see Mirdal, 1999, for instance). However, it is naturally correct to determine whether a psychological background can be identified for such symptoms. In some circumstances, inexplicable pain and physical sensations may be symptoms of depression.

Background and medical history

When diagnosing psychopathology, knowledge is needed about the education and previous occupation of elderly people. This is important in evaluating whether a poor test result should be interpreted as a sign of decline, or whether the result reflects a habitual and therefore unchanged state. A good number of elderly people have no particular education and may also suffer from dyslexia.

This illustrates why a psychological test cannot stand alone when diagnosing psychopathology – it needs to be compared with information about the previous functional level of the individual concerned, even though the test result may show symptoms corresponding to a given mental disorder. This is because fundamentally the performance itself is not the interesting parameter – the interesting thing is any change in relation to the previous situation.

In general the start and development of symptoms (medical history) have considerable diagnostic value. For instance, serious forgetfulness that develops within a week or two is an indicator not of Alzheimer's but of depression instead. In this connection, it is also important to collect knowledge about the individual's previous behaviour and coping abilities. For instance, was the individual concerned always mentally strong and happy in the past – have they suddenly started complaining and showing evidence of neurotic behaviour? Or have they always focused a great deal on their physical condition and complained regularly of the pain that they were in? If the answer to the first of these questions is in the affirmative, the individual in question may well be suffering from depression involving personality changes and strong agitation (agitated depression), rather than being in a mental crisis with neurotic traits.

In connection with the diagnosis of the causes of behavioural disorders in individuals suffering from dementia, information about the background and previous occupation of the people concerned may be extremely important. This can be illustrated by a clinical example: an elderly man suffering from severe dementia was referred for diagnosis because for some time he had been cutting down all the pot plants in the nursing home in which he lived. It was impossible to prevent him from doing this, and he could not provide any explanation of his behaviour. However, at a meeting with his wife it was revealed that he had been a lumberjack in Canada for his entire working life. The wife's interpretation was that he was still clearing the undergrowth in the forest – he was just doing this in new surroundings. This is not a unique example of the fact that a person's previous occupation can sometimes lead to bizarre behaviour in individuals suffering from dementia. The point is that it is a good idea to focus on the whole person, because doing so often makes bizarre behaviour comprehensible and therefore easier to accept and handle.

Finally, in charting the medical history of individuals it is important to find out whether the person concerned has suffered from mental illness previously and whether the current symptoms have been seen before. This is because a range of mental problems tend to reoccur or recidivate. Depression and paranoid complaints such as paraphrenia are examples of such problems. With regard to depression it also seems to be the case that each new episode increases the risk of reoccurrence. A similar situation may also apply to psychosomatic pain, which can become chronic after a number of years.

Information from the family and care staff

Information from the family or care staff may have great value when charting a person's medical history and pathology, not least when clients themselves do not have full insight into their problems. These sources of information can often provide very good descriptions of how the client has changed and what their development has been like. As a result, one of the regular routines at a number of geropsychiatry wards in Denmark involves calling a meeting involving family members and care staff as well as the patients themselves when a diagnosis is required. "Establishing the evolution, pattern, and impact of the deficits is the overall aim", as Hodges puts it (2004, p. 100).

The aim of such discussions with the family is to find out when the symptoms started, how they have developed over time, and which consequences they have in daily life both practically and socially. This information may be a great help with a view to distinguishing between various forms of dementia, the symptoms of which often vary most in the initial stages (ibid).

When discussing clients with care staff, it is important to remember that their descriptions may be influenced by their relationship with the clients concerned. This is true not least in connection with behavioural disorders in people suffering from dementia, which may be extremely hard to deal with and difficult for care staff to understand. Consequently, an attempt should be made to get behind descriptions of problems which employ interpretive concepts such as "aggressive" or "depressed". The first stage of diagnosis in this type of problem involves finding out what certain behaviour reveals about the client – not how it is perceived by other people. In this connection, it is often a good idea to ask for concrete examples of changes and problems.

Staff who work at rehabilitation wards for patients who have suffered brain damage should discuss patients with occupational therapists and physiotherapists both before and after examinations start. These professionals often have more practical contact with patients than psychologists do, so they may be able to provide a great many observations from their physiotherapy groups and from the daily lives of patients.

Medical records and previous examinations

Any available reports regarding previous examinations of the psychopathology of the elderly should of course be read. All previous assessments are of interest with a view to gaining a picture of developments and a better basis for evaluating the examinations you carry out. If clients have experienced long-term or repeated mental illness including admission to psychiatric hospital, their medical records will be highly relevant. If a case has been complicated, several working diagnoses will often be encountered. These may not all be equally reliable, and they may have influenced the interpretation (and thereby the treatment) of clients for some time after they were produced. So it is important not to rely solely on a description of the latest epicrisis,[1] but to look for concrete descriptions of the client's symptoms in the medical records. This is because the reason why cases land on the psychologist's desk is often that there is still some uncertainty regarding the nature and background of the disorder in question.

The clinical interview

All examinations should start with a thorough clinical interview. This interview will either render further examinations unnecessary (thereby saving the client a lot of difficulty and the professional staff a lot of time), or reveal the nature of the examinations that need to be carried out. It is important to start by establishing a good alliance with the client so he/she relaxes and starts to feel that they are involved in a joint project instead of feeling that they are being tested. If dementia is a possibility this initial good contact may be vital in determining whether an examination can be performed at all. This is because people suffering from dementia do not always sense that they have a problem – they have not asked anyone to come along and examine their memories. It is important (as quickly as possible) to gain an impression of the way the elderly client perceives the reason for their referral – partly to ensure that the interview is fruitful, and partly for diagnostic reasons (Hodges, 2004, p. 90).

Simple questions about the client's life history, employment and daily life can help to create good contact as well as providing an impression of the degree to which the client is able to participate in an interview. If the client is unable to take part in a reasonable conversation at this elementary level, it will often be more beneficial to ask the family for information rather than carrying out tests of the client:

If this clinical interview reveals significant cognitive deficits, with impairment of higher intellectual abilities, language, or both, it is not appropriate for investigators to let the patient go through a long and demanding testing procedure. Expected test performance must, in other words, be evaluated to arrive at an appropriate degree of test intervention.

Hestad et al., 1998, p. 266.

---

1 An epicrisis is partly a tool for use in registering the services provided by a ward, and partly a tool for communication between busy hospital wards or GPs. As a result, it presents a patient's data and problems briefly and factually. As a general rule it contains a brief summary of the reasons why the patient has been referred to the ward in question and the ward's own assessment and choice of treatment method. There is also a brief assessment of the effect of treatment and a final diagnosis forming the basis of future recommendations or referrals to other wards/bodies.

It may be an advantage to carry out the interview in the client's own home, and this is common practice in geropsychiatry. For one thing the client will quite literally be on familiar ground, making them feel more secure; and for another a great deal of information can be gleaned just by seeing the home in which they live. The state of the home may provide important indicators of the functional level of the client in ordinary daily life (this is known as "Observations of Daily Living"), and many observations may contribute to the clinical impression – including observation of the tea or coffee that will almost inevitably be served. One dramatic example of a home visit concerns a cat whose fur looked like a bottle brush because its owner (suffering from incipient dementia) had treated it for fleas using carpet cleaner! It was a shame for the cat, but it did provide the clinic with useful information.

As mentioned above, the client's own perception of their symptoms is a central factor, and it is important to focus on this aspect. Complaints about memory problems often reflect depression rather than incipient dementia. In such cases memory problems are often part of a wider picture of complaints involving physical distress and (as far as the rest of us can see) exaggerated anxiety. This kind of advanced picture of complaint is not seen so often in people suffering from dementia – they normally participate in testing with far greater enthusiasm than people who are depressed, and they have more obvious memory difficulties (see Eriksson, 2003, p. 22 for a more detailed study of the clinical differences between dementia and depression).

If the client is suffering from depression it is important to identify the degree of suffering, because this is vital with regard to the choice of treatment method and with a view to deciding whether the client should be referred to other bodies – including possible medical evaluation of the need for compulsory admission to psychiatric hospital either because the client needs treatment, or because the client may be a danger to himself/herself or others. In general, during the clinical interview it is necessary to examine the client's coping ability, which is relevant in order to assess which form of support is needed in the short and long term.

It is an advantage to base the clinical interview on a check list such as that shown in figure 1; but each interview should obviously be adapted to suit the client in question and their specific problem.

Psychological tests

In connection with psychopathology, psychological tests are a supplement to clinical assessment because they provide more objective measurements as well as increasing the perspective and depth of the clinical assessment and making the clinical work more disciplined and focused.

Some people would say that psychological tests constitute a replacement for professional observations of the client in their daily life – observations that are controlled by knowledge of basic mental functions just like the observations and training routines of occupational therapists, which are based on their knowledge of what is needed to function in ordinary daily life. Tests create a more highly structured situation in an attempt to identify the basic cognitive and personality mechanisms behind experience and behaviour. This is done in structured conditions in order to achieve a clearer and more varied picture. As a result, psychological tests sometimes seem remote from reality to non-professionals, who do not have the background required to understand that they should be regarded as scientific probes or samples. As Teasdale (1992, p. 124) points out, psychological tests provide samples of the whole range of a person's cognitive repertoire and personality.

A test result should not be regarded as an independent reality or answer from a predefined check list. This is because the results of tests need to be interpreted and seen in the light of a wider context if they are to make a meaningful contribution to the understanding of a human being and his problems. It is not enough to conclude that results differ from a given norm – the art is to understand what this difference reflects. So the use of psychological tests requires professional expertise and experience. In other words, psychological tests are not isolated phenomena with magical properties. They are tools which must be used with care – so the point made by Korchin (1976) is still relevant and thought-provoking: "Ultimately, the value and power of tests lie in the skill and knowledge of the clinician who uses them" (Korchin, 1976, p. 215).

The aim of psychological tests is to gain understanding of a patient's problems and to indicate possible solutions through treatment or mobilisation of networks and care staff. The tests themselves must be arranged to ensure that they match the problem in question, and consideration of the client must always be the overriding concern. So tests should only be carried out when there is a good reason for doing so – never as a matter of routine.

Screening tests

Screening tests are small tests which are easy to administer and calculate. They have been developed for clinical use, and are used a great deal in psychiatry to assess depression or dementia, among other things. Such tests may be a good supplement to individual clinical assessment, but they cannot stand alone. Folstein's Mini Mental Status Examination (MMSE, Folstein, 1975) is used extremely widely in connection with the diagnosis of dementia in Denmark and other countries. The MMSE consists of a series of questions and tasks involving orientation, memory recall, registration, language and writing, arithmetic and spatial skills in the form of reproducing a drawing. The maximum number of points in this simple test is 30, a score which healthy people can achieve in about five minutes. In terms of diagnosis the result expressed in figures is not as interesting as the type of error and difficulties that led to the result. One of the relevant aspects in this respect is the pattern of difficulties as a reflection of various pathologies. In this connection, it is worth noticing which difficulties elderly people encounter in performing specific tasks. In contrast to this qualitative aspect, the total number of points achieved in the test provides a quantitative measurement of the degree of dementia in question.

Healthy elderly people generally make a few mistakes in the test, but if people score less than 24 points further diagnosis is required. On the other hand, a score of 30 points does not mean that the presence of dementia has been disproved. Highly educated, talented individuals can often manage the test despite suffering from incipient dementia leading to changes in their abilities to manage daily life. This shows that small screening tests are superficial and cannot stand alone, thereby underlining the need for all-round assessment when diagnosing the psychopathology of the elderly. The strength of screening tests is that they do not take long and that they provide a first impression behind the façade often erected by individuals suffering from incipient dementia in order to conceal cognitive impairment. This is a natural reaction, a mental defence mechanism which should be treated with respect. But it is also a barrier that has to be overcome in order to obtain a diagnosis that can lead to the provision of the help that elderly people suffering from dementia need.

Cognitive test batteries

As mentioned above, psychological tests have been developed in order to achieve representative examples of mental functions in individuals by testing central cognitive areas. The same is true of tests of skills and neuropsychological test batteries whose aim is to provide a global picture of a person's cognitive function like that provided by the classic WAIS intelligence test. In Denmark the Glostrup test battery is widely used for dementia diagnosis (Fromholt, Pedersen, Lauridsen & Larsen, 1990); and in the field of neuropsychology in general Denmark has produced the Copenhagen University Hospital's Mental Status Test (Gade, 1994), which also exists in an expanded version (Gade, Mortensen & Bruhn, 1994).

Even though these test batteries are all standardised, the results achieved are still open to a good deal of interpretation. The raw data and figures may be clear enough; but the art is to determine what the figures and their special patterns reflect in the person being examined. This is done not only on the basis of an overall evaluation of the information and observations described above, but also based on the knowledge of pathologies possessed by the psychologist in question.

Personality tests

The Rorschach test is a classic personality test, and its projective method illustrates clearly the principle regarding the way in which psychological tests seek to produce representative samples of a greater whole. The method involves registering the pictures generated instantly in a person by the sight of a series of abstract figures or "ink blots". The assumption behind this test is that the multiple possible interpretations of the abstract figures will make the client use his/her most basic, characteristic and customary cognitive strategies to derive meaning from the new situation. The aim is to produce representative examples of the way in which the basic personality traits of the client concerned influence the way in which he/she copes with the world around them, and to determine whether any psychopathology is present.

The validity of the Rorschach test is widely disputed, and you need a great deal of experience to use it. In the fields of geropsychology and neuropsychology a range of other tests are often now used to assess personality traits which are easier to handle and more strongly based in the traditions of psychometrics. In Denmark the Minnesota Multiphasic Personality Inventory (MMPI) is used in particular (Hathaway & McKinley, 1989), as well as the Neuroticism Extraversion Openness Personality Inventory – Revised (NEO PI-R) (Costa & McCrae, 1992). Both of these inventories have now been translated into Danish.

Testing the elderly

Gerontology research reveals that the cognitive functions of elderly, healthy and active individuals are no different from those of young people. In other words, growing old does not make you stupid! But age does have an influence on motoric and sensory speed and accuracy, and flexibility and adaptability are also reduced with age (Lezak, 1995). Simply put, young people cope better under pressure of time and in stressful situations than elderly people. There may be major individual differences in these "benign" age-related changes, and it is of course important to be aware of this fact when testing elderly people.

One other important factor to remember is that the elderly often suffer from sight and/or hearing impairments, and it is vital to ask about this before starting tests so it can be taken into account when instructing test participants and selecting test materials. In this connection it is also important to mention that the test material should be clear and of a high standard. In general, old test material (faint photocopies or papers with coffee stains on them) should be avoided because they reduce the value of the test and give an unprofessional impression.

The performance of elderly people may be greatly influenced by tiredness or physical discomfort. So before starting a test it is important to ensure that the individual concerned is awake and ready, not suffering from any physical discomfort. Time should also be spent on explaining the purpose of the test and what is going to happen. It is important to ensure that elderly people understand the situation and that they are motivated for taking part so that they concentrate on the tasks and not on the situation. Otherwise you will not be measuring what you want to measure. "The goal of testing is always to obtain the best performance the patient is capable of producing" (Heaton & Heaton, 1981, from Lezak, 1995, p. 139).

Many elderly people are unused to psychological tests and may easily feel that they have been placed in a degrading examination situation. So it is important not to pressurise clients into trying to perform sub-tests which are clearly beyond their powers simply in order to obtain a figure reflecting the obvious. It is easy to pull the ground from beneath the feet of clients – the art is to discover the gaps without dropping the person concerned through them.

Clinicians vary in their approach when it comes to allowing the family to witness test procedures. On the one hand, attempts by the family to help the client or comment on their performance may confuse the issue. It may also be uncomfortable for the client to have their difficulties exposed to the family. On the other hand, the family may provide support for the client, who will no longer have to face a difficult situation on their own; and the family may gain more insight into the extent of the client's cognitive impairments. Practitioners should always obtain the acceptance of the client before allowing the family to witness test procedures. No matter where the test takes place (in the client's home or in the clinic), it is an advantage if two people carry it out. One investigator can then test the client in one room, while the other interviews the family in another. This is sometimes an advantage for the family because it enables them to provide more open, direct feedback regarding the client's difficulties than the feedback they may feel able to give when the client is present. The practice also provides more information for the medical records.

Reporting

The result of a psychological examination must be documented in a report describing the purpose and conditions of the examination, including the client's own perception of their difficulties, their motivation for taking part in the examination, their level of awareness and ability to cooperate, and their state of mind. The last three issues involve the psychologist's professional impression of the client (the clinical impression). The report must also include a documentation section in which the results of the tests used are described in such a way that the tests can be carried out again by any other psychologists who encounter the client at a later stage. This makes it possible to obtain a measurement of changes in the client's cognitive functions over time. Finally, the report should contain a conclusion in which the purpose of the examination is reviewed. This conclusion must be based on the conditions described and on the results and observations mentioned previously in the report, ensuring that the overall picture is given the scientific flavour that enriches and adds new angles to the clinical assessment. The conclusion should be expressed in a manner indicating possible action – or at least pointing towards the future. This is because the purpose of a psychological examination is to proceed with a case on a better foundation than previously – often with the contributions of other groups of professionals. In this respect examinations can help to resolve doubts, create a more multi-faceted understanding of the client's difficulties, or indicate new paths for treatment. Test results should never be over-interpreted of course, but guidelines for action may also consist of a proposal for retesting at a later date.

Naturally, clients are entitled to receive an account of the results of examinations. These results should be expressed in a language that clients understand, and clients must be given the opportunity to ask questions.

In general it is important to remember the ethical considerations associated with the testing of other people. These considerations are described as follows in the instructions provided for psychologists at the psychiatric hospital in Holstebro, Denmark:

Examinations involving tests are often significant events for patients – they may be a strain and they may be perceived as good and fruitful. The main thing is to explain why a test is being performed and how it may benefit the patient's treatment in future. It is also important to ensure that the patient is well informed and that he/she understands and agrees with what is to happen. And finally, it is very important that the test results are communicated to the patient with care, so that they may be received as positively as possible with patients feeling the minimum amount of stigmatisation.

Lund, 2003.

Pathologies

In order to work with the diagnosis of psychopathology in geropsychiatry, it is necessary to be familiar with the various pathologies of dementia; and neuropsychologists also need knowledge of a wide range of other brain-damage syndromes following illness or trauma to the head (see Gade & Bruhn, 2004, for instance). This is because one of the purposes of cognitive and neuropsychological tests is to examine which syndromes may be present – and to what extent. In this connection the specialist will often supplement the regular test batteries with specific tests or include other tests that may be required in order to focus on specific problems:

A syndrome is (…) a useful working fiction which allows us to create some order out of the complexity of the patient's subjective complaints and the findings of our examinations. Knowledge of a variety of syndromes allows us to generate hypotheses about the nature of the disruptions of function in the individual case.

Walsh, 1994, p. 410.

This quotation makes it clear that the knowledge of the psychologist about syndromes constitutes a working hypothesis that directs our understanding and the procedure adopted, and that one important goal of psychological examinations is to provide an assessment of the relationship between reduced and retained skills in the individual patient.

In many respects, modern techniques employed to take pictures of the brain have made neuropsychological examinations superfluous when it comes to locating brain damage. However, neuropsychological examinations are still an important tool in identifying the consequences of brain damage, even though it is possible to make predictions about probable syndromes based on knowledge of the location of the damage in question. This is because owing to the complexity of the brain and various individual factors, different examples of damage that may seem identical may have very different consequences (see Eriksson, 2003, p. 18, for instance).

In the field of dementia, testing will focus partly on differential diagnostics and partly on guiding patients and their families. Identifying the relationship between lost and retained skills may help the family to decide whether their elderly relative should move to new accommodation, and what help is needed. Examinations may also be used to provide guidelines for staff when it comes to handling challenging behaviour in patients.

Rehabilitation after brain damage

Skills which are initially reduced following limited brain damage often improve with time, although this is not the case if dementia is involved. Naturally, the same applies to elderly people, and in such cases neuropsychological examinations are used as part of the rehabilitation process. A distinction is drawn between three stages in any such process:

1. The acute stage, in which the patient is often admitted to hospital in a confused and possibly life-threatening condition. At this stage the neuropsychologist can provide an initial, provisional assessment of the nature and extent of the damage, thereby helping to decide what is required in terms of subsequent treatment. One of the most important tasks of the psychologist is to help ensure that the correct type of adequate rehabilitation is prescribed.

2. At stage 2 the patient has improved so much that he or she can contribute to the rehabilitation process, although there may still be considerable reversible cognitive dysfunctions such as post-traumatic amnesia (PTA). At this stage the psychologist helps to identify the relationship between reduced and retained skills by carrying out clinical assessment and testing, so that rehabilitation can be planned in relation to the patient's current practical and mental resources. In this connection diagnosis comprises not only the patient's cognitive status but also their potential for rehabilitation, mental resources, degree of insight into their own problems and motivation.

3. At stage 3, on conclusion of rehabilitation, the psychologist also helps to plan the future steps to be taken after discharge from hospital. At this stage it is often still too soon to determine the final status of the patient, but the psychologist's diagnosis helps to plan future steps in terms of accommodation and further rehabilitation. The psychologist also helps to plan trials in the workplace for people of working age. During the transition from stage 2 to stage 3 the psychological diagnosis helps to ensure that certain important choices can be made with regard to the future of the elderly patient. So a diagnosis helps to point the patient into the future in the best possible way, which is one of the most important tasks involved in rehabilitation after brain damage.

Conclusion

In our culture working with the elderly has been an area of low status for many years. Why should we be interested in a group of the population who do not contribute to society, who will soon be dead, and who have already had their opportunities in life? A stage of life in which individuals are winding down instead of winding up! These may seem like cynical viewpoints, and yet they have sometimes been put forward when funding is allocated to different age groups. However, in recent decades major efforts have been made by various groups of professionals to put old age more firmly on the map of interesting forms of existence, both in Denmark and abroad. One of the major breakthroughs in Denmark was the establishment of the Centre for Gerontopsychology in Aarhus in 1991 (see Larsen, Bender & Torpdahl, 2006).

Clinically speaking there are plenty of challenges involved in working with the elderly, an area in which psychologists can gain experience of most forms of mental illness. There are also plenty of opportunities to gain experience of working with other groups of professionals with regard to diagnosis and treatment – both in the field of geropsychiatry and when it comes to rehabilitation after limited brain damage. In addition, there is the experience of existence and life as it is lived in this field that can be gained by observing the existential challenges that psychopathology in old age presents to elderly people and their families across multiple generations. Young clinicians may find this field to be a major challenge, and it is also thought-provoking on a personal level because we all hope to grow old one day.

The diagnosis of psychopathology in the elderly requires a multi-disciplinary approach with a view to laying the kind of mosaic that can lead to a useful understanding of the disorders and situation of elderly people. It also requires thorough knowledge of normal psychology in general and in the elderly in particular, thereby helping to put a stop to superficial interpretations and creating the space needed for distinctive, individual treatment when intervention is necessary. In addition, it requires good knowledge of the mental pathologies encountered in elderly people. And finally, it requires experience and a sure instinct. You cannot learn this by reading books – it only comes from concrete experience of elderly people who are ill, in situations in which you yourself play a role and accept a challenge. This is by no means the least exciting area of this field, and it can often prove enriching on a personal level as well.

REFERENCES

Costa, P.T. & McCrae, R.R. (1992). Normal personality assessment in clinical practice: The NEO Personality Inventory. *Psychological Assessment, 4,* 5-13.

Eriksson, H. (2003). *Neuropsykologi.* København: Hans Reitzels Forlag.

Folstein, M.F., Folstein, S.E. & McHugh, P.R. (1975). Mini-Mental State: A practical method for grading the state of patients for the clinician, *Journal of Psychiatric Research 12,* 189-198.

Fromholt, P., Pedersen, M., Lauridsen, I. og Larsen, S.F. (1990). *Kognitiv kapacitet hos ældre. En psykologisk undersøgelse af 400 75-årige danskere.* Institut for Statsvidenskab. Aarhus.

Fromholt, P. (1992). Gerontopsykologi. In: Gulmann, N.C. (Ed.), *Praktisk gerontopsykiatri.* København: Hans Reizels Forlag.

Gade, A.(1994). *RH Mental Status Undersøgelse.* København: Rigshospitalet.

Gade, A., Mortensen, E.L., & Bruhn, P. (2002). *Udvidet neuropsykologisk undersøgelse.* København: Rigshospitalet.

Gade, A. & Bruhn, P. (2004). Neuropsykologiske dysfunktioner. In: Poulson, O.B., Gjerris, F. & Sørensen, P.S. (Eds.), *Klinisk Neurologi og Neurokirugi.* København: FADL's forlag.

Gulmann, N.C. (2001). *Praktisk Gerontopsykiatri.* København: Hans Reitzels Forlag.

Hathaway, S.R. & Mckinley, J.C. (1989). The Minnesota Multiphasic Personality Inventory-2. Minneapolis: University of Minnesota Press.

Hestad, K., Ellertsen, B. og Kløve, H. (1998). Neuropsychological assessment in old age. In: Nordhus, I.H., VandenBos, G.R., Berg, S., & Fromholt, P. (Eds.), *Clinical Geropsychology.* Washington, DC: American Psychological Association.

Hodges, J.R. (2004). *Cognitive Assessment for Clinicians.* Oxford University Press.

Korchin, S.J. (1976). *Modern clinical psychology.* New York: Basic Books, Inc., Publishers New York.

Kasl-Godley, J.F., Gatz, M. & Fiske, A. (1998). Depression and depressive symptoms in old age. In: Nordhus, I.H., VandenBos, G.R., Berg, S. og Fromholt, P. (Eds.), *Clinical Geropsychology.* Washington, DC: American Psychological Association.

Larsen, L., Bender, L. & Torpdahl, P. (2006). Jubilæum: Center fylder rundt. *Psykolog Nyt,* 60 (20), 21.

Lazarus, R.S. (1998). Coping with aging: Individuality as a key to understanding. In: Nordhus, I.H., VandenBos, G.R., Berg, S. & Fromholt, P. (Eds.), *Clinical Geropsychology.* Washington, DC: American Psychological Association.

Lezak, M.D. (1995). *Neuropsychological Assessment.* New York: Oxford University Press.

Lund, C. (2003). *Intern instruks til behandlere ansat ved psykiatrisk afdeling, Holstebro Sygehus.* Holstebro: Psykiatrisk afdeling.

Mirdal, G. (1999). Mellem sundhed og sygdom: refleksioner over somatisering. *Psyke og Logos, 1* (20), 60-74.

Segal, D.L., Coolidge, F.L. & Hersen, M. (1998). Psychological Testing of older people In: Nordhus, I.H., VandenBos, G.R., Berg, S. & Fromholt, P. (Eds.), *Clinical Geropsychology.* Washington, DC: American Psychological Association.

Teasdale, T. (1992). Statistiske metoder i klinisk forskning. I: Østergaard, L. *Undersøgelsesmetoder i klinisk psykologi.* København: Munksgaard.

Walsh, K. (1994). *Neuropsychology. A clinical approach.* Edinburgh: Churchill Livingstone.

THE PERSON WITH DEMENTIA IN A PSYCHOLOGICAL PERSPECTIVE

Per Torpdahl & Lars Larsen

Summary

Historically speaking, the fact that the concept of dementia became synonymous with what became known as Alzheimer's disease at the start of the 20th century must be regarded as pure chance. The diagnostic criteria for this "new" form of dementia primarily covered symptoms of cognitive dysfunction. The identification of Alzheimer's disease was the beginning of what became known as the cognitive dementia paradigm. And even though the psychiatric characteristics of various forms of dementia have been the subject of increasing attention during the past 20 years, dementia research is still dominated by this cognitive paradigm.

However, it is both insufficient and unfruitful to understand dementia based solely on a neuroscientific approach. The phenotypical expression of dementia is a result of interaction between a range of factors specific to the individual involved, such as life history, personality, health and neuropathology on the one hand; and physical and socio-psychological environment on the other. Even though the specific individual factors are hard to change in a positive direction, the environment can be adapted to suit the individual instead – leading to a better match between demands, support and resources. This kind of match requires identification of the mental dysfunctions involved and the contextual needs arising as a result.

History of the concept of dementia

The term "dementia" means derangement or the loss of senses. In the 18th century the term was used clinically and legally to describe psychosocial conditions characterised by incompetence independently of age, reversibility or pathological causes. This broad use of the concept was gradually narrowed down, culminating at the end of the 19th century in what Berrios (1990) has called the cognitive paradigm, in which the term "dementia" was used to describe an irreversible cognitive disorder typically occurring in elderly patients suffering from memory loss.

In 1901 a 51-year-old woman named Auguste D was admitted to the state hospital in Frankfurt. She was suffering from cognitive impairment, auditive hallucinations, delusions, paranoia and aggressive behaviour. One of the hospital doctors, Alois Alzheimer, became interested in this unusual patient and started studying her case.

In 1903 Alzheimer started working for Emil Kraepelin in Munich, and when his former patient died in April 1906 her brain was sent to Munich for further study.

In November the same year Alzheimer presented the case at a psychiatry conference, publishing his findings the following year. In the original presentation Alzheimer discussed both cognitive and non-cognitive aspects of Auguste D's disorder. The results of the brain autopsy revealed the presence of plaques, tangles and arteriosclerotic changes in the brain.

Alzheimer was probably not seeking to describe a new brain disease, but to describe a case of unusually early senile dementia (as it was called in those days). But on the basis of this single case, in 1910 Kraepelin introduced the term Alzheimer's disease. His motivation for this premature introduction of a "new" brain disease probably came from high demands for performance and academic ambitions; and he even went as far as omitting important clinical characteristics of Auguste D's disorder (Berrios, 1990).

In fact, both the phenotypical and the neuropathological characteristics of Alzheimer's disease were already well known by 1910. And many of the leading brain researchers of the day objected to the new concept of dementia. The relatively unknown American researcher Fuller, who had drawn attention to the presence of neurofibrillary tangles in senile dementia before the introduction of the concept of Alzheimer's disease, wondered (like many of his colleagues) why a special term should be reserved for a phenomenon which simply seemed to be a feature of a more general age-related brain disorder (Berrios, 1990).

Even though the psychiatric characteristics of various forms of dementia have been the object of increasing attention in the past 20 years, a trend that can be illustrated by the introduction of the concept of BPSD (Behavioural and Psychological Symptoms of Dementia) in 1996 (Finkel, 2000), dementia research is still dominated by the cognitive paradigm. In fact the French psychiatrist Esquirol described symptoms resembling those of BPSD as long ago as the 1820s (Finkel, 2000).

Within the field of psychology dementia has also been regarded primarily as a cognitive disorder, as revealed in an excellent book on geropsychology entitled "The Psychology of Ageing" (Stuart-Hamilton, 1994), which focuses almost entirely on cognitive decline. This book also contains a very short section on the effects of ageing on carers, but says nothing about the personal experiences of people suffering from dementia and their need for contextual support.

However, as shown below other researchers have made significant phenomenological and socio-psychological contributions to this field.

Normal ageing, mild cognitive impairment or dementia?

The relationship between normal ageing, mild cognitive impairment and progressive dementia can be described as a continuum on a sliding scale.

Memory impairment is seen in roughly 25-50% of all healthy individuals living at home above the age of 75, a frequency which increases with age (Bruhn, 2005).

An increasing number of patients visiting clinics who are suffering from mild cognitive impairment (MCI) complain about memory problems, leading to the suspicion that they may be suffering from dementia. Even though the symptoms of MCI extend beyond normal age-related cognitive changes, they do not meet the criteria for dementia. Apart from cognitive impairment, unremarkable cognitive functions are also observed in such patients, who are able to function normally in daily life. It is estimated that each year 5-15% of all MCI patients will develop dementia. So this group of patients should be diagnosed on a regular basis by examining them at intervals of between six months and one year (Bruhn, 2005; DSAM, 2006).

Another dilemma involves the fact that about 60-70% of people with mild cognitive impairment develop dementia within a few years, which means that there are still 30-40% in the category of false positive diagnoses (people who do not develop dementia, but who are mistakenly regarded as suffering from dementia by their surroundings).

The early diagnosis of dementia is sometimes problematic because there is no treatment to cure the problem and the effectiveness of anti-dementia medicine seems to be limited (Pelosi, McNulty & Jackson, 2006). An early diagnosis may lead to reactions in the patient in the form of anxiety and emotional chaos, as well as threatening their identity and self-worth and affecting their family life.

Dementia

The primary symptoms of dementia are a change in brain function caused by the dysfunction or destruction and loss of brain cells. This results in a range of cognitive impairments comprising the following according to ICD-10 criteria: initial impairment of the memory (particularly with regard to new data); and impairment of other cognitive functions such as abstraction, thinking, planning and/or powers of judgement. But people suffering from dementia also possess a certain degree of consciousness. They also have impaired emotional control and motivation or social behaviour with more than one of the following symptoms: emotional lability, irritability, apathy and/or coarsened social behaviour. Finally, the condition must have lasted for more than six months (Bertelsen, 1995).

Dementia can be divided into mild dementia interfering with normal daily activities; moderate dementia requiring assistance in daily life; and severe dementia requiring continuous care and monitoring. Dementia can also be divided in different ways based on either neuropathology or clinical type, but in many cases a combination is involved (Engedal & Haugen, 2004; Hasselbalch & Stokholm, 2005).

Dementia results in the progressive loss of a range of central cognitive, emotional, behavioural and social functions, a loss which in a psychosocial perspective has wide-ranging consequences with regard to interaction between patients and their surroundings.

The signs of dementia become apparent in everyday actions and tasks. The loss of the ability to learn and memory loss may mean that patients find it difficult to remember names or faces. They forget things and tell the same story and ask the same questions repeatedly – even at extremely short intervals. They also find it difficult to remember which day, month and year it is.

Language impairments affecting the power of speech may lead to difficulties in recalling names or naming objects, speech may become incomprehensible, or patients may have difficulties pronouncing words. The development of dementia leads to the loss of practical skills: patients may forget to eat, have difficulty going to the toilet, or find it hard to get dressed and undressed. For instance, there is a risk that they will go outside without putting a coat on even in the winter. Perceptual difficulties may lead to problems in finding their way around or recognising familiar places. There is also a risk that their families suddenly seem like strangers. Their spouse might be seen as their mother, their daughter turns into their spouse or a sister, and so on.

We now know that there are a wide range of brain disorders that can cause dementia, but in practice a few of these dominate the picture.

Psychological domains influenced by dementia

In general terms, the psychological domains can be divided into: gnosis, memory, language, executive functions, personality and praxis.

- Gnosis is the ability to recognise complex sensory impressions. Gnosis comprises the processing of sensory impressions, perception, interpretation and understanding. The term used when dementia affects gnosis is *agnosia*.

- Memory is the ability to remember. Memory comprises learning, storing, recognition and recall. A distinction is drawn between short-term and long-term memory. The loss of memory functions is called *amnesia*.

- Language is the ability to understand and express spoken and written language. Language disorders are known as *aphasia*. Impressive-type aphasia is also known as Wernicke's aphasia, while expressive-type aphasia is called Broca's aphasia (Stuart-Hamilton, 2001).

- Executive functions are general regulating and controlling functions such as initiative, intentionality, planning, judgement, the ability to form a comprehensive overview and emotional control. The loss of these functions leads to psychological primitivising and the loss of social skills.

- Personality reflects the special characteristics of an individual which apply at any time and in all situations, such as emotional instability, extraversion, openness, agreeableness and conscientiousness (McCrae & Costa, 2003).

- Praxis comprises practical skills, automatic patterns of action and the co-ordination of movements. The loss of these skills is called *apraxia*.

The picture of dementia is often complicated by a range of secondary symptoms. Anxiety and depression are often evident, and the misunderstanding and misinterpretation of the intentions and reactions of other people may lead to a sense of helplessness and anger. The occurrence of delusions is also frequent during dementia.

There will always be a complex interaction between the area of the brain that has been affected, the personality and situational understanding of the person affected, and the way in which other people react to people suffering from dementia (Lauridsen & Eckermann, 2005).

The psychological and thereby cognitive and behavioural consequences of the disease vary, depending on which part of the brain is affected. Two forms of dementia can vary just as much as a neurosis and a psychosis, for instance – and they may require equally different programmes of treatment. This means that it is not sufficient to simply diagnose a problem as dementia. Patients and the people around them are entitled to expect the professional system to examine their problem carefully and collect the knowledge needed to provide psychological, pedagogical and social guidance.

The diagnosis of the complex of problems connected with dementia requires knowledge of neuropsychology, development psychology and behavioural psychology, as well as requiring understanding of mental functions in a broader sense, including the perception and mastery of the problem by the elderly individual in question.

People suffering from dementia who possess good strategies to compensate for their problem can maintain their daily lives for longer than people who have similar problems but are less able to handle them. As a result, it is important to know not only the extent and nature of the problem concerned but also the way in which the individuals in question handle the problem (Fromholt, Bender & Torpdahl, 1993).

One important aspect of dementia is that memory problems are not always the central problem. Some forms of dementia in which other psychological processes break down can actually cause greater problems for dementia patients and the people around them. Experience shows that such dementia conditions are not acknowledged for a long time because the individuals concerned have other main symptoms than those normally connected with the concept of dementia.

Dementia of the Alzheimer Type (DAT)

It is estimated that about 60% of all cases of dementia are of the Alzheimer type. Alzheimer's disease has been defined in terms of neuropathology, but there are several different causes (both genetic and environmental). Traditionally a distinction has been drawn between early and late DAT. Patients with early DAT – also known as presenile dementia – normally experience the first symptoms at the age of 55-65, but occasionally symptoms start in the mid-30s. Patients with early DAT constitute a very small proportion of all cases. A diagnostic distinction based on an age limit of 65 years is arbitrary, and the similarities between the two varieties are greater than the differences (Eriksson, 2003).

The borderline between Alzheimer's and many other forms of dementia is unclear, and the overlap with vascular dementia is particularly striking.

DAT is an atrophic disorder involving damage primarily to the parietal lobe and the temporal lobe, as well as to the frontal lobe to a lesser extent – even though damage to the frontal lobe becomes more typical with increasing age. The average life expectancy from the time symptoms commence is about 15 years; but the earlier the symptoms start, the faster the disease progresses.

Characteristic symptoms are:

• Loss of both short-term and long-term memory
• Loss of episodic and autobiographical memory

- Visuospatial problems and reduced orientation ability
- Apraxia and the breakdown of everyday functions
- Aphasia – expressive and (in time) impressive aphasia
- Depending on which hemisphere the lesions are most pronounced in, aphasia or apraxia may be more or less dominant

DAT is also often accompanied by depression, delusions and confabulation.

The prevalence of DAT increases exponentially with age. The incidence is 1% for 65-80 year-olds (Gulmann, 2001) and about 10% (Eriksson, 2003) after this age. The lifetime risk is about 20-30%, which means that 20-30% of the population suffer from dementia during the final years of their life (Gulmann, 2001).

DAT is neuropathologically and pathophysiologically characterised by various pathological proteins: amyloids, tau protein, presenilin and the neurotransmitter substances acetylcholine and glutamate. Characteristic microscopic lesions of the cerebral cortex are senile plaques with precipitated β-amyloid and neuro-fibrillary degeneration, which involves an accumulation of abnormal, tangled fibrils in the form of phosphorylated tau. In the nucleus basalis of Meynart, which has branched axons to the cortex, there is widespread neuron loss of 50-80%. Early pathological changes in the hippocampus and the parahippo-campal gyrus seem to be an important indicator of the subsequent development of DAT (Scheltens, 1999). There also seems to be an inflammatory element. The genetic mutation of chromosomes 21, 14 and 1 has been observed. These rarer, dominant hereditary cases are primarily found in presenile patients.

There are also other risk factors such as serious head trauma and (not least) great age.

DAT is also called perception dementia because agnostic problems are so characteristic of this form of dementia (Gulmann, 2001). Agnostic disturbances and the accompanying reduction in visuospatial abilities lead to considerable problems with regard to spatial orientation, even in familiar surroundings. Agnosia and apraxia lead to increasing helplessness and an increasing need for care, even though actual physical degeneration does not occur until a late stage of the disease. Unlike most other forms of dementia, DAT typically involves very early compromising of the memory (first the episodic memory and then the semantic memory). People suffering from DAT retain a certain amount of insight into their medical condition and a certain amount of judgement until a late stage of the disease; and their personality and social skills are not affected until a late stage either. Nominal aphasia is a characteristic language disorder.

Frontotemporal dementia (FTD) is a form of dementia that occurs in various types with an early debut and rapid progression. Hereditary factors play a greater role than they do in DAT, with mutation in the tau gene in chromosome 17 or 9, although this only explains a small proportion of cases (Hasselbalch & Stokholm, 2005). In FTD the memory is not affected as badly, but there are problems with regard to flexible thinking and planning. FTD patients show evidence of stereotypical behaviour, perseveration and behaviour limitations involving an uncritical attitude, uncontrolled behaviour or opposite apathy. Average life expectancy after the debut is 5-10 years. Sub-groups of FTD have been discovered in which the above-mentioned characteristics are not registered until later in the process, but in which language disorders are the primary symptom. What is involved is semantic dementia (with patients gradually losing knowledge about language and concepts), and progressive aphasia (in which the ability to speak and write is affected).

FTD is also known as executive dementia (Gulmann, 2001). Patients may display primitive, impulsive and unplanned behaviour. Their insight into their problem and their powers of judgement are greatly reduced, while their memory is often relatively well preserved in the early stages of the disease. Perseverance behaviour and stereotyped language use are characteristic of this form of dementia. Early, significant changes in personality are always seen in frontal forms of dementia – typically in the form of reduced sociability and empathy. Uncontrolled, impulsive behaviour combined with a well-preserved physical condition constitute a major challenge for the people involved with FTD patients. The dominance of the cognitive paradigm and the idea that dementia primarily affects the memory may be the reason why both care staff and families find it difficult to understand and accept manifestations of FTD. Problem-causing behaviour owing to the compromised intentions of FTD patients may be misinterpreted as an expression of deliberate thoughtlessness.

Lewy body dementia (LBD) is a form of dementia that has not been explored as thoroughly as DAT, and the criteria for LBD were not proposed until 1996 even though so-called Lewy bodies in neurons were described by Friederich Lewy as long ago as 1913. LBD is observed almost exclusively in people aged 60 or more, with a frequency of 10-20% (Hasselbalch & Stokholm, 2005). However, these figures are a little uncertain because the limits to LBD have not been defined precisely (Gulmann, 2001).

LBD leads to changes in both the cortical and the subcortical areas of the brain. The particular pathological characteristics are neurons with Lewy bodies. LBD is an aggressive form of dementia which affects the brain more generally than other forms of dementia, as well as having a shorter average life expectancy after the initial symptoms have been registered. Apart from the symptoms (which may resemble DAT symptoms to some extent), subcortical signs also become evident such as Parkinsonism and a tendency to fall, as well as fluctuating consciousness involving periods of confusion and hallucinations. Patients with LBD may have problems in tolerating anti-psychotic medicine, which in such cases causes severe extra-pyramidal side-effects even in small doses.

LBD's most prominent characteristics are general slowness, lethargy in mental processes and exhaustion. A low level of both physical and mental activity is also evident. People suffering from LBD seem to lack initiative, to be apathetic and indifferent; and one way to describe LBD in general terms is by referring to it as attention dementia. There are personality changes: lower extraversion and less sense of conscience. There is considerable variation with regard to the insight of patients into their problem – and with regard to their powers of judgement. Other frequent symptoms are reduced powers of recall, dysarthria (a motor speech disorder) and early physical impairment.

Vascular dementia (VaD) causes about 20-25% of all cases of dementia, and is due to blood clots and vascular problems such as arteriosclerosis, often leading to the formation of multiple brain infarcts. There are various forms of VaD. Multi-infarct dementia (MID) is a consequence of embolism or thrombosis in the vessels of the brain. This type of dementia is observed frequently in patients with heart disease, in patients with long-term hypertension that has not been treated optimally, and/or in patients with diabetes mellitus. Apart from symptoms of dementia, VaD patients may suffer from focal neurological disorders such as paresis.

Psycho-motoric lethargy and an excessive frequency of depression and/or psychotic symptoms are observed in the subcortical form. Vascular dementia is characterised by uneven progression and widely varying remaining life expectancy.

Gulmann (2001) has described VaD as "scattered dementia". The functional disorders that are observed depend entirely on which part of the brain is damaged. This form of dementia is the most unpredictable of them all. Apart from frequent aphasia and early physical impairment, patients suffering from VaD vary considerably with regard to gnosis, memory, executive functions and personality.

Dementia caused by other brain diseases

Apart from occasional signs of reversible dementia in people suffering from somatic and psychiatric disorders, dementia does also occur as a consequence of neurological diseases – although only at various times and in various forms.

In general dementia is observed in cases of brain disease if major areas of the temporal structure of the brain or central areas corresponding to the peri-ventricular area are affected.

Dementia occurs in connection with *Parkinson's disease*: about 10% of such patients experience learning and memory difficulties as well as failures of orientation ability. Their language and executive abilities may be intact. A number of elderly patients with Parkinson's disease experience periods of confusion, which may be caused by pharmaceuticals which have a central dopaminergic or anticholinergic effect – including anti-Parkinson's pharmaceuticals in particular. In addition to the characteristic subcortical symptoms, dementia symptoms can also be observed in patients suffering from *Huntington's chorea*. Such patients may have no insight into their difficulties, as well as having entirely unrealistic ideas about their own abilities. *Multiple sclerosis* is another neurological disorder in which dementia may occur to a varying degree. The primary symptoms are a lack of concentration and reduced psycho-motoric tempo as well as tiredness. *Creutzfeldt-Jacob disease*, which occurs in several varieties with a very early and later debut respectively, is a terminal disease with a rapid progression involving neurological symptoms, dementia and confusion. Dementia may also occur in cases of encephalitis (caused by herpes virus, for instance), *syphilis* and *AIDS*. *Tumours* in the brain may also lead to states of dementia, and in such cases the symptomatology will depend on the location of the problem. *Alcohol dementia*, also known as *Korsakoff's psychosis*, which is characterised primarily by amnesia, may be due not only to the constant intake of alcohol but also to a lack of thiamine (vitamin B1) caused by malnutrition. In some cases the symptoms of dementia are reversible if the alcohol abuse is terminated in time.

Normal pressure hydrocephalus, which may occur due to unknown reasons or many years after a major head trauma and subarachnoid haemorrhage, is another cause of reversible dementia symptoms. Urine incontinence and ataxia (a malfunction of muscle coordination) are observed as well as signs of dementia. Endocrine diseases such as *thyroid disorders* may also lead to cognitive disorders. Both hypothyroidism and hyperthyroidism may result in forgetfulness, disorientation and increased latency time. *Depressions* may also cause signs of dementia which are also known as pseudo-dementia. Patients experience concentration, learning and memory problems, whereas their language and practical skills remain intact.

The contextual needs of people suffering from dementia

In order to help individuals suffering from dementia to maintain the best possible functional level and life quality, it is vital not only to gain clarity regarding the nature and progression of the specific dementia problem in question, but also to identify the contextual needs of the patient concerned. In this connection, contextual needs should be understood in a broad sense, ranging from the physical environment at one end of the scale to communicative needs at the other. This section deals primarily with the latter.

The British psychologist Tom Kitwood has pointed out that cases of dementia cannot be viewed solely from a neuropathological perspective. It is important that carers understand that dementia is the result of a series of person-specific factors such as life history, personality, health, neuropathology and socio-psychological environment (Kitwood, 1993, 1999). In treatment contexts the last of these factors is particularly interesting for psychology, since this is where we find the largest potential for treatment and thus the best opportunities for helping the patient in question. The life history, personality and neuropathology of persons suffering from dementia are difficult to influence, and nor can we prevent a progressive somatic decline even though a complete somatic diagnosis and sufficient efforts may increase life quality. But it is possible to change the environment.

In extension of Kurt Lewin's point that behaviour is a result of interaction between the individual and the environment (Lewin, 1935), the American psychologist Mortimer Powell Lawton (1973) has claimed that the behaviour and wellbeing of persons suffering from dementia are a function of the interaction between their resources and the demands and support of the environment: f (individual resources, demands of the environment) = behaviour. It is difficult to influence individual resources in a positive direction, so the context must be adapted to suit the individual in question with a view to achieving a better match between demands, support and resources. This approach to each individual case of dementia means that each person suffering from dementia is regarded as an individual who may exhibit difficult behaviour owing to their illness, rather than as an individual who is difficult by definition. It is difficult to change the basic characteristics of an individual, but behaviour can be influenced. This distinction is vital with a view to treating people suffering from dementia as more than just cases of a disease. Careful, individually tailored adjustments of context generally have a considerable positive effect on problematic behaviour, the life quality of people suffering from dementia, and the burden placed on the people caring for them.

Psychological disorders and contextual needs

This section outlines a number of contextual needs generated by a variety of mental dysfunctions. It is important to remember that mental dysfunctions and the needs arising in this connection change as the disease progresses (Larsen & Kabel, 2002). As a result, ongoing evaluation and possibly re-evaluation are necessary.

Perception
The ability to perceive the world around us using our sight, hearing and senses of smell and touch may be affected by dementia. When these abilities fail, the foundations on which people suffering from dementia interact with their surroundings become distorted. Interaction with the world around us is only possible if we perceive the world with reasonable accuracy. Inaccurate and occasionally erroneous perceptions will lead to a wide range of misunderstandings. Such misunderstandings will potentially bring people suffering from dementia into conflict with their surroundings, unless these surroundings support them and compensate for their reduced perceptions.

Communication between two people works best when they know each other. However, if people suffering from dementia and the people who care for them are to benefit from any such prior knowledge of each other, it is important that persons with dementia are given the opportunity to identify the people caring for them correctly. When their powers of perception are reduced, it is often difficult for people with dementia to recognise carers who they actually know well. So they need such carers to compensate for this by giving them various opportunities to perceive them correctly. This can be done by sending different signals which can be perceived by different senses. Their sight can be stimulated by body language, gestures, clothing and hairstyle. Their hearing can be stimulated by speech, language use and intonation. Their sense of smell can be stimulated by familiar creams and perfumes. And their sense of touch can be stimulated by shaking hands and other forms of physical contact.

Fundamentally carers cannot automatically assume that they have been recognised – so it is always a good idea to introduce yourself at the beginning of any new interaction. It is also important to be aware that emotional contact increases the chance of correct identification and recognition.

People with dementia whose powers of perception have been reduced need help from the physical layout and organisation of their immediate surroundings. So it is important to make these surroundings as simple as possible. The presence of a great number of objects in a room may confuse people with dementia. Objects will be perceived more clearly if they have a colour different from that of their background, and people with dementia will often perceive dark areas against a light background as holes.

Memory

Memory can be divided roughly into learning, storing, recognition and recall. When people's memory starts to fail, it is important to remember that memory loss is a phenomenon that varies considerably from one individual to the next. Some persons with dementia with subcortical brain damage will find recollection particularly difficult, while others with cortical damage such as DAT and FTD find it harder to learn and store things in their memories. Agnosia in people with DAT also leads to difficulties in recognising things.

People with memory problems should not be asked factual questions. If they are asked a great number of questions they may soon feel that they are being examined in a subject for which they are insufficiently prepared. Anyone who has ever been in this situation will recognise the sense of anxiety that it can provoke. Being asked a great number of questions may lead to a degree of anxiety that may in itself cause the memory of the person with dementia to be even poorer than it really is. In addition, you risk exposing their inadequacies. So it may be a good idea to avoid questions starting with "Do you remember …?" Other questions to be avoided are those starting with "When?", "Who?" and "What?" Instead, it is better to wait until people with dementia say something themselves – or to tell them something and provide them with relevant guidelines for carrying on some form of dialogue. This requires great knowledge of their life history.

If it is necessary to ask a question, it is an advantage to use emotionally related questions rather than factual ones. For instance, it may be better to say "Are you hungry?" rather than "Have you had your breakfast?" This will enable them to relate to their immediate feelings instead of trying to remember events from the past. And finally, it is possible to jog people's memory with song, music and particular odours. Naturally, it is important to have good knowledge of their preferences and history in this respect. Not all music or all odours may be connected with happy memories for the individual concerned.

Language

Dementia may cause impressive or expressive language dysfunctions, and it is important to be aware of the degree of expressive or impressive aphasia in question. When people with dementia are suffering primarily from expressive aphasia, there is a danger that carers and others will automatically assume that they find understanding things just as hard as speaking. The risk is that carers will, as it were, talk down to people suffering from expressive aphasia. On the other hand, there is a risk that carers will talk above the heads of people suffering from impressive aphasia if they assume that their understanding of language is just as good as their speech. Impressive language problems are sometimes mistaken for deafness because such patients ask people to repeat things that they have just said. However, this wish for repetition is not necessarily due to the fact that such patients cannot hear what has been said – the problem may be that they cannot understand the content of what has been said. This can often be remedied by simplifying your language and trying to use different words.

Many people with dementia suffer from both expressive and impressive aphasia, although not necessarily to the same degree.

During linguistic communication people suffering from dementia need to have (and to retain) eye contact so both the partners in communication are focused and can benefit from supplementary non-verbal signals in the form of body language and gestures. It is vital to allow plenty of time and never to start a conversation unless you have the time needed to complete it. Impressive aphasia problems can be alleviated if carers catch the attention of dementia sufferers before they start speaking, and if they use simple, clear language employing short words and sentences.

Expressive aphasia problems can be alleviated if carers show that they are interested in trying to understand and if they allow people with dementia to express themselves. If it is not possible to understand what the person with dementia is trying to say, carers can try to guess what they mean – but should avoid correcting them.

Powers of judgement

The powers of judgement constitute a vital executive function when it comes to mastering interaction with your environment. Effective powers of judgement become apparent in the ability to assess your own potential and limitations (and those of others) realistically. Planning and the calculation of consequences also depend on intact powers of judgement. The everyday lives of elderly people can be improved for a long time if they have good insight into their problems as well as the ability to compensate for them, but the result may also be that other people fail to appreciate the true extent of these problems. Many people with dementia have failing powers of judgement, constituting a major problem for the people around them. Failing powers of judgement often go hand-in-hand with a lack of acknowledgement of illness, and people suffering from dementia often act on the basis of an unrealistic idea of their own abilities and potential. The result is inevitable. Without help and support their interaction with their surroundings will fail, often leading to anger, irritation and conflict.

The task facing carers involves helping people with dementia to overcome their functional difficulties – but how do you help people to judge things if they do not want any help? This is a central dilemma in the care offered to people with dementia (Ulrich, 2000). If the need for help is not met and people with dementia are allowed to make their own decisions, they will be left to their own unrealistic assessments and resulting fiasco and chaos. This situation can easily turn into neglect. But if you try to help persons with dementia to make judgements when they do not want any help, you may be transgressing their limits.

The solution involves finding a compromise in which carers with intact powers of judgement, and based on the long-term interests of people suffering from dementia, steer the situation in the right direction with all due consideration and acknowledgement of the experiences and feelings of the person concerned (Larsen & Sørensen, 2002). However, this is often easier said than done.

Based on thorough knowledge of the individual concerned, carers must try to gain a good overview of the situations in which reduced powers of judgement typically become evident. Once this has been done it is normally possible to think ahead and prevent the difficult situations from arising again. It may be necessary to construct clear rules, stability and consistency which may cause difficulties at the moment but which will in the long term benefit the person with dementia. Such measures by carers can be characterised as a necessary "loving custodialism" (Riis, 1999).

Individually adapted limits must be set up and some protection must be provided when people with dementia display behaviour that is inconsistent with their own interests or which results in serious discomfort or risk for their surroundings. The best way of achieving these goals is by being fair, firm and friendly – and by avoiding any attempts to reason with the people concerned or discuss the matter in question. People suffering from dementia will always lose a discussion and will be unable to follow a line of argument anyway – so their only possible reaction (apart from resignation) will be anger. It is often difficult for both families and care staff to set limits for other adults. However, the need to set limits and regulate behaviour becomes apparent in the long term because people with reduced powers of judgement become attached particularly strongly to carers who understand the importance of retaining a necessary structure in everyday life – whereas they grow confused in the company of people who fail to appreciate how important this is.

Personality
Changes of personality are linked with both reversible and irreversible pathological conditions in the brain. Relatively stable personality traits are observed during the normal process of ageing and in cases of moderate somatic disorders; whereas in reversible conditions involving delirium, substance abuse problems, pharmaceutically induced problems and mental illness changes of behaviour and personality are sometimes evident (McCrae & Costa, 2003; Costa, Met-

ter & McCrae, 1994; Gulmann, 2001; Kunik, Yudofsky, Silver & Hales, 1994; Hirschfeld, Klerman, Clayton et al., 1983; Kramer, 1997).

Major irreversible changes of personality may be due to frontal and subcortical brain damage (Chatterjee, Strauss, Smyth & Whitehouse, 1992; Hawkins & Trobst, 2000; Costa & McCrae, 2000; Golden & Golden, 2003; Finkel, 1997; Neary & Snowdon, 1996; Lebert, Pasquier & Petit, 1995). These changes will typically be expressed in the form of increased emotional lability and reduced social understanding and interest, as well as the tendency towards primitive, instinctive behaviour. So pathological changes, particularly in the form of greater emotional instability and reduced agreeableness and consideration, will be very different from normal age-related changes with the opposite tendency (Larsen & Winsløv, 2005).

In cases of personality change it is important to provide a manageable and well-structured daily life which has a meaningful content and which is neither over-stimulated nor under-stimulated. Owing to the risk of increased emotional lability, there is a risk of over-stimulation, and it may sometimes be necessary to shelter the person with dementia from this in an environment of low stimulation. It is also important to remember that reduced sociability and a reduced sense of conscience – including irritability, aggression and the failure to keep appointments – are not a reflection of bad will on the part of the person suffering from dementia but a result of the illness.

In caring for the elderly it is common practice to adapt the care provided with due respect for the life history of the individuals concerned. However, when pathological personality changes are involved it is important to gain a picture of the way in which the morbid personality can be distinguished from the pre-morbid personality, in order to prevent the implementation of care measures that are in direct conflict with the personality in question.

For families, whose relationship with the person with dementia is based on experience of the pre-morbid personality, the pathological changes can be extremely difficult to bear. In this respect there is a need to inform families that dementia involves not only memory loss but also changes in behaviour and personality.

Praxis

The praxis function should be seen in connection with other cognitive functions such as memory and the senses. In general terms, dementia results in a breakdown of over-learned, automatic patterns of action with a reduced or terminated ability to manoeuvre objects or carry out appropriate movements. In daily life such difficulties may influence not only the way in which the person with dementia performs and handles various tasks, but also the demands which it is reasonable for their surroundings to make on them. The person with dementia may have forgotten how to perform an action; or he may remember patterns of action but can only move clumsily. Sometimes there is a mixture of executive and perception dementia, with persons trying to use a toothbrush as a razor or stirring their coffee with a lipstick. In an attempt to compensate for these difficulties they may stop performing many daily activities in an attempt to avoid making mistakes, explaining this behaviour by saying that they are no longer interested in the activities in question. Early symptoms are that more complicated activities are affected, such as knitting and operating the television or coffee machine.

When we interact with people who are experiencing practical difficulties, problems may arise if we fail to adjust our demands regarding the practical contributions they are expected to make. At worst, they may become angry and aggressive. Naturally, nobody is interested in increasing the frustration often present in persons suffering from dementia when it becomes apparent that they

TABLE 1. Characteristics of various forms of dementia

	DAT	FLD	VaD	Subcortical	LBD[1]
General	Perception dementia	Executive dementia	Scattered dementia	Lethargy dementia	Attention dementia
Agnosia	Early	Very late	Varying	Late	Early, particularly visual
Amnesia	Distinct	Slightly reduced	Uneven	Recall	Slight, particularly visual
Aphasia	Nominal aphasia	Stereotypical	Often	Dysarthria	Dysarthria, verbal flow
Executive disorders	Late	Early; structure, plan	Varying	Alternating	Early; lethargy, perseveration
Personality changes	Late	Early	Observed sometimes	Some reduction	Varying
Apraxia	Early	Early	Varying	Late	Early
Contextual needs	Recognisability, manageability	Structure, "loving custodialism"	Individual, varying	Structure, activities	Low stimulation, recognisability, manageability

Inspired by Gulmann, 2001, p. 109.

1 Both cortical and subcortical lesions

are incapable of performing various forms of practical activity. This does not mean that they cannot carry out any form of praxis – instead, it means that carers must try to find out what they can still manage to do, and how they can be helped to realise this remaining potential thanks to the provision of a little support. For instance, if their procedural memory is more intact than other forms of memory, people with dementia will know what to use a washing-up brush for – although they may find it very hard to put the crockery away once it has been washed up because this involves a more complex process.

Table 1 above contains a summary of various forms of dementia, their symptoms, and the contextual needs which they imply.

What about the spouses?

People suffering from dementia induce grief (the experience of loss), anxiety, anger, shame, guilt and a loss of motivation in their spouses. These problems may have an impact on the entire social environment, which worsens the situation, behaviour and life quality of the person with dementia and increases the risk that a vicious circle will be established. The role allocated to the spouse changes, and the spouse needs to make greater efforts in various areas. The new situation may make it difficult for spouses to maintain their own daily lives, friends and interests. There will also be changes in the way a couple spend their time together, and for dementia sufferers the old and the new will coincide (Nordhus, 1995; Torpdahl, 1999). Spouses normally feel great responsibility for the person with dementia, and may find it difficult to let go in certain situations. Both spouses may once have promised each other that neither of them would end their days in a nursing home as long as the other spouse was still physically and mentally capable.

Spouses are normally responsible for contact with the public authorities, including arguing for any help and support that may be needed to make everyday activities possible. In certain periods spouses will experience emotionally harrowing situations, and they will also experience loss. The burden placed on their daily lives will vary, and in general they will be expected to demonstrate great flexibility as far as the care of the person with dementia is concerned.

For spouses there are various ways of handling this change in life situation. Some people try to gain control of the situation by looking for information, trying to obtain help and providing practical care. Others try to understand and explain the fact that dementia is an illness for which their spouse is not to blame (Ingebretsen, 1995). Some spouses refuse to accept the seriousness of the situation and mistakenly continue to make the same high demands on the person with dementia that they have always made. Others are better at focusing on the things that their spouse can still manage with a little support and help. And others try to think, plan and act on behalf of the person with dementia in an attempt to maintain the family's previous functional level.

Spouses see themselves as supporters and carers. This may make spouses reduce their own expectations with regard to acknowledgement and support, or they may look for appreciation elsewhere and revise their picture of their relationship with the person with dementia. Others try to adapt by using their ability to change family roles and the way they communicate.

A great number of things start to take place on the terms of the person with dementia, but it is also important to be aware of the opportunities of spouses for obtaining help to manage their own reactions such as sorrow, bitterness, love, compassion, exhaustion or resignation. In addition, spouses will need an explanation of the extent, nature and expected progression of the form of dementia concerned.

Spouses often ask for good advice about how to act in relation to the person with dementia, and the following guidelines may be useful in this connection:

1. Make suitable demands on the person with dementia – demands that allow for the range of personal and everyday problems that they encounter.

2. Do not over-stimulate the person with dementia – this may lead to unnecessarily restless behaviour in the form of anger or direct violence, particularly when he might not understand what you are trying to get him to do.

3. Create a good structure in daily life – there may be situations in which spouses have to assume responsibility for planning the activities of the person with dementia because they are completely unable to judge their situation.

4. Take good care of yourself – remember to set limits when things get too tough. Spouses are entitled to receive help to manage a person with dementia on a daily basis.

Final remarks and perspectives

This chapter has provided a historical introduction to the concept of dementia, identified various forms of dementia, and indicated the need to understand dementia as more than just a cognitive disorder.

Based on identification of the level of dysfunction in persons with dementia, medical staff and carers can create a good overview of the contextual needs of the people concerned. These needs constitute the foundations of individually adapted socio-psychological adjustments of the context of people with dementia with a view to increasing their sense of wellbeing, life quality and social interaction with their surroundings.

Contextual adjustments are the most potent form of treatment in relation to people with dementia, so it is important that professionals working with dementia (doctors, nurses, care staff and other groups of professionals) learn to carry out a systematic identification of contextual needs and adjust the context accordingly.

Geropsychologists play an important role when it comes to communicating knowledge about this important supplement to the classical neuroscientific dementia paradigm.

Acknowledgements

We should like to thank geropsychiatrist Nils Chr. Gulmann and geropsychologist Lise Bender for reading the manuscript of this chapter and providing constructive comments.

REFERENCES

Berrios, G.E. (1990). Alzheimer's disease: A conceptual history. *International Journal of Geriatric Psychiatry, 5*, 355-365.

Bertelsen, A. (1995). *WHO ICD-10 Psykiske lidelser og adfærdsmæssige forstyrrelser. Klassifikation og Diagnostiske kriterier*. København: Munksgaard.

Bruhn, P. (2005). Neuropsykologiske forstyrrelser ved demens. In: S.G. Hasselbalch, N. Engelbreht & O. Thage, *Forstå demens*. København: Lindhardt og Ringhof Forlag A/S og Alzheimerforeningen.

Chatterjee, A., Strauss, M.E., Smyth, K.A., & Whitehouse, P.J. (1992). Personality Changes in Alzheimers-Disease. *Archives of Neurology, 49*, 486-491.

Costa, P.T. & McCrae, R.R. (2000). Comtemporary personality psychology. In: C.E. Coffey & J.L. Cummings (Eds.), *Textbook of geriatric psychiatry*. 2. ed., 453-462, Washington, D.C.: American Psychiatric Press.

Costa, P.T., Metter, E.J., & McCrae, R.R. (1994). Personality Stability and Its Contribution to Successful Aging. *Journal of Geriatric Psychiatry, 27*, 41-59.

DSAM (2006). *Demens i almen praksis. Udredning, diagnostik, behandling, opfølgning. Klinisk vejledning*. Dansk Selskab for Almen Medicin i samarbejde med Fonden for tidsskrift for praktisk lægegerning. Lægeforeningens forlag.

Engedal, K. & Haugen, P.K. (2004). *Demens. Fakta og udfordringer.* Oslo: Nasjonalt Kompetanse-senter for aldersdemens.

Eriksson, H. (2003). *Neuropsykologi – Normalfunktion, demensformer og afgrænsede hjerneskader.* København: Hans Reitzels Forlag, kap. 20.

Finkel, S. (1997). Behavioural and psychological signs and symptoms of dementia. *International Journal of Geriatric Psychiatry, 12,* 1060-1061.

Finkel, S. (2000). Introduction to Behavioural and Psychological Symptoms of Dementia (BPSD). *International Journal of Geriatric Psychiatry, 15,* 2-4.

Fromholt, P., Bender, L. & Torpdahl, P. (1993). Den demente og den professionelle – psykologens vinkel. *Gerontologi og Samfund, 3,* 46-48.

Golden, Z. & Golden, C. (2003). Impact of Brain Injury Severity on Personality Dysfunction. *International Journal of Neuroscience, 113,* 733-745.

Gulmann. N.C. (2001). *Praktisk gerontopsykiatri.* København: Hans Reitzels Forlag.

Hawkins, K.A. & Trobst, K.K. (2000). Frontal lobe dysfunction and aggression: Conceptual issues and research findings. *Aggression and Violent Behavior, 5,* 147-157.

Hasselbalch, S.G. & Stokholm, J. (2005). Demenssygdomme. In: S.G. Hasselbalch, N. Engelbreht & O. Thage, *Forstå demens.* København: Lindhardt og Ringhof Forlag A/S og Alzheimerforeningen.

Hirschfeld, R.M.A., Klerman, G.L., Clayton, P.J., Keller, MacDonald-Scott, P. & Larkin, B.H. (1983). Assessing Personality: Effects of depressive states on trait measurement. *American Journal of Psychiatry, 140,* 695-699.

Ingebretsen, R. (1995). Demens på nært hold – mestring i parforhold og familier. In: P. E. Solem, R. Ingebretsen, K. Lyng & Aa-M. Nygård, *Demens i psykologisk belysning.* København: Hans Reitzels Forlag.

Kitwood, T. (1993). Person and Process in Dementia. *International Journal of Geriatric Psychiatry, 8 (7),* 541-545.

Kitwood, T. (1999). *En revurdering af demens.* Frederikshavn: Dafolo.

Kramer, A.M. (1997). Rehabilitation care and outcomes from the patient's perspective. *Medical Care, 35,* 48-57.

Kunik, M.E., Yudofsky, S.C., Silver, J.M., & Hales, R.E. (1994). Pharmacological Approach to Management of Agitation Associated with Dementia. *Journal of Clinical Psychiatry, 55,* 13-17.

Larsen, L. & Kabel, S. (2002). Terapeutisk kommunikation i praksis. *Demens Nyt, 29,* 3-6. Aalborg Institut for Pensions- og Ældrepolitik, tidl. Formidlingscenter Nord.

Larsen, L. & Sørensen. L.U. (2002). Samtale mellem ligeværdige. *Sygeplejersken, 29,* 16-21.

Larsen, L. & Winsløv, J.-H. (2005). Stadig mig selv efter alle disse år – om den aldrende person-lighed. In: Larsen, L. & Winsløv, J.H. (Eds.), Tema: Gerontopsykologi. *Nordisk Psykologi, 57 (1),* 21-46.

Lauridsen, I. & Eckermann, A. (2005). At mestre demens. In: S.G. Hasselbalch, N. Engelbreht & O. Thage, *Forstå demens.* København: Lindhardt & Ringhof Forlag A/S and Alzheimerforeningen.

Lawton, M.P. & Nehemow, L. (1973). Ecology and the Aging Process. In: *C. Eisdorfer & M.P. Lawton (Eds.), The Psychology of Adult Development and Aging.* Washington, D.C.: American Psychological Association.

Lebert, F., Pasquier, F., & Petit, H. (1995). Personality traits and frontal lobe dementia. *International Journal of Geriatric Psychiatry, 10*, 1047-1049.

Lewin, K. (1935). *A Dynamic Theory of Personality – Selected Papers of Kurt Lewin*. New York: Mc-Graw-Hill Book Company Inc., kap. 1.

McCrae, R.R. & Costa, P.T. (2003). *Personality in Adulthood: A Five Factor Theory Perspective*. New York: Guilford Press.

Neary, D. & Snowden, J. (1996). Fronto-temporal dementia: Nosology, neuropsychology, and neuropathology. *Brain and Cognition, 31*, 176-187.

Nordhus, I.H. (1995). Parter i samspil – pårørende i demensprocessen. In: P.E. Solem et al., *Demens i psykologisk belysning*. København: Hans Reitzels Forlag.

Pelosi, A.J., McNulty, S.V. & Jackson, G.A. (2006). Role of cholinesterase inhibitors in dementia care needs rethinking. *British Medical Journal, 333*, 491-493.

Riis. P. (1999). Svækkelse og etik. In: P. Fromholt, J. Hjort-Hansen, D. Høeg & A. Viidik (Eds). *Svækkelse i alderdommen – Omsorg og etik i svækkelsesforløbet*. Frederikshavn: Dafolo.

Scheltens, P. (1999). Early diagnosis of dementia: neuroimaging. *Journal of Neurology, 246*, 16-20.

Stuart-Hamilton, I. (2001). *Aldringens psykologi – grundbog i gerontopsykologi*. København: Gyldendalske Boghandel, Nordisk Forlag.

Torpdahl, P. (1999). Problemer med samvær og kommunikation med demente. *Psykinfo Nyt, 2*, 8-9.

Ulrich. G. (2000). Omsorg og anerkendelse: Et etisk perspektiv på problemer vedrørende behandlingen af gamle demente i hjemmet og i den offentlige plejesektor. In: Ersbøl. E. (Ed.), *Dementes menneskerettigheder – etik og ret i Danmark*. København: Det Danske Center for Menneskerettigheder.

THE PSYCHIATRY OF DEMENTIA – FROM A PSYCHOLOGICAL PERSPECTIVE

Gitte Kragshave & Anna Aamand

Summary

It is only in recent decades that the psychiatry of dementia has become a focus area in research and clinical practice. This chapter contains an explanation of the concept of Behavioural and Psychological Symptoms of Dementia (BPSD), as well as exploring selected research themes. There is broad agreement that any explanatory model for BPSD must contain a great number of interacting factors, but diagnostic practice does not reflect the current multi-faceted theoretical understanding of the problem. Current practice is dominated by a form of diagnosis that rests on a biomedical framework of understanding, whose purpose is to create the foundations for medical intervention. This chapter supports the argument that a satisfactory diagnosis standard must also include a form of diagnosis that rests on a phenomenological framework of understanding, with the purpose of creating the foundations for psychosocial intervention. In this connection the concept of challenging behaviour is presented, and a central person-centred model of dementia is explained.

The conclusion is that psychosocial diagnosis should be regarded as a complement to medical diagnosis, and should be implemented as part of the standard for good clinical practice.

The first Alzheimer's patient

Nearly one hundred years ago, Alois Alzheimer described the symptoms of the woman whose disease later carried his name as follows:

> The first sign of illness in this 51-year-old woman was jealousy of her husband. This was soon supplemented by rapidly progressing memory loss, she was no longer happy in her home, she moved all the objects in it and hid them; sometimes she thought that someone was trying to kill her, and she started screaming.

Since being transferred to a mental hospital she has become totally bewildered. She is confused with regard to time and place. Occasionally she says that she cannot understand everything and cannot find her way around. She sometimes regards the doctor as a visitor and apologises for failing to complete her work – on other occasions she screams that he is going to cut her up, or turns him away in a manner resembling a woman who fears he is going to violate her. Sometimes she is extremely distressed, dragging her bedclothes around, calling for her husband and daughter, and showing signs of auditive hallucinations. She often shouts for hours on end in a piercing voice.
Alzheimer, 1907, p. 147. Source: Gulmann, 2001, p. 82.

Alzheimer goes on to describe the familiar cognitive symptoms and neuropathological changes, but the interesting thing about this old casuistry today is the clear description of the psychiatric symptoms. No real interest was shown in this aspect of Alzheimer's disease and other forms of dementia for almost another century.

Behavioural and psychological symptoms of dementia (BPSD)

History of the concept
In 1996 the IPA (International Psychogeriatric Association) held a consensus conference focusing on the psychiatry of dementia (Finkel et al., 1996), which was attended by 60 leading dementia experts from 16 different countries. There was broad agreement that international research had focused for far too long purely on the cognitive symptoms of dementia, and that there was a need to include psychiatric symptoms of dementia in a holistic understanding of the nature of dementia. However, it was not easy to agree on a suitable term for use in this connection (Finkel, 2003). Expressions such as "behavioural disorders", "non-cognitive symptoms" and "neuropsychiatric symptoms" were considered but rejected; a fact which undoubtedly reflects the many different ways in which the nature of the phenomenon can be understood. However, a compromise agreement was reached finally and the term "Behavioural and Psychological Symptoms of Dementia" was adopted. This term is still used today, although not everyone has adopted the new terminology. For instance, a leading dementia researcher such as Jeffrey L. Cummings does not even mention the term in his book on the neuropsychiatry of dementia (Cummings, 2003); and the concept has been criticised openly for being too broad and imprecise in its content (Iersel et al., 2004). The birth of the concept has been inspiring for research and development, but the fact that it is something of an umbrella term does still create consensus problems.

Content of the concept

The consensus group mentioned above who created the concept of BPSD (Finkel et al., 1996) defined the evidence of BPSD as signs and symptoms of impaired perception, thought, mood or behaviour that occur frequently in patients suffering from dementia. A division into two main categories was suggested: psychological symptoms and behavioural symptoms. Psychological symptoms, which are generally identified on the basis of interviews with patients or their families, comprise anxiety, depressive mood, hallucinations and delusions. Behavioural symptoms, which are generally identified on the basis of observation of patient behaviour, comprise aggression, shouting, restlessness, agitation, wandering around, culturally unacceptable behaviour, sexual disinhibition, hoarding, swearing and clinging behaviour.

Looking at this list of various symptoms makes you want to add some new ones and arrange them into main groups. And it is true that different authors use slightly different symptoms and in particular different ways of arranging them (Cummings, 2003; Eriksson et al., 2004; Gulmann, 2001; Engedal & Haugen, 2004). In this presentation we shall use the Danish geropsychiatrist Nils Gulmann's proposed subdivisions of BPSD:

Proposed subdivisions of BPSD

Psychological symptoms
Emotional disorders:
  Apathy, depression, irritability, anxiety
  The emotional dysregulation syndrome
 Agnostic misidentification
 Confabulation
Psychotic symptoms:
  Hallucinations, delusions

Behavioural disorders
Activity disorders:
  Restlessness (trailing, shadowing, checking)
  Unplanned wandering
  Compulsive actions (vandalism, occupational delirium)
  Infringement of territory, absenteeism
Restlessness at night
Anger:
  Verbal
  Physical aggression
Shouting behaviour
Sexual disorders
Uncleanliness

These symptoms will only be described briefly here. For further insight, please see Gulmann's own text (Gulmann, 2001, pp. 80-94).

1. Psychological symptoms

Apathy is regarded by some authors as a psychological symptom, and by others as a behavioural symptom. Apathy is the lack of motivation and emotional commitment. The symptom is not connected with subjective suffering and must not be confused with depression. *Depression* in accordance with ICD-10 criteria often occurs in combination with dementia, and there are a great number of dementia sufferers who are occasionally *sad* and *irritable* without meeting the criteria for depression. *Anxiety* may occur in the form of anxiety about being left alone or worrying about forthcoming events. The term *emotional dysregulation syndrome* is taken to mean emotional incontinence, normally in the form of compulsive weeping; but it may also occur in the form of compulsive laughter. *Agnostic misidentification* may resemble hallucinations; but the patient's unrealistic experiences are due to the perception disorders that accompany certain types of dementia. Characteristic symptoms are mirror agnosia (patients perceive their mirror image as someone they do not know), and picture agnosia (people on television or in pictures are perceived as real people who are present). Such patients may also fail to recognise close relatives or their own homes, or think that they know people who are actually complete strangers. There are also certain complex forms in which partial recognition by patients leads to the idea that their spouse or home has been replaced with a fake copy or produced in several versions. *Confabulation* may resemble delusions, but like agnostic misidentification it depends on the primary symptoms of dementia, including confusion regarding time and place. In their own understanding, such patients typically live in a situation which was once real (back home with their long-dead parents, or back in their old jobs). The commonest forms of *hallucinations* are visual and auditory hallucinations, the content of which often includes phantom visitors such as animals, children, relatives or other people in the patient's home. There may be a sliding scale involved here leading to misidentification. Genuine *delusions* differ from confabulations because they have never been real at any time in the patient's life. One typical delusion is that patients believe that someone has stolen things from them, whereas in fact they have forgotten where they put these things.

2. Behavioural symptoms

Behavioural symptoms in BPSD differ from psychological symptoms in several respects. The central question is how such symptoms should be categorised and described, and it is always the surroundings and not the patients themselves who define any given example of behaviour as a behavioural symptom. *Restlessness* is referred to in the literature as "agitation", an unclear concept that contains a range of very different phenomena. Clinging behaviour occurs when people suffering from dementia follow their carers around like a shadow, and is also referred to as "trailing, shadowing and checking". *Unplanned wandering* means that people with dementia often wander around in their waking hours, something which may also lead to *the infringement of territory*. This occurs typically in a nursing home when they walk into the rooms of other residents. *Occupational delirium* occurs when people with dementia agnostically/apractically try to recreate former working situations. *Absenteeism* from their home or nursing home may have an entirely different background in the understanding of dementia sufferers of the situation. *Restlessness at night* sometimes indicates that the brain can no longer regulate the daily rhythm. *Anger* may be shown in many different ways. It can be verbal or physical, and physical aggression may be either predictable or unpredictable. *Shouting* is nearly always connected with the loss of the ability to walk. *Sexual disorders* generally result in the loss of all sexual inhibitions, and are observed in men in particular. And *uncleanliness* (covering yourself in faeces, for instance) may be due to agnostic disorders.

BPSD: Selected research themes

During the past ten years a wide range of studies of BPSD have been carried out, primarily in connection with Alzheimer's disease. Unfortunately, the occurrence of BPSD in connection with other forms of dementia has been examined far less.

The occurrence of at least one BPSD symptom in major groups of dementia patients is reported to be 64-84% (Gulmann, 2001; Eriksson et al., 2004; Cummings, 2003), and in most people several symptoms occur simultaneously. In one summary article (Finkel, 2003), the occurrence of various sub-categories of BPSD is as follows: 10-73% of all dementia patients have delusions; and 12-53% of all Alzheimer's patients have hallucinations, while up to 20% suffer from actual depression and far more than this have depressive characteristics without complying with all the criteria for depression. Behavioural symptoms are all dealt with under the single heading of "agitation", and Finkel does not state any frequency for this group of symptoms. The wide dispersion in the occurrence of BPSD symptoms probably reflects the unclear borderlines between the individual groups of symptoms and the lack of consensus regarding their content.

A number of researchers have been interested in finding out whether it is possible to use factor analysis to identify groups of symptoms which behave like syndromes (occurring at the same time in the same patient). In one study a measuring instrument known as the Present Behavioural Examination was used in a mixed group of Alzheimer's patients and people suffering from vascular dementia, and factors were found for aggressive behaviour, motoric hyperactivity and depression. But no factor was found for psychosis (McShane, 2000). In another study using a measuring instrument known as the Neuropsychiatric Inventory in a group of Alzheimer's patients, factors were found for hyperactivity, psychosis, anxiety and both heightened mood and depressive mood/apathy. Apathy was in fact the most widespread BPSD symptom in this group, as well as being the only BPSD symptom which had a demonstrable connection with cognitive functional level. Increased apathy was found in connection with the decline of cognitive functional level (Spaletta et al., 2004).

Some studies have focused on whether there is a connection between the type of BPSD symptom and the type of dementia in question. In one summary article Luxenburg (2000) points out that patients with vascular dementia exhibit a higher occurrence of depressive symptoms and more frequent problems distinguishing between day and night than patients with Alzheimer's disease. In Lewy Body dementia there is a particularly frequent occurrence of visual hallucinations; and in frontotemporal dementia there is an excessive frequency of impulsive and compulsive behaviour. The clearest connection is the connection between disinhibition and frontotemporal dementia; but on the whole there is a very considerable overlap between the various types of dementia and BPSD symptoms (Cummings, 2003).

During the past ten years a number of longitudinal studies of the natural development of BPSD symptoms in Alzheimer's patients have been carried out. The patients involved have been observed at intervals to monitor their BPSD symptoms; and whereas their cognitive development has definitely decreased each time it has been measured, the occurrence of BPSD has been far more varied. Differences between these studies in terms of time intervals, patient populations and measuring instruments have contributed to this complex picture. However, the studies agree that BPSD can occur in all stages of the disease, and that there is great individual variation. Psychotic and depressive symptoms have a fluctuating course over time, while behavioural symptoms are more persistent once they have occurred (Devanand et al., 1997; Eustace,

2002). Individual patients with dementia may experience one or more period with BPSD symptoms (Hope et al., 1999), and they may also switch from one group of BPSD symptoms to another (Ballard et al., 2001). One study proves that a small group of patients with Alzheimer's disease (8.5%) do not develop BPSD symptoms at all, despite being observed over a period of three years (Devanand et al., 1997).

As revealed by the research in this field described above, the conclusion is rather complicated. Knowledge of a dementia diagnosis or the stage of dementia in question is not in itself sufficient to predict the way in which BPSD symptoms will develop in individual patients – with the exception of the particular behavioural characteristics applying to frontotemporal dementia (Engedal & Haugen, 2004).

Framework of understanding and various types of diagnosis

There is broad agreement that an explanatory model for BPSD must contain a great number of contributing factors such as the type of dementia involved, the personality and life history of the patient in question, the environment and the patient's interaction with their surroundings, and any possible somatic illnesses and side-effects of medicines (Gulmann, 2001; Engedal & Haugen, 2004; Eriksson et al., 2004). However, holistic diagnosis reflecting the complicated theoretical understanding outlined above is rarely carried out in clinical practice. Even in the secondary health service, which has a specialist function and is obliged to accept complicated cases, holistic diagnosis is more the exception than the rule. There is no tradition for holistic diagnosis yet.

1. **Diagnosis with a view to medical intervention**
   The commonest form of diagnosis of BPSD – and the minimum diagnosis required – focuses first on gaining a medical overview of any somatic illnesses that may be present and the side-effects of any medicine being administered, since these factors may lead to delirious conditions either causing BPSD symptoms or making them worse. In this connection it may be necessary to prescribe, discontinue or change somatic medicine. It is also important that the doctor involved gains a good basis for assessing the diagnosis and deciding whether psychopharmaceuticals should be prescribed. This can be done by carrying out a purely clinical assessment; but it is now common practice to supplement the clinical assessment by applying one or more assessment scales capable of generating a symptom profile, a quantitative measurement of the severity of the symptoms, and in some cases a measurement of the degree of burden placed on carers.

In Denmark the scales used most widely are the Neuropsychiatric Inventory (NPI), the scale of Behavioral Pathology in Alzheimer's Disease (BEHAVE-AD), and the Cohen-Mansfield Agitation Inventory (CMAI). For a survey of BPSD assessment scales, please see Eriksson et al. (2004). The framework of understanding on which this type of BPSD diagnosis is based is biomedical; or to use an expression from a report on BPSD in a Scandinavian perspective, you could also say that the framework of understanding is "at organ level" (Eriksson et al., 2004, p. 49).

Even though a thorough assessment is made of the patient's condition, the doctor may find it very difficult to make a decision regarding the prescription of psychopharmaceuticals, particularly if the BPSD symptoms in question cannot be categorised under the traditional psychiatric groups of symptoms (depression or psychosis) but actually belong under the behavioural symptoms. There is little evidence for the effect of psychopharmaceuticals on behavioural symptoms, and the effect on actual psychiatric symptoms is uncertain and must always be balanced against the risk of serious side-effects (Gulmann, 2004). So for a large group of patients with BPSD, there is a need for a supplementary type of diagnosis which can form the basis of more specific psychosocial measures.

2. Diagnosis with a view to psychosocial intervention

A number of psychologists have pointed out that basically an entirely different type of diagnosis is required with a view to replacing or supplementing psychopharmaceutical treatment with psychosocial intervention (Bird, 1999 and 2003; Stokes, 1996 and 2000; Kitwood, 1996). The basic framework of understanding involved here is phenomenological, and the terminology is different. In this kind of approach it is preferable to refer to people as "individuals" rather than "patients". However, the language used is far from consistent because the work involved often takes place in the health system, where people are traditionally called patients. Instead of BPSD people refer to "challenging behaviour", which is defined as any form of behaviour in connection with dementia that causes suffering or danger to the patient and/or others (Bird, 2003). Challenging behaviour is typically abnormal behaviour, but it is not the objectively abnormal nature of the behaviour that determines whether it can be defined as "challenging". Instead, the deciding factor is whether anyone – the person suffering from dementia or anyone else – is affected negatively by it. Two objectively identical forms of behaviour may be regarded as challenging in one care environment and neutral in another; and the background of behaviour may vary considerably depending on the individual and context in question. People suffering from dementia are regarded as both acting and reacting in relation to internal and external influences, and this is true whether or not their dementia has robbed them of significant aspects of cognitive function. Any possible challenging behaviour is seen not only as a symptom of dementia but also as a potential gateway providing access to their subjective experiences. The behaviour may be an attempt to make a statement, communicate needs, or adapt to the environment and dementia disabilities. In this way the phenomenological framework of understanding resembles an implicit form of phenomenology. As shown above, the term "challenging behaviour" places the behaviour of people suffering from dementia in a concrete social framework with concrete relations to other people. And it is also in relation to the individual, concrete context that challenging behaviour must be diagnosed.

Even though psychosocial diagnosis must be concrete and individual, it is important that it can be carried out systematically. So it is useful to have a model for diagnosis comprising all the areas needed to understand the individual background for a given form of behaviour. The British psychologist Tom Kitwood should be mentioned in this connection. His ideas about dementia have had great international influence. In connection with psychosocial diagnosis it is his dementia model in particular (the so-called dementia equation) that is of interest (Kitwood, 1996). In this model he expresses (highly instructively) the need to combine various points of view and professional approaches in the following manner:

KITWOOD'S MODEL OF DEMENTIA
$$D = P + B + H + NI + SP$$

D	stands for dementia (as the condition occurs – in other words, both primary dementia symptoms and BPSD)
P	stands for the premorbid personality
B	is the biography or life history of the person concerned
H	stands for physical health (somatic status, illnesses, effects and side-effects of the medicine administered)
NI	refers to neuropathology
SP	stands for social psychology: environmental conditions and the interaction between the person suffering from dementia and care staff/families

In this model there are a number of factors which cannot be changed but which need to be known anyway. These are the premorbid personality (P), life history (B), and the type, extent and location of the cerebral neuropathology in question (NI). The factors that can be influenced are physical health (H, cf. medical intervention) and social psychology (SP, cf. psychosocial intervention). In other words, this model can be used for holistic diagnosis.

Based on the model's socio-psychological dimension, Kitwood and his staff developed a method known as Dementia Care Mapping which is now used to develop care practice in nursing homes (Høeg, 2005). This is not a model for the psychosocial diagnosis of BPSD, so it will not be dealt with any further here.

We will now briefly describe the way in which Michael Bird (1999 and 2003) and Graham Stokes (1996 and 2000) work with the psychosocial diagnosis of challenging behaviour. Their point of departure is an assessment of whether behaviour is associated with suffering or danger for the person with dementia or others. If this is the case, detailed information is gathered regarding the person concerned, their environment, and the interaction between individual and environment. People with dementia are often undervalued as sources of information. Contact with the people concerned will always be possible, perhaps in the form of listening to them or empathetic contact, which can be accompanied by the observation of behaviour. Otherwise their immediate family and care staff who know them well can help by providing information. More details are added to the description of challenging behaviour, and a conclusion is drawn as to whether it occurs in particular situations or varies depending on the way in which care tasks are performed. Various registration charts can be used to gain a good overview and provide the opportunity for quantifying your observations. Traditional scales of evaluation are not very suitable for this purpose because their description of behaviour is limited to the symptom level and lacks information about the context of the behaviour in question. Stokes (2000) uses registration charts to map behaviour, and the Norwegian nurse Kirsti Solheim (1999) has also published suitable charts for this purpose. Ideally, psychosocial diagnosis will generate understanding of the complicated individual background to any given challenging behaviour and result in the formulation of potential actions that can be tried out subsequently. Bird (2003) points out that the success of psychosocial intervention may become apparent in two ways which are in principle different from each other: challenging behaviour may disappear or be reduced considerably, and/or the ability of carers to cope with it may increase. In many cases both occur at the same time, thereby removing tension between the two parties. Psychosocial intervention targets not only people suffering from dementia but also their surroundings, which is why the psychologist cannot simply collect information and submit a report regarding his/her findings. The result of diagnosis must also be communicated to the people who are responsible for the care of people with dementia, and the psychologist must take responsibility for drawing up a psychosocial intervention and following up on the result.

A number of psychologists working with the elderly have been inspired by Kitwood's dementia model. In the UK Ian James has developed a practice with regard to persons with dementia who exhibit challenging behaviour involving the systematic study of all the factors in Kitwood's model with a view to drawing up a hypothesis regarding the experience that lies behind such behaviour. Ian James's work has been described by Ballard et al. (2001); and to give an impression of the primarily phenomenological approach involved, here is a summary of some of the major features of one of the cases in question, taken from Ballard et al. (2001):

> The patient was a 79-year-old widower suffering from Alzheimer's disease who moved into a residential home four months ago. His physical health was generally good and he did not need any medicine. He displayed challenging behaviour in the form of aggressiveness, and he wandered around the home constantly. A detailed description of his behaviour revealed that his aggressiveness was linked to situations in which other people invade his private sphere, for instance by entering his room without knocking or by giving him a hug. His restlessness culminated one morning when he tried to get out into the garden, which he could see through the window. He was able to explain to the psychologist that he missed his son. Premorbidly he was described as a quiet man with no intimate friends, a man who valued good order and discipline. A number of staff had left the home recently, and the current key-worker was not very familiar with his background and level of well-being. An assessment resulted in the staff showing greater respect and refraining from being over-familiar with him. They managed to persuade his son to visit him more often, and every day after breakfast the patient was allowed to go for a walk in the garden on his own. The result of the all-round psycho-social intervention was that his aggressiveness was reduced considerably; but even though he clearly enjoyed his walk around the garden each morning he was still restless. However, the staff no longer regarded his behaviour as challenging.
>
> Ballard et al., 2001, pp. 100-106.

The authors of this chapter have also been inspired to try and convert Kitwood's dementia model for practical application. We carried out a psychological study of ten geropsychiatric patients who had been admitted to hospital suffering from severe dementia and challenging behaviour. The study procedure was based on factors P and NI in Kitwood's dementia model – and also to some extent on factor B – and consisted of a semi-instructed interview with the closest family members regarding the premorbid personality of the patients and a neuropsychological study using the Severe Impairment Battery (Saxton et al., 2002). The result of diagnosis was communicated to care staff based on the expectation that knowledge of the premorbid personality of dementia patients and a neuropsychological picture of their dementia could improve the ability of the staff to support their personal identity and their remaining cognitive function and compensate for lost functions in their daily contact with patients. Our experience was that the study proved to be an extremely suitable point of departure for a subsequent dialogue with staff – there was an increased holistic understanding of the individual background to the challenging behaviour of patients, and an increased understanding of the fact that care services must be tailored individually to suit the person involved (Kragshave & Aamand, 2001). Subsequently one of the authors of this chapter has worked alongside nurses in one local area to develop a partnership between a geropsychologist and a specialist nurse working closely with care staff to diagnose patients with severe dementia and challenging behaviour in the style of Kitwood – this is known as a "care clinic". The medical part of the diagnosis is communicated at the care clinic, after which staff concentrate on the psychosocial part of the diagnosis with a view to tailoring a psychosocial intervention (Kragshave, Kimmbech & Niljendahl, 2003). This approach was developed at a geropsychiatric ward, but has subsequently been applied to problematic cases in which care clinics are set up involving psychologists and district nurses from the geropsychiatric team.

Concluding remarks

The psychiatry of dementia has only become an area of focus in research and clinical practice during recent decades. The history of its development has been characterised by a biomedical framework of understanding; but research shows that this framework is inadequate. The fact is that there is a considerable overlap between different types of dementia in terms of the degree of BPSD symptoms involved, and studies have revealed considerable variation in the occurrence and progress of BPSD symptoms in patients suffering from clearly progressive cognitive functional losses. There is also broad agreement in principle that any explanatory model for BPSD must also contain factors which are outside the biomedical framework of understanding. However, despite this agreement current clinical diagnosis practice is still dominated by the biomedical framework of understanding, in which the focus is placed on creating the basis for medical intervention.

There is a need for a supplementary framework of understanding capable of accounting for individual variations and the complicated overall picture with a view to creating the basis for psychosocial intervention. The phenomenological framework of understanding and accompanying psychosocial diagnosis practice are relevant in this connection. The focus on the symptoms of BPSD can be replaced by the concept of challenging behaviour. It is not the objectively abnormal nature of behaviour that determines whether it can be defined as "challenging". Instead, the deciding factor is whether anyone – the person suffering from dementia or anyone else – is affected negatively by it. Such behaviour is seen not only as a symptom of dementia but also as a potential gateway providing access to the subjective experiences of persons with dementia. The behaviour may be an attempt to make a statement, communicate needs, or adapt to the environment and dementia disabilities. In this way the term "challenging behaviour" places the behaviour of people suffering from dementia in a concrete social framework with concrete relations to other people. And it is also in relation to the individual concrete context that challenging behaviour must be understood – and diagnosed. Psychosocial intervention, therefore, also becomes an immediate consequence of psychosocial diagnosis.

Many psychological sub-disciplines such as neuropsychology, personality psychology, social psychology and behaviour therapy are relevant and necessary in order to understand the individual background of challenging behaviour. Psychosocial intervention is directed both at people with dementia and at their surroundings, so the psychologist cannot simply collect information and submit a report regarding his/her findings. The result of diagnosis must also be communicated to the people who are responsible for the care of people with dementia, and the psychologist must take responsibility for drawing up a psychosocial intervention and following up on the result.

Psychosocial diagnosis should be regarded as a complement to medical diagnosis, with the two aspects joining forces to produce a holistic diagnosis and the basis of both medical and psychosocial intervention. The establishment of a tradition for holistic diagnosis will help to give a clearer indication for the use of psychopharmaceuticals in dementia psychiatry. It will also help to meet the needs of people with BPSD who are typically unable to express their needs or make demands regarding examination and treatment. In our view, diagnosis with a view to psychosocial intervention is an area of development which should be given higher priority, an area which should be implemented as a central part of the standard for good clinical practice.

REFERENCES

Alzheimer A. (1907). Über eine eigenartige Erkrankung der Hirnrinde. *Allgemeine Zeitschrift für Psychiatrie, 64*, 146-148.

Ballard, C., O'Brien, J., James, I. & Swann, A. (2001) *Dementia: management of behavioural and psychological symptoms.* Oxford.

Bird, M. (1999). Challenging behaviour in dementia: A critical role for psychology. *Australian Psychologist, 34*, 144-148.

Bird, M. (2003). Psychiatric and behavioural problems: Psychosocial approaches. In: Mulligan R, Van der Linden M (Eds.), *Clinical management of early Alzheimers disease: A Handbook.* Lawrence Erlbaum Associates Publishers, 143-167.

Cummings, J.L. (2003). *The Neuropsychiatry of Alzheimer's Disease and Related Dementias.* London and New York: Taylor & Francis.

Devanand, D.P., Jacobs, D.M., Tang, M.X., Castillo-Castaneda, C del, Sano, M., Marder, K., Bell, K., Bylsma, F.W., Brandt, J., Albert, M. & Stern, Y. (1997).The course of psychopathologic features in mild to moderate Alzheimers disease. *Archives of General Psychiatry, 54*, 257-63.

Engedal, K. & Haugen, P.K. (2004). *Demens, fakta og utfordringer.* Norge, Nationalt kompetansesenter for aldersdemens.

Eriksson, S., Minthon, L., Moksnes, K.M., Saarela, T., Sandman, P.O., Snaedal, J., Karlsson, I. & BPSD referencegruppen (2004). *BPSD i et nordisk perspektiv.* Dansk udgave ved Kirsten Abelskov. Janssen-Cilag.

Eustace, A., Coen, R., Walsh, C., Cunningham, C.J., Walsh, J.B., Coakley, D. & Lawlor, B.A. (2002). A longitudinal evaluation of behavioral and psychological symptoms of probable Alzheimers disease. *International Journal of Geriatric Psychiatry, 17* (10), 968-73.

Finkel, S. (2003). Behavioral and psychologic symptoms of dementia. *Clinical Geriatric Medicine, 19* (4), 799-824. Review.

Finkel, S.I., Costa eSilva, J., Cohen, G., Miller, S. & Sartorius, N. (1996). Behavioral and psychological signs and symptoms of dementia: a consensus statement on current knowledge and implications for research and treatment. *International Psychogeriatrics, 8 (3)*, 497-500.

Gulmann, N.C. (2001). *Praktisk gerontopsykiatri.* 3. udgave, København: Hans Reitzels Forlag.

Gulmann, N.C. (2004) Demenspsykiatri efter Sundhedsstyrelsens udmelding om antipsykotika og demens – hvad nu? *www.laegemagasinet.dk, 7*, 1-6.

Hope, T., Keene, J., Fairburn, C.G., Jacoby, R. & McShane, R. (1999). Natural history of behavioural changes and psychiatric symptoms in Alzheimers disease. A longitudinal study. *British Journal of Psychiatry, 174*, 39-44.

Høeg, D. (2005). Hvad er Dementia Care Mapping? www.aeldreviden.dk, *Alderens nye sider, 8 (1)*, 1-4.

Iersel, M. van, Koopmans, R., Zuidema, S. & Rikkert, M.O. (2004). Do not use "BPSD" if you want to be cited. *International Journal of Geriatric Psychiatry, 19*, 803-4.

Kitwood, T. (1996). A dialectical framework for dementia. In: Woods, R.T. (Ed). *Handbook of the clinical psychology of ageing.* New York: Wiley & Sons, 267-282.

Kragshave, G. & Aamand, A. (2001). Svær demens og problemskabende adfærd. *Psykolog Nyt, 5*, 3-9.

Kragshave, G., Kimmbech, A.M. & Niljendahl, T. (2003). Nyt plejeredskab i gerontopsykiatrien. *Sygeplejersken, 7,* 22.

McShane, R. (2000). What are the syndromes of behavioral and psychological symptoms of dementia? *International Psychogeriatrics, 12,* 147-153.

Saxton, J., Mcgonicle, K.L., Swihart, A.A. & Boller, F. (2002). *The Severe Impairment Battery.* (Dansk oversættelse ved Gitte Kragshave). København: Psykologisk Forlag.

Solheim, K. (1999). *Demensguide.* København: Hans Reitzels Forlag.

Spaletta, G., Baldinetti, F., Buccione, I., Fadda, L., Perri, R., Scalmana, S., Serra, L. & Caltagirone, C. (2004). Cognition and behavior are independent and heterogenous dimensions in Alzheimers Disease. *Journal of Neurology, 251* (6), 688-95.

Stokes, G. (1996). Challenging behaviour in dementia: A psychological approach. In: Woods, R.T. (Ed.), *Handbook of the clinical psychology of ageing.* Wiley & Sons. New York, 601-628.

Stokes, G. (2000). *Challenging behaviour in dementia.* UK: Winslow Press.

DEPRESSION IN LATE LIFE

Karen Munk

Summary

The aim of this chapter is to show on the one hand that depression in healthy elderly people is no more common than depression in younger people, and on the other that age-related depression is a complicated disorder which has many diagnostic pitfalls. This is because somatic illness and many forms of loss in life accumulate as we grow older, and because depression often has an atypical symptom profile. It is also a disorder that must be taken extremely seriously by clinicians dealing with the elderly, because age-related depression has been proved to be a separate risk factor involved in death – not only owing to the increased risk of suicide, but also in connection with cardio-vascular diseases and cancer. Owing to this complicated interaction with somatic conditions and the side-effects of pharmaceutical treatment, it is important that psychologists treating age-related depression have greater knowledge of somatic factors than is normally required. Aggressive, inter-disciplinary diagnostics is necessary when dealing with elderly people suffering from a low level of wellbeing.

Introduction

From the perspective of young people, the idea of being old may seem depressing because you know that you are approaching the end of your life. So it is interesting to note that depression is no more frequent in elderly people *living in their own homes* than in young people (Kørner, 1998; Blazer, 2003).

However, depressive disorders in the elderly constitute a difficult area that requires all the clinicians involved to display a good deal of caution and possess a good deal of knowledge. Depression is a tricky disorder to deal with at any time in life, but the potential pitfalls increase as we grow older. This is owing to a range of factors linked in particular with age and the way age is perceived by the rest of the world. One of the difficulties seems to be that it is hard to imagine that elderly people who do not feel good are actually suffering from depression (Djernes, Gulmann, Abelskov et al., 1998). Another difficulty involves implementing and carrying out an adequate course of treatment (Harmann & Reynolds, 2000; Karel & Henrichsen, 2000; Gottfries & Karlsson, 2001). For instance, it is a well-known fact that a correct diagnosis does not necessarily ensure that patients are ever given treatment (Gulmann, 2001).

Even though it has become clear during the past 20 years that most elderly people are healthier and live longer than they did just a few decades ago, it is still the case that illness accumulates in the oldest section of the population in a negative interaction with the process of ageing (Jeune, Avlund & Kirk, 2006). In addition, even though the elderly are healthier and live longer than they did in the past, they still have to be prepared to leave this life in the near future. The rest of the world often regards any feelings of sadness in the elderly as a natural result of these facts of life, rather than as anything which should be regarded as an illness. And this is one of the main reasons why depression in the elderly is often overlooked.

In addition, some people seem to expect that it is natural for the elderly to behave in a peculiar manner, and that "old age" is not something that can be treated. And finally, another reason why depression in the elderly is often overlooked is that it has a more varied symptom profile in the elderly than in young and middle-aged people (Djernes et al., 1998).

However, it has been proved that depression is a separate risk factor connected with death – not only in cases of suicide but also in general, particularly in cases of cardio-vascular diseases and cancer (Gulmann, 2001; House, Knapp, Bamford et al., 2001). Among other things, it is important to remember that elderly people with poor health very easily get into a fatal vicious circle of insufficient nutrition and fluid intake. There are also many other costs involved in overlooking depression because it is painful for both patients and their families when the mood, cognitive function, thought processes, energy levels and executive abilities of patients are affected negatively. The psychosocial consequences are isolation and a reduced level of activity (Bird & Parslow, 2002). Overlooking depression is also expensive for society, because these patients are major users of the health services owing to the large number of subjective somatic disorders from which they suffer – due partly to the lower pain threshold applying in connection with depression (Reynolds, 1999).

In order to illustrate an array of clinical pitfalls related to late-life depression, as, for example, to make the correct diagnosis, to give an adjusted treatment and prevent a vicious circle evolving which would make the patient even more fragile, I present in the following a real-life case on the catastrophic result of wrong clinical practice:

A 76-year-old woman is admitted as an acute patient in a medical department with a social-medical diagnosis (*causa socialis*) because for months she has been lying in bed in an overheated bedroom complaining about a lack of appetite, dizziness and general discomfort. Six months previously she was widowed after a long and happy marriage. She had been sole carer for her husband (a cancer patient) almost until he died. They had no children. Shortly after her husband died she took to her bed and developed diffuse somatic disorders, complaining that she could not manage anything and that she was worried about her financial situation. There were no observations of her crying over the loss of her husband. She had enjoyed good health previously apart from a certain amount of calcification around her heart. She has a fragile network: a nephew and his wife (living at a great distance) and a small group of friends living nearby (the same age as her, and also in poor health), who help her to the best of their ability. Reluctantly (and under pressure from her nephew), the municipality agrees to arrange visits from a home help and installs an alarm system for the district nurses. The woman is also registered for the municipal meals-on-wheels service. Her GP and the district nurses make statements about her which sometimes reflect a lack of sensitivity ("she refuses to do anything") and sometimes display understanding of her situation ("she can't live without her husband"), explaining that her condition has been caused by grief. During the first six months after the death of husband she loses 1/3 of her body weight as well as several teeth, and she starts to look like a 90-year-old. After brief admission to hospital for a somatic examination nothing is found apart from the usual calcification around her heart, and she is discharged again and sent back to her own home despite the protests of her nephew – who reports her weight loss and rapidly ageing appearance to the staff. A distant member of the family (a doctor) hears about her case and issues the diagnosis *melancholic depressive single episode of a serious nature*. Antidepressive treatment is started, although she only takes her medicine following pressure by her nephew, and after 14 days her appetite begins to improve. She starts getting out of bed more, is able to start reading again (something which she loves), and agrees to start physical training on a daily basis. Her weight increases a little, but after six months of treatment her physical condition has not improved and she still suffers from some anxiety. She is not examined by her GP until there is an emergency (she has a fall). She is admitted to the orthopaedic department because she complains of pain in one of her hips. A small crack in this hip is found but does not require treatment. After four days in the department her nephew is told to come immediately because the staff have found her delirious with small pupils and irregular respiration. When her nephew arrives at the hospital after a drive of several hours she is still alive – but she has been transferred to the intensive-care department, where the doctor on duty has prescribed anti-morphine treatment because he thinks that she has had an overdose of painkillers in the orthopaedic department. Her nephew, who also has a medical training, inspects her medical records to see how much medicine she has been given over the last few days and finds out that painkillers have been administered without taking her age and general condition into account. He also discovers that she has been given more than the full adult dose. The woman slowly wakes up again, but several days later she is still in a delirious condition. After a brief period of rehabilitation she is discharged and admitted on a temporary basis to the local nursing home. Even though she grows constantly weaker, after a few weeks she demands to be sent home, where she is found dead three months later (two years after the death of her husband).

The concept of depression

The research literature does not agree completely as to how depression should be defined (Gulmann, 2001; Blazer, 2003). The atypical versions of the disorder that occur in elderly people add to the confusion; and the fact that organic brain disorders and somatic complaints which can also cause depression increase with age makes defining the concept even more difficult. The problem is whether depression with a direct somatic etiology should be included or not (Munk, 2007).

Throughout the history of psychiatry it has typically been the case that a pragmatic range of sub-categories has been created whenever clinicians need to distinguish between different types of depression. This has led to the existence of so many sub-types of depression that the recent literature proposes (as far as age-related depression is concerned) abandoning the idea of this being a well-defined illness and starting to regard it as a spectrum disorder with a varying symptomatology, etiology and strength (Lebowitz, Pearson, Schneider et al., 1997; Sable, Dunn & Zisook, 2002). It has also been proposed that the situation could be simplified by only distinguishing between somatic and mental symptoms (Blazer, 2003).

The following criteria have been used in the clinical literature (Bertelsen, 1996; Gulmann, 2001):

1. *Etiology*, understood in terms of hereditary and environmental factors ("endogenous" versus "psychogenous/neurotic/primary"); in terms of the side-effects of chemical substances such as medicine and alcohol ("secondary"); or in terms of biochemical disturbances caused by organic illness ("organic").

2. *Spectrum of unusual symptoms* ("atypical", "agitated").

3. *Duration of symptoms* ("chronic"; "dysthymic": lasting more than two years; "periodic" or "single episodic" lasting at least two weeks).

4. *Severity* (in ICD-10 terms: "mild", "moderate", "severe"; or in DSM-IV terms: "mild" and "severe". Or finally "sub-clinical depression", which does not comply with the criteria for depression in the two diagnostic systems).

5. *With or without mania* ("bipolar" versus "unipolar").

6. *With or without psychotic symptoms* (delusions and/or auditive hallucinations).

7. *With or without somatic symptoms* ("melancholia": weight loss, reduced appetite and energy, interrupted sleep patterns, motoric restlessness or lethargy).

8. *Age at first episode* ("early debut" versus "late debut": before or after the age of 64).

Apart from the terms "endogenous" and "psychogenous", all these terms are still used – probably because they are informative. In relation to age-related depression, the criterion called "age at first episode" attracts particular attention. Geropsychiatrists disagree about whether it is meaningful to distinguish between early and late debut, and this distinction is not used at all in a great deal of geropsychiatry research literature. The reason for this seems to be disagreement about whether organic depression should be included (Kørner, 1998). Organic depression is a condition caused by damage to the brain or by other somatic illnesses influencing the function of the brain. In relation to the ICD-10 diagnosis system, which is used in Danish geropsychiatry, organic depression is a separate diagnosis with no age criteria which is different from affective mental disorders (Bertelsen, 1996). The people who support this line regard age criteria as a misunderstanding because co-morbid depression (which is depression related to somatic illness) occurs at all ages and is difficult to treat whatever the age of the patient concerned. But they do concede that the melancholic syndrome seems to be related to great age (Blazer, 1998). On the other hand, geropsychiatrists who support the idea of age criteria claim that somatic conditions become increasingly dominant with increasing age, and that the symptoms tend to be "age-coloured" in depressions with a late debut notwithstanding the etiology in question (Gulmann, 2001). One of the things they suggest is that there might be a dynamic interplay between silent strokes (minor cerebral haemorrhages or blood clots, also known as vascular catastro-

phes) and psychosocial stress, making rehabilitation more difficult (Baldwin
& O'Brien, 2002). Silent vascular catastrophes are primarily a phenomenon
which is linked with old age. The conclusion of this debate is probably that the
borderline between organic conditions and other forms of depression is more
indistinct and harder to draw in elderly patients, even though this is the ideal
goal of the ICD-10 system. It is also the case that ¾ of the depressive patients
seen in geropsychiatry clinics have a late debut, so these considerations do seem
relevant (ibid.) As a result, one could ask whether the official diagnosis system
is of any assistance in gerontology clinics. However, trained geropsychiatrists
say that this is the case. Once clinicians have had the idea that a depression
might be involved, the ICD-10 system provides useful assistance in the diagnosis process. This should be taken to mean that under the atypical, misleading surface of symptoms the symptoms of depression described in ICD-10 do
actually exist (Kragh-Sørensen & Stage, 1996; Gulmann, 2001). But the fact
that there is a discrepancy between the immediate, atypical symptomatology
of elderly patients and the classical symptoms of depression does constitute a
challenge to the ICD-10 system.

The ICD-10 system divides the depression diagnosis into sub-types using
the following seven dimensions:

- Core symptoms and accompanying symptoms (lasting at least two weeks,
  table 1)
- With or without mania
- With or without melancholy (table 2)
- With or without psychotic symptoms (hallucinations and/or delusions)
- Degree of severity (depending on the number of symptoms, table 3)
- Frequency of reoccural ("periodic": with an interval of at least two months)
- Chronicity (symptoms lasting at least two years)

It should be emphasised that lowering of mood does not necessarily occur in
mild and moderate depression (table 1 and 3), which may constitute a diagnostic trap.

Disagreement about the expediency of distinguishing between early and late
debut is also apparent with regard to the way that etiology and prevalence are
understood. However, it is worth remembering that clinical practice does need
to take the close interaction between the body/brain/psyche of old people much
more seriously than the diagnosis system proposes – for instance in connection
with the diagnosis and treatment of somatic conditions and the reconsideration
of any pharmaceutical intake, all of which may have an influence on the mental
state of old patients (Gulmann, 2001). In the rest of this chapter a distinction

TABLE 1. Core symptoms and accompanying symptoms of depression according to the ICD-10 system

	ICD-10
Core symptoms	1. Lowering of mood 2. Reduced enjoyment or interest 3. Reduced energy or increased tiredness
Accompanying symptoms	1. Reduced self-confidence or self-esteem 2. Feelings of worthlessness or guilt 3. Thoughts of death or suicide 4. Difficulty in thinking or concentrating 5. Agitation or inhibition 6. Sleep disturbance 7. Changes in appetite or weight

TABLE 2. Melancholia syndrome

At least four of the following symptoms
1. Reduced enjoyment or interest 2. Reduced emotional activity 3. Waking early in the mornings (>2 hours before normal) 4. Depression worst in the morning 5. Inhibition or agitation 6. Reduced appetite 7. Weight loss (>5% of your weight in one month) 8. Reduced libido

TABLE 3. Definitions of severity in the ICD-10 system

Type and number of symptoms	
Two core symptoms and at least two accompanying symptoms	Mild depression
Two core symptoms and at least four accompanying symptoms	Moderate depression
Three core symptoms and at least five accompanying symptoms	Severe depression

will be drawn between depressions with an early or late debut respectively, since there also seem to be other differences (including etiological ones).

Etiology

Depression with an early debut
With regard to the reasons for depression with an early debut (not including depression associated with bipolar illness), there have been a number of major differences in the past with regard to the way Danish psychologists and psychiatrists have perceived the etiology involved (Hougaard, 1999). Psychiatry researchers have claimed that depressive single episodes with an early debut are a hereditary illness because a number of studies state that first-degree relatives of people suffering from depression have a greater probability of suffering from the same problem (Wasylenki, 1980; Nielsen, 1999; Gulmann, 2001). The illness makes its presence felt primarily in the form of biochemical disorders in the brain, and is susceptible to pharmacological treatment. On the other hand, psychology researchers have claimed that it is primarily the combination of dysfunctional thoughts and stressful life circumstances that provokes depressive disorders, and that only bipolar disorders are hereditary. It has been demonstrated that bipolar patients who have recovered are free of dysfunctional, depressive thoughts – unlike people suffering from unipolar depression, who carry the seed of the next episode inside them. It has also been shown that people who suffer from depressive episodes tend to have accumulated negative events during the course of their lives, which may help to explain the increased risk in first-degree relatives. From this perspective the fact that anti-depressive medicine seems to have a certain effect is explained based on the close interaction between mind and brain, since it is assumed that depressive disorders have a biochemical correlation in the brain (Nielsen, 1995; 1999). A third etiological model is the stress-vulnerability model, which unites the two perspectives and deals with the dynamic interplay between biological conditions and all types of stressful life conditions (von Knorring, 1996). In this model, biological vulnerability is understood to mean more than mere hereditary vulnerability. What is involved is acquired biological vulnerability in the form of the consequences of birth complications, brain damage, hormonal disorders, chemical substances such as alcohol and medicine, and age-related changes. In this model, biological vulnerability is seen not as a fixed entity but as something that is changeable during a lifetime – something that can be increased by physical illness and reduced (for instance) by the discontinuation of medicine intake if depression is a side-effect of the substance concerned. Psychosocial stress includes development traumas such as early separation, disturbances in parent-child relations,

the experience of helplessness during upbringing, and social traumas such as the loss of relatives due to death, divorce, unemployment or a poor financial situation. In general, the feeling of a lack of control in important areas of life seems to be a risk factor.

Depression with a late debut
The question of inheritance has not been a subject for disagreement to the same extent with regard to age-related depression with a late debut. In these cases there is agreement that hereditary factors do not play any role in the occurrence of the disorder (Wasylenki, 1980; Kørner, 2000). To a large extent, etiologically speaking the problem resembles the vulnerability-stress model apart from hereditary vulnerability. According to a number of authors, depression with a late debut is best understood as a group of clinical syndromes or a spectrum disturbance with many types of etiologies (Lebowitz et al., 1997; Sable et al., 2002). Other authors prefer to refer to it as a disorder with a high prevalence of co-morbidity. Increasing age means that somatic illnesses and their pharmacological treatment play an increasing role in an intricate interaction with depression (Kørner, 2000). The development of the disorder is complicated and the mechanisms involved are hard to understand completely. Sometimes depression occurs before medical illness, and sometimes it occurs afterwards. There also seems to be an interplay between medicine and depression that strengthens both factors. In principle the following potential causal connections can be identified (Kørner, 1998):

1. Depression could be a biochemical and/or psychological reaction to somatic illness.

2. Depression could be a psychological reaction to pharmaceutical treatment.

3. Depression could be a biochemical side-effect of pharmaceutical treatment.

4. Depression could be a cause of or contribution to somatic illness.

In one sub-group of depressed elderly people the problem indicates the onset of dementia, with depression being a so-called "prodromal" symptom of dementia (Sable et al., 2002). Depression also frequently accompanies the following somatic illnesses in the elderly: vascular catastrophes in the brain or heart, cancer, Parkinson's disease, diabetes mellitus, rheumatoid arthritis and other painful complaints. In recent years people have also started talking about *vascular depression*, which seems to unite several of the somatic disorders that are related to the vascular system (Baldwin & O'Brien, 2002). This connection has also been found in young people, but the frequency of vascular disorders increases with age because they are disorders which normally accumulate during the course of a lifetime. In the elderly the white matter in the brain may be damaged by small vascular catastrophes (small blood clots, for instance), which seem to be associated not only with dementia but also with depression – although the causal mechanisms involved are not yet understood (Gottfries & Karlsson, 2001; Baldwin & O'Brien, 2002). It seems as if the prevention of vascular disorders can reduce not just the frequency of somatic illness in the elderly, but also the frequency of mental illness.

Researchers have also discussed whether great age itself plays a role; but the conclusion is that co-variation with great age is involved, frequently followed by physical illness and psychosocial loss (Kørner, 2000). However, it has been pointed out that depression with melancholia has a later debut than depression without (Blazer, 2003); and that depression with a late debut also has "age-coloured symptoms" (Gulmann, 2001).

But the complex etiological interaction involved here consists of more than just medical factors. A range of psychological factors are also involved such as anxiety disorders, the loss of relatives, being divorced, a poor financial situation, and conflicts in the family leading to a lack of social support in life (Kørner, 1998; Sable et al., 2002). One particular stress factor for elderly married people is the burden of being the informal carer for an infirm spouse who is often suffering from dementia. Elderly women live longer than their husbands on average (both because women live longer than men, and because they often marry men who are older than they are); so this tends to be a gender-specific fate affecting women in particular (Kørner, 1998). In addition, people with certain personality traits rendering them poorly equipped to deal with the limitations of old age (ambitious, perfectionist and eccentric people) seem to risk age-related depression (Reynolds, 1997; Gulmann, 2001). One central concept in relation to psychosocially induced depression seems to be *social disintegration*, and it is important to remember this fact in treatment contexts (Munk, 2007). In a recently published longitudinal study, it was shown that the relationship between social integration and depression may have its own "evil" dynamics. Depression can be caused by stress factors in life, but depression can also cause new problems involving social context, financial situation and health – thereby leading to a vicious circle (Moos, Schutte, Brennan et al., 2005). Not surprisingly, it has been shown that stress factors occurring in many areas of life at the same time increase the risk of developing a chronic depressive condition (ibid.) So we can conclude that social factors are extremely important. Conventional wisdom in the field of gerontology states that a supportive social network throughout life, a stimulating environment, a good financial situation and a healthy lifestyle all give better opportunities for living a long life and avoiding a high frequency of illness (including mental disorders) in old age (Hobman, 1978; Nowlin, 1985; Avlund, 2004). It is also the case that the same favourable social conditions mean a better prognosis for elderly people who are affected (against all the odds) by age-related depression; whereas isolated elderly people and elderly people whose families adopt an unfriendly and critical attitude ("Why don't you just pull yourself together?") have a poorer prognosis (Gulmann, 2001).

Prevalence

From a gerontology point of view the most important questions in relation to prevalence are whether the occurrence of depression and its gender distribution change during the course of life. For many reasons, knowledge of the epidemiology of depression has not been clear and consistent (Blazer, 2003). The results depend on the people being studied and the way in which depression is defined and measured. For instance, no distinction is drawn between early and late debut in prevalence studies. To avoid mixing results with organic conditions, there was also a tendency in the past to exclude somatically ill elderly people and the oldest subjects from prevalence studies (Sable et al., 2002). The oldest subjects represent a particular problem: it is easy to diagnose them as suffering from the melancholic syndrome owing to their physical infirmity and resulting lack of energy. However, relatively new 100-year studies show that depression does not necessarily accompany old age. The oldest person ever registered (Jeanne Marie Calment, who died at the age of 122) and one of the oldest men (Danish-American Chris Mortensen, who died at the age of 115) were not depressed. They were both blessed with good spirits, and despite serious infirmities they both enjoyed the few hedonistic pleasures that life still had to offer: good food, chocolate and a good cigar (Jeune, 2002).

There are a great number of measurement problems in this area, resulting in misunderstandings with regard to the association between age, gender and affective disorders: typically it has been claimed that the prevalence of such disorders increases after middle age, and that women are more depressed than men. However, it has been shown that the effects of age and gender disappear when somatic illness, other health aspects and social problems are included (Kørner, 1998; Blazer, 2003). In other words, age and gender are not in themselves etiological factors. Instead, it is the risk profile that changes with age and gender. It is important in this respect to remember that prevalence figures are not fixed entities because society and risk profiles are variable. So the important aspect to focus on is always the risk profile. However, there is one conclusion that can be drawn from prevalence studies in all countries: no matter how healthy they are, elderly people living in their own homes have the same prevalence of moderate to severe depression as young adults (2-4%); while residents of nursing homes and elderly people in hospital have a somewhat higher prevalence (up to 20% has been registered in American studies) (Blazer, 2003). One thing that has surprised researchers is the evidence of unchanged prevalence in adulthood when depressions with a late debut actually do occur. This is explained by pointing out that depression which reoccurs after an early debut is a disorder with a poor prognosis (some of the people suffering from depression with an early debut die before they reach old age). So the unchanged prevalence can be explained by changes in the population (Blazer, 1998). However, there is a general increase in mild depression and depressive symptoms (sub-clinical depression) in the elderly – although once again this is largest in people in hospital and residents of nursing homes (figures up to 35% have been registered) (Reynolds, 1997; Blazer, 2003). The highest prevalence of depressive symptoms has been found in people of great age (+85) (Blazer, 2003). Some authors have pointed out that sub-clinical depression and organic depression are common diagnostic categories in infirm elderly people, which should give these diagnoses a more dominant position in everyday clinical practice (Schneider, Kruse, Nehen et al., 2000).

As far as gender differences are concerned, most studies show a higher prevalence among women over the course of a lifetime, although the gender differences become narrower at great age (Ayuso-Mateos, Vázquez-BarQuero, Dowrick et al., 2001). However, with regard to suicide the gender differences are reversed after the age of 75: at the moment the frequency of suicide among Danish men above the age of 75 is three times as high as that of women (Sundhedsstyrelsen, 2005). In general, the number of successful suicides increases with age (Sable et al., 2002; Blazer, 2003).

Symptoms – the old, depressed patient
It has already been mentioned that it can be difficult to diagnose depression, particularly depression with a late debut. The two main problems are 1) actually having the idea that an elderly person who does not feel good may be suffering from depression; and 2) distinguishing between depression, organic conditions such as dementia, and grief. As mentioned above, there may be good reasons why elderly people are in a bad mood or feel "normally" depressed. There is a tendency to draw excessively sharp borderlines between normality and pathology. For instance, it has been proved that 20% of elderly widows/widowers meet the criteria for moderate to severe depression two months after losing their spouse. For one-third of these people the condition lasts at least one year; and

depressed, grieving elderly people generally have a higher frequency of illness and greater risk of death (Sable et al., 2002).

It is assumed that the more varied symptomatology of depression with a late debut is connected with a more varied etiology. It should also be mentioned that anxiety disorders earlier in life also seem to play a role in the varied profile. Patients who suffered from anxiety or insomnia at a younger age, or who were preoccupied with physical sensations or prone to mild phobias, risk developing hypochondria-type depression in old age; while people who suffered from compulsive thoughts when they were younger risk developing anxiety-type depressions (Wasylenki, 1980).

To help clinicians to identify depression in old age, a group of Danish gero-psychiatrists have constructed a typology of five sub-types: *demential, hypo-chondric, neurotic, eretic (anger and irritability) and classical depression* (Djernes, Gulmann, Abelskov et al., 1998).

Old people suffering from depression with a late debut have a tendency to be irritable. They complain about somatic symptoms, they are anxious, and they function poorly cognitively. They display reduced initiative, take less care of themselves and complain of pain. They tend to become substance abusers and suffer from compulsive thoughts, social isolation, guilt and paranoia. They often focus on somatic symptoms and deny vigorously that they are depressed. The consequence of this is that depressed elderly people are often regarded as suffering from dementia, hypochondria or anxiety – or else they may simply be regarded as hopeless cases arousing no sympathy in their surroundings (Djernes et al., 1998; Gulmann, 2001). However, it is important to remember that even though their clinical characteristics are atypical, the typical daily fluctuations (feeling worse in the mornings but brighter in the evenings) will be present, and that the ICD-10 criteria do constitute a useful diagnostic tool for systematic searching once a suspicion has been aroused (Kragh-Sørensen & Stage, 1996).

Distinguishing between pharmaceutical problems and depression

Once the suspicion of depression has been aroused, it is important (as far as possible) to exclude organic causes of the disorder. Greater pharmaceutical knowledge is required in connection with the psychological treatment of the elderly than is normally the case. As mentioned above, a range of organic disorders, pharmaceuticals and alcohol can cause depression, and the failure to exclude these factors before starting anti-depressive treatment (psychological treatment and/or medicine) would obviously be incorrect. So if depression is suspected, careful consideration of any medicine that is being taken can be the first step in treatment. In addition, it is important to remember that the optimum pharmaceutical treatment of somatic disorders undoubtedly improves the general condition of patients. Sable, Dunn & Zisook (2002, p. 22) also recommend the following guidelines in relation to diagnosing depression in elderly patients who are taking medicine:

- Never assume that major depression is a normal response to aging or medical illness. Optimizing treatment of existing medical conditions and discontinuing any medications that may be associated with depression are rational initial steps, but aggressive treatment of the depressive episode is warranted if symptoms persist.

- If it is unclear whether somatic symptoms are caused by medical illness or depression, focus on psychological symptoms such as dysphoria, anhedonia, low self-esteem, and feelings of hopelessness or worthlessness. Certain behavioral symptoms such as social withdrawal, brooding, and pessimism may help distinguish depression from medical illness.

- Obtain collateral history from family members, caregivers, and previous medical records, and reassess frequently. Particularly in patients aged 80 and older, it is often the family or caregivers who notice the signs of depression. Loss of interest in activities, social withdrawal, irritability, and somatic complaints are common features in this older population.

The problem involved in the decline of cognitive functional abilities is another complication. Is a depressive executive dysfunctional syndrome resulting in poor powers of concentration causing memory loss involved? Or is this an early stage in the development of Alzheimer's disease? In the past, failures of cognitive function in connection with depression were called pseudo-dementia because the condition is reversible. However, we now know that even though such patients recover completely from their depressive disorder, 20% of them develop dementia (Sable et al., 2002). But it is also worth remembering that 80% of them actually have a good prognosis, serving to underline the importance of diagnostics and aggressive treatment. The similarities between Alzheimer's disease and depression (with a late debut) are: poor powers of concentration, poor memory, low energy levels, reduced interest, social withdrawal, irritability, psycho-motoric lethargy or hyperactivity. A number of authors have listed a series of tips enabling clinicians to distinguish between the two conditions (Gulmann, 2001; Sable et al., 2002). However, such distinctions require intensive monitoring using a series of rating scales:

- Slow (dementia) or rapid (depression) development of symptoms
- Late (dementia) or early (depression) approach to doctor asking for help
- Anger (depression)
- Persistent complaints about poor memory (depression)
- Attempt to conceal poor memory (dementia)
- Persistent poor function (dementia)
- Fluctuation in symptoms during the day (depression)
- Presence of aphasia (language disorders) and apraxia (lack of ability to carry out practical actions) (vascular dementia)

However, it is always possible that both syndromes may be present at the same time.

Distinguishing between grief and depression

The experience of loss is an inevitable fact of life in old age, so it is important that clinicians can distinguish between grief and depression. However, it is also important to remember that both may be present at the same time: depressed patients requiring treatment could of course be suffering from deep grief as well, even though the depressive symptoms overshadow the evidence of this grief (cf. the case outlined above). They may be suffering from one or both of these disorders. Unlike people suffering from grief alone, typical depressive patients do not weep and they have a permanently lowered mood (apart from possible fluctuations during the day combined with anger and anxiety). They are unable to talk about neutral topics and suffer from perseveration, a lack of realism and self-centredness (Gulmann, 2001). It is a good idea to focus on the lack of ability to change the subject (perseveration) in particular, since this is a typical difference between depression and the state of grief.

Conclusion

Aggressive diagnostics is vital when elderly people have a low level of wellbeing. A nihilistic attitude such as "It's just their age" is both unprofessional and dangerous. Depression in the elderly can be cured in the vast majority of cases if a persistent, broad programme of treatment is implemented.

REFERENCES

Avlund, K. (2004). *Disability in old age. Longitudinal population-based studies of the disablement process* (doctoral thesis). København: Munksgaard.

Ayuso-Mateos, J.L., Vázquez-BarQuero, J.L., Dowrick, C., Lehtinen, V., Dalgard, O.S., Casey, P., Wilkinson, C., Lasa, L. Page, H., Dunn, G., Wilkinson, G. & the ODIN Group (2001). Depressive disorders in Europe: prevalence figures from the ODIN study. *British Journal of Psychiatry, 179*, 308-316.

Baldwin, R.C. & O'Brien, J. (2002). Vascular basis of late-onset depressive disorder. *British Journal of Psychiatry, 180 (2)*, 157-160.

Bertelsen, A. (1996). *Psykiske Lidelser og Adfærdsmæssige Forstyrrelser. Klassifikation og Diagnostiske kriterier.* WHO ICD-10. København: Munksgaard.

Bird, M.J.& Parslow, R.A. (2002). Potential for community programs to prevent depression in older people. *Medical Journal of Australia, 177 (7)*, 85-86.

Blazer, D.G. (1998). Late Life Affective Disorders. *Archives of Gerontology and Geriatrics-Supplement 6*, 43-47.

Blazer, D.G. (2003). Depression in Late Life: Review and Commentary. *Journal of Gerontology. Medical Sciences, 58A (3)*, 240-265.

Djernes, J.K., Gulmann, N.K., Abelskov, K.E., Juul-Nielsen, S. & Sørensen, L.U. (1998). Symptomprofil ved indlæggelseskrævende depression hos ældre, relateret til kliniske undergrupper. En genvej til forbedret diagnostik. *Ugeskrift for Læger, 160 (47)*, 6820-6823.

Gottfries, C.G. & Karlsson, I. (2001). Depression och ångest hos äldre fortfarende underdiagnostiserade. *Läkartidningen, 98 (8)*, 821-827.

Gulmann, N.C. (2001). *Praktisk Gerontopsykiatri.* København: Hans Reitzels Forlag.

Harmann, J.S. & Reynolds III, C.F. (2000). Removing the Barrieres to Effective Depression Treatment in Old Age. *Journal of American Geriatrics Society, 48*: 1012-1013.

Hobman, D. (1978). *The Social Challenge of Ageing.* London: Croom Helm.

Hougaard, E. (1999): Forbeholdt de lette tilfælde? *Psykolog Nyt, 10*, 6-13.

House, A., Knapp, P., Bamford, J., Vail, A. (2001): Mortality at 12 and 24 Months After Stroke May Be Associated With Depressive Symptoms at 1 Month. *Stroke, 32*, 696-701.

Jeune, B. (2002). *Længe leve!? Om udforskningen af det lange liv.* København: Fremad.

Jeune, B., Avlund, K. & Kirk, H. (2006). Sundhed og funktionsevne i det aldrende samfund år 2030. I: J.H. Petersen (Red.): *Det aldrende samfund 2030.* Rapport fra styregruppen for det strategiske fremsyn om det aldrende samfund 2030. Det Strategiske Forskningsråd, Forskningsstyrelsen, 50-79.

Karel, M.J. & Hinrichsen, G. (2000). Treatment of Depression in Late Life: Psychotherapeutic Interventions. *Clinical Psychology Review, 20 (6)*, 707-729.

Knorring von, L. (1996). Depression. En allvarlig, livslång men behandlingsbar sjukdom. *Nordisk Medicin, 111*, 259-63.

Kragh-Sørensen, P. & Stage, K.B. (1996). Behandling af depression hos ældre. *Nordisk Medicin, 111*, 267-70.

Kørner, E.A. (1998). *Forekomst af depression hos ældre over 65 år i Karlebo Kommune.* Ph.d.-afhandling. København: Foreningen af Danske Lægestuderendes Forlag.

Kørner, E.A. (2000). Depression hos ældre. Fokus på diagnosen. *Ugeskrift for Læger, 162, (18),* 2543-2545.

Lebowitz, B.D., Pearson, J.L., Schneider, L.S., Reynolds III, C.F., Alexopoulos, G.S., Bruce, M.L., Conwell, Y., Katz, I.R., Meyers, B.S., Morrison, M.F., Mossey, J., Niederehe, G., Parmelee, P. (1997). Diagnosis and Treatment of Depression in Late Life. Consensus Statement Update. *Journal of the American Medical Association, 278 (14).*

Moos, R.H., Schuttte, K.K., Brennan, P.L. & Moos, B.S. (2005). The Interplay Between Life Stressors and Depressive Symptoms among Older Adults. *Journal of Gerontology: Psychological Sciences. 60B (4),* 199-206.

Munk, K. (2007). *Late-life Depression. Also a field for Psychotherapists! Part One.* In: *Nordic Psychology,* Vol. 59, no. 1, May, pp. 7-26.

Nielsen, T. (1995). *Depression. Psykologisk forståelse og behandling.* København: Dansk psykologisk Forlag.

Nielsen, T. (1999). Er depression en hjernesygdom? *Psykolog Nyt, 12,* 3-8.

Nowlin, J.B. (1985). Introduction. In: E. Palmore, E.W. Busse, G.L. Maddox, Nowlin, J.B. & I.C. Siegler (Eds.), *Normal Aging III.* Durham: Duke University Press.

Reynolds III, C.F. (1997). Treatment of Major Depression in Later Life: A Life Cycle Perspective. *Psychiatric Quaterly, 68 (3).*

Reynolds III, C.F., Dew, M.A., Frank, E., Begley, A.E., Miller, M.D., Cornes, C., Mazumdar, S., Perel, J. M., & Kupfer, D.J. (1998). Effects of Age at Onset of First Lifetime Episode of Recurrent Major Depression on Treatment response and Illness Course in Elderly Patients. *American Journal of Psychiatry, 155 (6),* 795-799.

Reynolds III, C.F. (1999). What Are the Best Teatments for Depression in Old Age? *Harvard Mental Health Letter, 15 (12),* p8, 1p.

Sable, J.A., Dunn, L.B. & Zisook, S. (2002). Late-life depression. How to identify its symptoms and Provide effective treatment. *Geriatrics, 57 (2).*

Schneider, G., Kruse, A., Nehen, H-G, Senf, W & Heuft, G. (2000). The Prevalence and Differential Diagnosis Syndromes in Inpatients 60 Years and Older. *Psychotherapy and Psychosomatics, 69,* 251-260.

Sundhedsstyrelsen (2005). *Nye tal fra Sundhedsstyrelsen, 9 (5).*

Wasylenki, D. (1980). Depression in the elderly. *CMAJ (Canadian Medical Association Journal), 122,* 525-532.

PARAPHRENIA IN THE ELDERLY

Lise Bender & Lars Larsen

Summary

A good number of elderly people who have not displayed psychiatric symptoms previously in their lives develop psychotic symptoms in old age without any evidence of organic causes. These people are often in good physical condition; but their symptoms are very fixed and highly developed delusions (they think they are being persecuted and harassed by other people) which dominate their thoughts and actions. These psychotic symptoms with no evident organic cause can be called paraphrenia.

The etiology and pathogenetic mechanisms of paraphrenia have not been clearly identified. Its etiology is probably multi-factorial, with several risk factors being associated with the disorder without any of them being identified as the primary cause. However, an isolated lifestyle and the lack of social correction, in combination with reduced source monitoring, must be assumed to be significant factors in the development of paraphrenic ideas.

Introduction

The concept of psychosis is used to describe conditions in which people lose the ability to assess the reality of their experiences, ideas and behaviour. The most obvious signs of a psychotic condition are delusions and hallucinations. Psychoses can occur in all elderly people and are not uncommon in old people. Psychoses in the elderly often occur due to a reduced cerebral capacity in cases of dementia or as the result of apoplexy. When the ability of the brain to perceive and process sensory impressions is impaired, the basis is created for misinterpretations which may develop into genuine delusions. Such cases are known as organic psychoses. However, a number of elderly people who have not previously displayed psychiatric symptoms develop psychotic symptoms in old age without any organic reasons being apparent.

The symptoms of these elderly people, who are often in good physical condition, are highly fixed and well-developed delusions about persecution and harassment which dominate their thinking and actions. In more serious cases these symptoms are accompanied by hallucinatory experiences. The main theme is a sense of invasion of their personal territory and integrity. The presumed persecution takes place only in or around their home, and their delusory systems are surprisingly similar. These elderly people do not acknowledge their illness at all, so requests for help often come from people around them who are concerned about their ongoing and obviously unrealistic complaints that someone is spying on them, tapping their phones, stealing from them, or exposing them to noise, radiation, electrical rays and other similar problems.

These psychotic symptoms with no obvious organic cause can be called paraphrenia.

The concept of paraphrenia

The term "paraphrenia" comes from the Greek words *para* (which means "next to") and *phrenos* (which means "reason"). The concept of paraphrenia was originally introduced by Emil Kraepelin in 1909 to describe a particular kind of paranoid psychosis in which, from a clinical viewpoint, patients displayed exciting, colourful and often pleasurable delusions, as well as retaining a relatively intact emotional life (in contrast to schizophrenia, Naguib, 1991). The diagnosis paraphrenia was quickly replaced by a variant of schizophrenia; but in 1955 it was re-adopted by Roth as a descriptive diagnosis with the addition "late-onset" paraphrenia based on the following criteria (ibid.):

• Onset of symptoms after the age of 60
• Predominance of women
• Delusions
• Hallucinations
• Schizoid or pre-morbid paranoid personality structure
• Absence of dementia or primary affective disorder

Over the years there has been a great deal of disagreement about whether paraphrenia should be regarded as a separate illness or as late-onset schizophrenia (Almeida, Howard & Levy, 1992). Paraphrenia is no longer included in the ICD-10 categories as a separate illness – instead, it is categorised under chronic, long-term psychoses. The international literature now tends to prefer the term "late-onset schizophrenia" (Rabins, 1999). However, not everyone agrees that the concept of paraphrenia should be removed from the psychiatric taxonomy (Munro, 1987; Almeida et al., 1992; Abelskov, 1999; Gulmann, 2001). In practice the diagnosis paraphrenia is still used in Denmark by many geropsychiatrists (Gulmann, 2001).

Clinical examples

Casuistry

The old lady on the third floor confides in her family and home help, whispering that the other residents in the block are sending radiation up into her flat. This radiation affects her legs and makes it hard to walk, which is why she now stays indoors. It also prevents her from sleeping in her bed, so she has to spend her nights in an armchair padded with cushions to prevent the rays from reaching her. She has complained to the caretaker and the police, but nobody takes her seriously. Nobody seems to care that she is being harassed by someone who wants to take over her flat. She provides countless examples of harassment to support her claims, varying from noise and malodorous fumes to people breaking into her flat when she is not home. They move her things around, ruin them or even steal them, and they have bugged her flat with hidden microphones so they can listen to her telephone conversations.

Her daughter says that she has become senile, but her son-in-law says she has gone crazy. The home help registers that her client is suffering from dementia. And they all try to make the old lady see sense – with the best intentions, but in vain.

The case outlined above is an artificially constructed example based on various ideas and experiences that can be encountered in the clinic, and it represents a classic example of the symptomatology of paraphrenia. The presumed persecution takes place in or around the patient's home, and there is a surprising degree of similarity from one patient to the next. It is also worth pointing out that despite their delusions, patients suffering from paraphrenia are usually able to maintain their daily routines and may seem perfectly normal and unremarkable when talking about other things. They do normally express a certain amount of concern and anxiety, but their emotional reaction is often indignation and a sense of injustice rather than fear and anxiety. Only in rare occurrences do patients suffering from paraphrenia feel that their lives and health are under threat. One other characteristic of paraphrenia patients is that they are not powerless. They think up counter-measures and strategies to use against their persecutors. These persecutors are often members of marginalised groups such as drug addicts, criminals, people who are mentally ill, foreigners or neighbours who patients say they know some secrets about – although this is all they know about them. Patients imagine that the purpose of the harassment is to drive them from their homes. They do not acknowledge that they have a problem at all – in other words, their subjective experiences are their reality. So they do not approach their doctor but complain to their families, the caretaker, the police and other authorities instead.

Prevalence

The prevalence of paraphrenia has been difficult to determine with any great accuracy. This is partly because there are cases of quiet paraphrenia which are never treated or registered. Although the figures are uncertain, the occurrence of paraphrenia has been described in 3-10% of the elderly in psychogeriatric wards in the US, the UK and Sweden. There are no figures for Denmark. In the US it is estimated that 4% of the elderly above the age of 65 have dominant delusions (Almeida et al., 1992), but it is unlikely that they can all be diagnosed as suffering from paraphrenia because delusions can occur in connection with other complaints as well (depression and dementia, for instance).

Paraphrenia is more frequent in women than in men. This gender distinction applies even though the figures are adjusted to allow for life expectancy, but so far no reason for this difference has been found.

Etiology

The etiology and pathogenetic mechanisms of paraphrenia have not been clearly identified by any means. As with most psychiatric disorders, the etiology is probably multi-factorial with several risk factors being associated with the disorder although it is not possible to identify any one cause as the main one. The literature on paraphrenia makes it clear that delusions occurring for the first time late in life must be attributed to a complex interaction with potential risk factors such as social isolation, pre-morbid deviant personality, sensory defects and age-related, structural cerebral changes leading to changes in the individual's vulnerability and the onset of paraphrenia (Almeida et al., 1992; Munro, 1991; Naguib, 1992). Studies of paraphrenia are associated with a good deal of uncertainty and methodological problems – partly owing to problems in relation to what is a clinically limited group of patients, and partly owing to difficulties in collecting valid information regarding hereditary tendencies and pre-morbid personality. A hereditary element in the form of an increased frequency of schizophrenia in the family has been demonstrated in some studies, but not in others.

During the development of dementia there are sometimes periods of paraphrenia-like psychotic symptoms. A number of studies have demonstrated an excessive frequency of both sub-cortical and cortifical atrophy in paraphrenia patients, but the evidence of cerebral changes has been inconsistent (Kay, 1999), and paraphrenia is not the same as dementia.

It is often claimed in the literature that people suffering from paraphrenia also had a deviant personality earlier in their lives in the form of a schizoid or paranoid personality structure, characterised by poor rapport with other people, touchiness and suspicion (Howard & Levy, 1993; Naguib, 1992). But not all studies reach the same result. For instance, the results of a study carried out by Howard and Levy (1993) do not support the hypothesis of pre-morbid personality deviance.

All the studies of paraphrenia agree that these patients generally live alone and have few social contacts (Naguib, 1992). People's social networks have a great influence on their wellbeing and health, and can reduce stress levels and generate a sense of security in elderly people in particular (Hagberg & Rennemark, 2005). Studies of normal people who are exposed to isolation have also revealed that isolation can result in a reduced sense of reality, delusions and hallucinations (Vernon, 1966). But even though social isolation constitutes a significant risk factor, paraphrenia does not occur without other factors being present as well. After all, many elderly people live alone and are relatively isolated without developing the problem. Great age often results in sensory disorders. Sensory defects, particularly hearing or sight impairment leading to uncertainty and communication difficulties may exacerbate isolation and form the background leading to paranoid conditions (Parnas, 2000). Studies have also shown an excessive presence of hearing impairment in paraphrenia patients compared with control groups of the same age, whereas sight impairment as a risk factor seems less prevalent (Naguib, 1992). Obviously, it is easy to misinterpret what other people are talking about if you only hear snatches of what they are saying. However, not all paraphrenia patients have hearing impairments.

The fact that paraphrenia patients maintain so many "normal" mental abilities (if we ignore their "abnormal" ideas) makes it interesting to focus on the psychological mechanisms and the inner connections between their patterns of thought and action. And it was interest in this particular angle that formed the point of departure for the only Danish study of paraphrenia carried out so far.

A Danish study

This study included 20 elderly people aged 76-90 (average age 82). There were 19 women and one man, all of whom had been referred to a geropsychiatric ward owing to paraphrenia symptoms (Fromholt, Bender, Elleberg, 1998; Bender, 1998).

The criteria for inclusion were as follows:

- Paranoia linked to their home with or without hallucinations
- Absence of primary affective disorder
- No obvious signs of dementia
- Onset of symptoms after the age of 60

All these individuals were examined in their own homes by a psychologist based on a semi-structured interview guide. A coping-analysis model was used inspired by Lazarus (1984, 1991). This method made it possible to distinguish between different dimensions in the patterns of thought and action of these paraphrenia patients, such as the subjective meaning attributed by the patients to their imaginary experiences (for instance how threatening these experiences were, or how much control they felt they had over the situation), their choice of coping strategies, and the effect of the coping strategies used.

Based on this study, the clinical picture of paraphrenia can be illustrated as follows:

Patient's experiences	Emotional reactions	Coping strategies
Someone has stolen from me Someone has moved my possessions Someone has ruined my things Someone is spying on me I am being bugged I am being exposed to noise I am being exposed to radiation or electrical rays I am being exposed to smells, toxic fumes	Anger, indignation Obsessed by thoughts that the persecution must stop Anxiety increasing to unease and fear in the severest cases	Approach the police, caretaker, various authorities Change locks Hide possessions Put up black-out curtains Open windows to air the place Try to move

The conclusion of this study of paraphrenia interviewees was that they were actually acting rationally and logically based on their subjective interpretation of the situation. Or in other words, psychologically speaking they were using normal coping strategies. In general they displayed great variation in their efforts to protect themselves from their imaginary persecutors. For instance, they changed their locks if they felt that people were entering their home; they hid their possessions; and they worked out various methods of protecting themselves from noise, radiation and malodorous fumes. Most of them had approached the caretaker, the police and other authorities asking for help to stop their persecutors. On the other hand they rarely approached their presumed persecutors, who were described in general as people of low status such as criminals, drug addicts or people who were mentally ill. In most cases the people involved were neighbours with whom the paraphrenia patients had no personal relationship.

Psychologically speaking these paraphrenia patients also displayed natural emotional reactions to their experiences based on the subjective significance they attributed to them. The predominant emotional reactions were expressed in the form of indignation, anger and a sense of invasion of privacy, accompanied by demands that the persecution should cease. Most of them expressed slight unease and anxiety. Six of the interviewees expressed anxiety because they felt their health and their lives were under threat. Two of these six felt so threatened that they no longer dared to remain in their own homes, which led to their admission to a geropsychiatric ward.

From a psychological perspective it is interesting to note that the "madness" of paraphrenia patients is largely limited to their perceptions and interpretations of the world around them; whereas the coping strategies used are primarily normal in relation to the world of their imaginations.

The most striking common denominator among the interviewees was their lonely and isolated lifestyle, which influenced their current life situation. In normal lives, interaction between people takes place in a continuous process of feedback with experiences and impressions being exchanged and corrected if they are inconsistent with reality. Elderly people who live alone with few opportunities for social contact do not have the same opportunities to test their sense of reality on a continuous basis, and therefore run a greater risk of developing mistaken conclusions and actual delusions. The ability to distinguish between internal thoughts and external events (known as "source monitoring", Mitchell et al., 1986) is also important here. Empirical studies have shown that this ability does become impaired to a certain extent with age (Larsson et al., 1994).

An isolated lifestyle and the lack of social correction, combined with reduced source monitoring, must be assumed to be significant in the development of paraphrenia. Old people who lead isolated lives may do so because they have always had an unusual personality structure – but this is not necessarily the case. It is often claimed that elderly people who develop paraphrenia have always been suspicious, touchy and poor at establishing rapport. In our study there was no available information about the possibly deviant lives of the interviewees, and their life stories were not noticeably different from other representatives of the same generation who did not suffer from paraphrenia. Some of them may have had a habitual schizoid personality judging by their level of rapport, while the others varied from being lively extroverts to having a more withdrawn personality type.

The fact that paraphrenia patients insist on the truth of their delusions despite the attempts of the world around them to correct them might indicate that psycho-dynamic forces also play a major role – perhaps these delusions have a particular function in the lives of people with paraphrenia (protection from painful experiences of loneliness and emptiness, for instance). Viewing these cases from a functional angle, paraphrenia patients might "benefit" from their symptoms both because they provide new content in otherwise empty lives, and because they result in people paying them more attention.

Treatment

Treatment can almost always be provided without admission to hospital, and involves three stages:

1. Establishing a therapeutic relationship
2. Long-term treatment with antipsychotic medicine
3. Strengthening the network of paraphrenia patients

Psychopharmaceutical treatment
Paraphrenia patients often reject medicine because they lack insight into their illness.

However, antipsychotic medicine may be a necessary feature of treatment. Experience shows that a small dose of antipsychotic medicine will remove or moderate people's delusions, and most people can be persuaded to accept pharmaceutical treatment providing that a good rapport can be established with them.

The risk of side-effects resulting from antipsychotic medicine (limitation of normal functions and resources, for instance) is considerable in the elderly, so it is necessary to balance the advantages and disadvantages of initiating pharmaceutical treatment in each individual case. When the experiences of paraphrenia patients become too violent, provoking too much anxiety, there is good reason for pharmaceutical treatment; but as a main principle treatment should aim primarily to put an end to the loneliness and isolation and try to create an alternative content in the lives of paraphrenia patients which can displace their delusions.

Psychological treatment

In general it is not difficult to establish therapeutic contact with paraphrenia patients if you respect their experiences and listen to and understand their ideas and notions without having any major ambitions about correcting their thinking.

One of the characteristics of paraphrenia patients is that they feel insulted if you try to challenge their imaginary world – which for them is the real world. Attempts to correct them or provide counter-arguments will inevitably make them provide additional evidence, thereby intensifying their "madness". Consequently, it is important that the people around them (family and carers, for instance) understand the underlying psychological mechanisms of paraphrenia, because paraphrenia patients may react with anger and rejection if you challenge their credibility. This does not mean that you need to accept their ideas unconditionally and say that they are right. Instead, it is necessary to demonstrate understanding of their feelings and situation. Paraphrenia patients are normally pleased to have some human contact, and once you have established a good alliance with them they are often easy to distract. In your interaction with them it is a good idea to support their healthy side by talking about their memories and interests, for instance. If you manage to establish a good network the imaginary experiences will often take up less space in their consciousness. But it is rarely a good idea to comply with their wish to move to different accommodation. This will only be a temporary solution because their sense of persecution will soon begin again.

Concluding remarks

In this chapter we have attempted to outline the nature of paraphrenia, identifying some of the differential diagnostics in relation to schizophrenia and the psychotic symptoms of dementia. We have also pointed out some potential etiological factors and described encounters with paraphrenia patients in the clinic.

There is no one conclusive theory explaining why elderly people who have not been psychotic previously start having delusions. The tendency to have unrealistic thoughts, including the formation of delusions, is potentially inherent in the psyche of all human beings – perhaps as an adaptive component in our interaction with the world around us.

Previous research into paraphrenia has identified a number of risk factors which are assumed to contribute to the onset of the problem. However, the significance of these individual factors and their interaction has not been fully illuminated. At the same time, the extent to which the ageing process increases the vulnerability of the individual is uncertain.

The only Danish study carried out so far showed that paraphrenia patients availed themselves of normal coping strategies and generally exhibited great creativity in their attempts to protect themselves from imaginary persecutors. They also displayed natural emotional reactions to their experiences based on the subjective significance they attached to these experiences. Their dominant emotional reactions were indignation, anger and a sense of injustice accompanied by demands that the persecution should cease. The most significant common denominator was their lonely and isolated lifestyle, indicating that the absence of social correction and reality checks, in combination with reduced source monitoring, may be significant factors in the development of paraphrenic ideas.

The clinical picture of paraphrenia is extremely characteristic, and there is a surprising similarity from one patient to the next – indicating the necessity to reintroduce the paraphrenia diagnosis as a separate illness. Increased knowledge of this relatively common, late-onset psychotic disorder would increase the opportunities for early diagnosis and intervention before the symptoms become too manifest.

REFERENCES

Abelskov K. (1999). Paraphrenia: The Scandinavian View. I: Howard, R., Rabins, P.V. & Castle, D.J. (Eds.). *Late onset Schizophrenia*. Petersfield, UK and Philadelphia, USA: Wrightons Biomedical Publishing LTD.

Almeida, O.P., Howard, R.J., Førstl, H. & Levy, R. (1992). Late paraphrenia: A review. *International Journal of Geratic Psychiatry, 7,* 543-548.

Almeida, O.P., Levy, R., Howard, R.J. & David A.S. (1996). Insight and paranoid disorders in late life (late paraphrenia). *International Journal of Geriatric Psychiatry, 11,* 653-658.

Bender, L. (1998). De forrykte gamle – parafreni. *Gerontologi og samfund, 14 (3),* 62-63.

Fromholt, P., Bender, L. Elleberg, B. (1998). Coping with a Paraphrenic World in Late Life. *Journal of Clinical Geropsychology, 5,* 301-308.

Gulmann, N. (1992). *Praktisk Gerontopsykiatri*. København: Hans Reitzels Forlag.

Howard, R. & Levy, R. (1993). Personality structure in the paranoid psychoses of later life. *European Journal of Psychiatry, 8,* 59-66.

Kay, D.W.K. (1999). The English Language Literature on Late Paraphrenia from the 1950s. In: Howard, R., Rabins, P.V. & Castle, J. (Eds.), *Late onset Schizophrenia*. Petersfield, UK and Philadelphia, USA: Wrightons Biomedical Publishing LTD.

Larsson, M. & Backman, L. (1994). Did I unplug the iron or did I only look at it? External source monitoring across the adult life span. Aging. *Clinical Experimental Research, 6,* 35-42.

Lazarus, R.S. (1991). *Emotion & Adaption*. New York: Springer Publishing Company.

Lazarus, R.S. & Folkman, S. (1984). *Stress, Appraisal and Coping*. New York: Springer Publishing Company.

Mitchell, D.B., Reed Hunt, R. Smitt, F.A. (1986). The Generation Effect and Reality Monitoring: Evidence from Dementia and Normal Aging. *Journal of Gerontology, 41*, 79-84.

Munro, A. (1991). A Plea for Paraphrenia. *Canadian Journal of Psychiatry, 36*, 667-672.

Naguib, M., Levy, R. (1991). Paranoid states in the elderly and late paraphrenia. In: Jacoby, R. & Oppenheimer, L.C. (Eds.), *Psychiatry in the Elderly*. Oxford University Press.

Naguib, M. (1992). Paranoid disorders. In: Arie, T. (Ed.), *Recent Advances in Psychogeriatrics*. London: Churchill Livingstone.

Parnas, J. (2000). Paranoide tilstande. In: Hemmingsen, R., Parnas, J., Gjerris, A., Kragh-Sørensen, P. & Reisby, N. (Eds.), *Klinisk psykiatri*. København: Munksgård.

Rabins, P.V. (1999). Schizophrenia beginning in Late Life. In: Howard, R., Rabins, P.V., Castle, D.J. (Eds.), *Late Onset Schizophrenia*. Petersfield, UK and Philadelphia, USA: Wrightson Biomedical Publishing LTD.

Vernon, J. (1966). *Inside the Black Room. Studies in Sensory Deprevation*. Middlesex, England: Penguin Books.

CONTRIBUTORS

Bender, Lise, MSc (Psychology), recently retired, was a geropsychology specialist at the Center for Geropsychology, Aarhus University Hospital, Risskov.

Hartmann, Peter, MSc (Psychology), PhD, is Chief Psychometrician at Hogrefe Psykologisk Forlag, Copenhagen.

Kragshave, Gitte, MSc (Psychology), specialist in geropsychology and psychotherapy, Psychiatric Hospital, Dianalund.

Larsen, Lars, MSc (Psychology), PhD, Associate Professor, Head of Research Unit for the Psychology of Aging (RUPA), Department of Psychology, Aarhus University.

Mehlsen, Mimi Y., MSc (Psychology), PhD, Associate Professor, Department of Psychology and Behavioural Sciences, Aarhus University.

Mortensen, Erik Lykke, MSc (Psychology), Associate Professor, head of Institute for Health Science, Copenhagen University.

Munk, Karen P., MSc (Psychology), PhD, Associate Professor, Centre for Health, Humanity and Culture, Department for Culture and Society, Aarhus University.

Solem, Per Erik, MSc (Psychology), Norwegian Institute for Research on Upbringing, Welfare and Aging, Oslo.

Seilman, Uffe, PhD, is a specialist in neuropsychology at the Neurological Department, Aalborg Hospital – Aarhus University Hospital.

Torpdahl, Per, MSc (Psychology), geropsychology specialist, Center for Geropsychology, Aarhus University Hospital, Risskov.

Winsløv, Jan-Henrik, MSc (Psychology), Center for Suicide Prevention, Aalborg Psychiatric Hospital – Aarhus University Hospital.

Aamand, Anna, MSc (Psychology), is a private consultant and geropsychology specialist.